W9-BUD-082

Comic Relief

New Directions in Aesthetics

Series editors: Dominic McIver Lopes, University of British Columbia, and Berys Gaut, University of St Andrews

Blackwell's New Directions in Aesthetics series highlights ambitious single- and multiple-author books that confront the most intriguing and pressing problems in aesthetics and the philosophy of art today. Each book is written in a way that advances understanding of the subject at hand and is accessible to upper-undergraduate and graduate students.

Comic Relief

A Comprehensive Philosophy of Humor

John Morreall

Foreword by Robert Mankoff,
Cartoon Editor of The New Yorker

WILEY-BLACKWELL

A John Wiley & Sons, Ltd., Publication

This edition first published 2009
© 2009 John Morreall

Blackwell Publishing was acquired by John Wiley & Sons in February 2007.
Blackwell's publishing program has been merged with Wiley's global Scientific,
Technical, and Medical business to form Wiley-Blackwell.

Registered Office
John Wiley & Sons Ltd, The Atrium, Southern Gate, Chichester, West Sussex,
PO19 8SQ, United Kingdom

Editorial Offices
350 Main Street, Malden, MA 02148-5020, USA
9600 Garsington Road, Oxford, OX4 2DQ, UK
The Atrium, Southern Gate, Chichester, West Sussex, PO19 8SQ, UK

For details of our global editorial offices, for customer services, and for information
about how to apply for permission to reuse the copyright material in this book please
see our website at www.wiley.com/wiley-blackwell.

The right of John Morreall to be identified as the author of this work has been asserted
in accordance with the Copyright, Designs and Patents Act 1988.

Library of Congress Cataloging-in-Publication Data

Morreall, John, 1947–
   Comic relief : a comprehensive philosophy of humor / John Morreall ; foreword by
Robert Mankoff.
      p. cm. — (New directions in aesthetics)
   Includes bibliographical references and index.
   ISBN 978-1-4051-9612-3 (alk. paper)
1. Wit and humor–Philosophy.   I. Title.
   PN6149.P5M67 2009
   809'.7—dc22

                                                                            2009007420

A catalogue record for this book is available from the British Library.

Set in 10/12.5pt Galliard by Graphicraft Ltd, Hong Kong
Printed and bound in Malaysia by Vivar Printing Sdn Bhd

4   2013

For Jordan,
who'll probably cure cancer and Alzheimer's
before all these issues get resolved

Contents

Foreword
Robert Mankoff

People tell me I have the best job in the world. They're wrong, because actually I have the best *jobs* in the world. For my day job, I'm cartoon editor of *The New Yorker* magazine, which means I get to see over one thousand cartoons, every week, from the best cartoonists there are. From those thousand, I get to pick the best of the best – the crème de la crème, de la crème de la crème, if you will. I also moonlight as a cartoonist for *The New Yorker*, contributing over nine hundred cartoons to the magazine since 1977. By the way, as a cartoonist, I use the pen name Mankoff, which, coincidentally, is the same as my real name.

However, as much fun as these jobs are, I take cartoons, and the humor they represent, very seriously – or, at least, very semi-seriously. I have to, because surveys done by *The New Yorker* magazine show that 98 percent of its readers view the cartoons first and the other 2 percent are lying.

Now, that last statement is itself a lie, but you didn't think of it as a lie, because you knew it was a joke, which, in this case, though not literally true, expresses through exaggeration ("98 percent of its readers") and fabrication ("2 percent are lying") a truthful insight. Further analysis of this joke might classify it as a certain type, a "one liner" that has the structure of a "set-up" and a "punch line." Still further analysis might bring to mind the famous quip of E. B. White: "Analyzing humor is like dissecting a frog. Few people are interested and the frog dies of it." Well, he was joking too, but was he also on to the truth?

Perhaps he was, back then, some 60 years ago, but times have changed. In the first place, a search on Google brings up 196,000 results for "frog dissection," so a lot of people are interested in the topic, plus, there are even virtual frog dissection kits online, which means, *mirabile dictu*, the frog lives!

Secondly, as fascinating as frog dissection is, and with all due respect to its legion of pithy devotees, the search results it brings up are quite meager when compared to the staggering 25,000,000 you get for "humor analysis."

So, compared to the frog, interest in humor is definitely an elephant. Unfortunately, in the past, it has been the proverbial elephant in the room of human experience, ignored by the social sciences, whose attention was focused on the twin 800-pound gorillas of aggression and depression. Lately that has changed with a growing understanding that attention must be paid to positive feelings like humor that not only make life enjoyable, but endurable and comprehensible as well.

Of course, this turn of events has enraged the 800-pound gorilla of aggression, and caused his depressive twin to go into such a deep funk that even the antics of the funny elephant couldn't alleviate it – that is, until he accidentally stepped on the frog, which caused everyone to burst into laughter, except the frog, who was already burst.

The hilarity quickly came to an end, however, when a bunch of glum blind men wandered in from another proverb by way of the department of social sciences to examine the elephant. Each glumly sought to explain it from within their particular discipline, which they did to their own satisfaction, but not to each other's, or, I might add, to someone like myself, for whom humor pays the rent.

What they, and I, and you need is an interdisciplinary approach. Fortunately we have it in this book, *Comic Relief: A Comprehensive Philosophy of Humor*, by that interdisciplinarian nonpareil, John Morreall.

John is a philosopher by training who combines the temperament of a scholar with the timing of a stand-up comedian. This book entertains as it educates us in what we find funny and why. It is both comprehensive and comprehensible. I guarantee you'll find it interesting and informative. If you don't, then, well, I'll warrantee it, and if that doesn't work for you, there's always the fascinating field of frog dissection to explore.

Preface

In college I stumbled into the philosophy of laughter and humor while looking for Aristotle's *Politics* in the stacks. Where it should have been was his *Problems*. Opening that book at random, I lighted on the question, "Why is it that no one can tickle himself?" A few seconds later I moved on to, "Why are drunks more easily moved to tears?" but the Tickle Question had lodged in my brain. Ten years later, as an assistant professor looking for a new research topic, Aristotle's question came back to me, triggering many more about laughter and humor. The big one was why humor is so important in ordinary life, but so neglected or frowned upon in traditional philosophy.[1] In *Taking Laughter Seriously* (1983), I wrestled with that and a dozen other questions about laughter and humor. That book is still in print and has been translated into Japanese and Turkish.

I went on to collect what traditional philosophers have said about laughter and humor, and put it together with contemporary essays, in *The Philosophy of Laughter and Humor* (1987). That book brought some media attention, which led to invitations from medical and business groups to talk about the benefits of humor. So, printing up 500 business cards, I became a humor consultant to the likes of AT&T, IBM, and the IRS. That led to a practical book, *Humor Works* (1997). Then, following my wife's career, I joined a department of religion, where I started off with a course on humor in Zen. That got me thinking about humor as a world-view, and its competitors, especially what literary people call the Tragic Vision. So I wrote *Comedy, Tragedy, and Religion* (1999).

This book returns to the philosophy of humor. The philosophy of X asks what X is and how X fits into human life; it describes X and assesses it. We'll be asking some standard questions such as whether humor has an essence and when it's wrong to laugh. But we'll also consider neglected questions such as why humor is associated with the odd facial expressions and breathing patterns known as laughter; why laughter is contagious; and whether comedy is as valuable as tragedy. While most academic treatments of humor concentrate on fictional texts such as jokes, I will favor humor that we create spontaneously, as in conversation, and that we find in real situations. And to make sure my descriptions and assessments are reasonable, I will test them against lots of real examples.

The central idea of this book is that in humor we experience a sudden change of mental state – a cognitive shift, I call it – that would be disturbing under normal conditions, that is, if we took it seriously. Disengaged from ordinary concerns, however, we take it playfully and enjoy it. Humans, along with the apes that have learned a language, are the only animals who can do this, I argue, because we are the rational animals.

We'll focus on the playful disengagement in humor as we explore issues in psychology, aesthetics, and ethics. In psychology, comic disengagement differentiates amusement from standard emotions. In aesthetics, it explains why humor is so often an aesthetic experience, and it helps us contrast comedy with tragedy. In ethics, comic disengagement is the key to understanding both harmful humor and beneficial humor. In a chapter on philosophy and comedy, I'll argue that most philosophers have been either obtuse or perverse in not recognizing the value of comic disengagement, since they advocate a similar kind of disengagement.

Early in the writing of this book, I put "Comprehensive" in the subtitle to remind myself that I was aiming for at least three kinds of explanations. First, I wanted to clarify the concepts of laughter, amusement, and humor. Secondly, I wanted to provide two causal explanations: a psychological account of what causes what in amusement, and an evolutionary account of what in early humans led to humor, and how it then developed. That evolutionary explanation, being based on the survival value of humor, would lead to a third kind of explanation – an evaluation of the benefits humor has had for our species. To what extent I've succeeded in any of these explanations, I leave to you to determine.

Acknowledgments

Chapter 1

No Laughing Matter

The Traditional Rejection of Humor and Traditional Theories of Humor

PLEASE ENJOY THIS CULTURALLY, ETHNICALLY, RELIGIOUSLY, AND POLITICALLY CORRECT CARTOON RESPONSIBLY. THANK YOU.

SHAW

Humor, Anarchy, and Aggression

Of all the things human beings do or experience, laughing may be the funniest – funny strange, that is, not funny ha-ha. Something happens or someone says a few words, and our eyebrows and cheeks go up, as the muscles around our eyes tighten. The corners of our mouths curl upward, baring our upper teeth. Our diaphragms move up and down in spasms, expelling air from our lungs and making staccato vocal sounds. If the laughter is intense, it takes over our whole bodies. We bend over and hold our stomachs. Our eyes tear. If we had been drinking something, it dribbles out our noses. We may wet our pants. Almost every part of our bodies is involved, but none with any apparent purpose. We are out of control in a way unmatched by any other state short of neurological disease. And – funniest of all – the whole experience is exquisitely pleasurable! As Woody Allen said of stand-up comedy, it's the most fun you can have with your clothes on.

Not only is laughter biologically odd, but the activities that elicit it are anomalous. When we're out for a laugh, we break social conventions right and left. We exaggerate wildly, express emotions we don't feel, and insult people we care about. In practical jokes, we lie to friends and cause them inconvenience, even pain. During the ancient Roman winter festival of Saturnalia, masters waited on servants, sexual rules were openly violated, and religious rituals were lampooned. Medieval Europe saw similar anarchy during the Feast of Fools and the Feast of Asses, which were organized by minor clerics after Christmas. The bishop was deposed, and replaced with a boy. At St. Omer, they wore women's clothes and recited the divine office mockingly, with howls. At the Franciscan church in Antibes, they held their prayer books upside-down, wore spectacles made from orange peels, and burned soles of old shoes, instead of incense, in the censers.[1] Today, during Mardi Gras and Carnival, people dress in outlandish costumes and do things forbidden during the rest of the year, sometimes leading to violence.

In everyday humor between friends, too, there is considerable breaking of social conventions. Consider five of the conversational rules formulated by Paul Grice:

1. Do not say what you believe to be false.
2. Do not say that for which you lack adequate evidence.
3. Avoid obscurity of expression.
4. Avoid ambiguity.
5. Be brief.[2]

Rule 1 is broken to create humor when we exaggerate wildly, say the opposite of what we think, or "pull someone's leg." Its violation is a staple of comedians like George Carlin:

Legal Murder Once a Month
You can talk about capital punishment all you want, but I don't think you can leave everything up to the government. Citizens should be willing to take personal responsibility. Every now and then you've got to do the right thing, and go out and kill someone on your own. I believe the killing of human beings is just one more function of government that needs to be privatized. I say this because I believe most people know at least one other person they wish were dead. One other person whose death would make their life a little easier . . . It's a natural human instinct. . . . Don't run from it.[3]

Grice's second rule is violated for laughs when we present fantasies as if they were reasonable hypotheses. If there are rumors at work about two colleagues having an affair, we might say, "Remember on Monday when nobody could find either of them – I bet they were downstairs making hot monkey love in the boiler room."

We can create humor by breaking Rule 3 when someone asks us an embarrassing question and we give an obviously vague or confusing answer. "You want to know why my report contradicts the Census Bureau? Well, we used a new database that is so secret I'm not at liberty to reveal its name."

Violating Rule 4 is the mechanism of most jokes, as Victor Raskin showed in *Semantic Mechanisms of Humor*.[4] A comment, a story, or a question-and-answer exchange starts off with an assumed interpretation for a phrase, but then at the punch line, switches to a second, usually opposite interpretation. A simple example is Mae West's line, "Marriage is a great institution – but I'm not ready for an institution."

Rule 5 is broken in comic harangues, such as those of Roseanne Barr and Lewis Black.

Not only does humor break rules of conversation, but it often expresses contempt or even hostility toward someone, appropriately called the "butt" of the joke. Starting in childhood, we learn to make fun of people by imitating their speech patterns, facial expressions, and gestures in ways that make them look awkward, stupid, pompous, etc. To be mocked and laughed at can be taken as seriously as a physical attack would be, as the 2006 worldwide controversy over the Danish cartoons about the Prophet Muhammad showed.

The Superiority Theory: Humor as Anti-social

With all the ways in which laughter and humor involve the loss of self-control and the breaking of social rules, it's not surprising that most societies have been suspicious of them and have often rejected them. This rejection is clear in the two great sources of Western culture: Greek philosophy and the Bible.

The moral code of Protagoras had the warning, "Be not possessed by irrepressible mirth," and Epictetus's *Enchiridion* advises, "Let not your laughter be loud, frequent, or unrestrained."[5] Both these philosophers, their followers said, never laughed at all.

Plato, the most influential ancient critic of laughter, saw it as an emotion that overrides rational self-control. In the *Republic*, he said that the Guardians of the state should avoid laughter, "for ordinarily when one abandons himself to violent laughter, his condition provokes a violent reaction."[6] Plato was especially disturbed by the passages in the *Iliad* and the *Odyssey* where Mount Olympus was said to "ring with the laughter of the gods." He protested that "if anyone represents men of worth as overpowered by laughter we must not accept it, much less if gods."[7]

The contempt or hostility in humor, which Ronald de Sousa has dubbed its *phthonic* dimension,[8] also bothered Plato. Laughter feels good, he admitted, but the pleasure is mixed with malice towards those being laughed at.[9]

In the Bible, too, laughter is usually represented as an expression of hostility.[10] Proverbs 26:18–19 warns that, "A man who deceives another and then says, 'It was only a joke,' is like a madman shooting at random his deadly darts and arrows."

The only way God is described as laughing in the Bible is scornfully: "The kings of the earth stand ready, and the rulers conspire together against the Lord and his anointed king. . . . The Lord who sits enthroned in heaven laughs them to scorn; then he rebukes them in anger, he threatens them in his wrath." (Psalms 2:2–5)

God's prophet Elijah also laughs as a warm-up to aggression. After he ridicules the priests of Baal for their god's powerlessness, he has them slain (1 Kings 18:27). In the Bible, ridicule is offensive enough to carry the death penalty, as when a group of children laugh at the prophet Elisha for being bald:

> He went up from there to Bethel and, as he was on his way, some small
> boys came out of the city and jeered at him, saying, "Get along with you,

bald head, get along." He turned round and looked at them and he cursed then in the name of the lord; and two she-bears came out of a wood and mauled forty-two of them. (2 Kings 2:23)

Early Christian thinkers brought together these negative assessments of laughter from both Greek and biblical sources. Like Plato and the Stoics, they were bothered by the loss of self-control in laughter. According to Basil the Great, "raucous laughter and uncontrollable shaking of the body are not indications of a well-regulated soul, or of personal dignity, or self-mastery."[11] And, like Plato, they associated laughter with aggression. John Chrysostom warned that,

> Laughter often gives birth to foul discourse, and foul discourse to actions still more foul. Often from words and laughter proceed railing and insult; and from railing and insult, blows and wounds; and from blows and wounds, slaughter and murder. If, then, you would take good counsel for yourself, avoid not merely foul words and foul deeds, or blows and wounds and murders, but unseasonable laughter itself.[12]

An ideal place to find Christian attacks on laughter is in the institution that most emphasized self-control and social harmony – the monastery. The oldest monastic rule – of Pachom of Egypt in the fourth century – forbade joking.[13] The Rule of St. Benedict, the foundation of Western monastic codes, enjoined monks to "prefer moderation in speech and speak no foolish chatter, nothing just to provoke laughter; do not love immoderate or boisterous laughter." In Benedict's Ladder of Humility, Step Ten was a restraint against laughter, and Step Eleven a warning against joking.[14] The monastery of Columban in Ireland assigned these punishments: "He who smiles in the service . . . six strokes; if he breaks out in the noise of laughter, a special fast unless it has happened pardonably."[15] One of the strongest condemnations of laughter came from the Syrian abbot Ephraem: "Laughter is the beginning of the destruction of the soul, o monk; when you notice something of that, know that you have arrived at the depth of the evil. Then do not cease to pray God, that he might rescue you from this death."[16]

Apart from the monastic tradition, perhaps the Christian group which most emphasized self-control and social harmony was the Puritans, and so it is not surprising that they wrote tracts against laughter and comedy. One by William Prynne condemned comedy as incompatible with the sobriety of good Christians, who should not be "immoderately tickled with mere lascivious vanities, or . . . lash out in excessive cachinnations in the public view of dissolute graceless persons."[17] When the Puritans came to rule England under Cromwell, they outlawed comedy. Plato would have been pleased.

In the seventeenth century, too, Plato's critique of laughter as expressing our delight in the shortcomings of other people was extended by Thomas Hobbes. For him, people are prone to this kind of delight because they are naturally individualistic and competitive. In the *Leviathan*, he says, "I put for a general inclination of all mankind, a perpetual and restless desire for Power after Power, that ceaseth only in Death."[18] The original state of the human race, before government, he said, would have been a "war of all against all."[19] In our competition with each other, we relish events that show ourselves to be winning, or others losing, and if our perception of our superiority comes over us quickly, we are likely to laugh.

> Sudden glory, is the passion which makes those grimaces called laughter; and is caused either by some sudden act of their own, that pleases them; or by the apprehension of some deformed thing in another, by comparison whereof they suddenly applaud themselves. And it is incident most to them, that are conscious of the fewest abilities in themselves; who are forced to keep themselves in their own favor by observing the imperfections of other men. And therefore much laughter at the defects of others, is a sign of pusillanimity. For of great minds, one of the proper works is, to help and free others from scorn; and to compare themselves only with the most able.[20]

Before the Enlightenment, Plato and Hobbes's idea that laughter is an expression of feelings of superiority was the only widely circulated understanding of laughter. Today it is called the "Superiority Theory." Its modern adherents include Roger Scruton, who analyses amusement as an "attentive demolition" of a person or something connected with a person. "If people dislike being laughed at," Scruton says, "it is surely because laughter devalues its object in the subject's eyes."[21]

In linking Plato, Hobbes, and Scruton with the term "Superiority Theory," we should be careful not to attribute too much agreement to them. Like the "Incongruity Theory" and "Relief Theory," which we'll consider shortly, "Superiority Theory" is a term of art meant to capture one feature shared by accounts of laughter that differ in other respects. It is not, like "Sense Data Theory" or "Dialectical Materialism," a name adopted by a group of thinkers consciously participating in a tradition. All it means is that these thinkers claimed that laughter expresses feelings of superiority.

Discussing a philosopher under the "Superiority Theory," further-more, does not rule out discussing them under "Incongruity Theory" or "Relief Theory." As Victor Raskin notes, the three theories "character-ize the complex phenomenon of humor from very different angles and do not at all contradict each other – rather they seem to supplement each other quite nicely."[22] Jerrold Levinson explains how the accounts of laughter in Henri Bergson, Arthur Schopenhauer, and Herbert Spencer all had elements of both the Superiority and the Incongruity Theory, and how Immanuel Kant's account, which is usually discussed under the Incongruity Theory, also has elements of the Relief Theory.[23]

We should also be careful in talking about theories of laughter and humor to distinguish different kinds of theories. Plato, Hobbes, and other philosophers before the twentieth century were mostly looking for the psychological causes of laughter and amusement. They asked what it is about certain things and situations that evokes laughter or amuse-ment. Advocates of the Superiority Theory said that when something evokes laughter, it is by revealing someone's inferiority to the person laughing.

Today, many philosophers are more concerned with conceptual ana-lysis than with causal explanation. In studying laughter, amusement, and humor, they try to make clear the concepts of each, asking, for example, what has to be true of something in order for it to count as amusing. Seeking necessary and sufficient conditions, they try to formulate de-finitions that cover all examples of amusement but no examples that are not amusement. Of course, it may turn out that part of the concept of amusement is that it is a response to certain kinds of stimuli. And so conceptual analysis and psychological explanation may intertwine.

In this chapter I will discuss the three traditional theories mostly as psychological accounts, which is how they were originally presented. But we will also ask whether they could provide rigorous definitions of amusement and humor. Now back to the first of the three, the Superiority Theory.

If the Superiority Theory is right, laughter would seem to have no place in a well-ordered society, for it would undermine cooperation, tolerance, and self-control. That is why when Plato imagined the ideal state, he wanted to severely restrict the performance of comedy. "We shall enjoin that such representations be left to slaves or hired aliens, and that they receive no serious consideration whatsoever. No free person, whether woman or man, shall be found taking lessons in them."[24] "No composer of comedy, iambic or lyric verse shall be permitted to hold any citizen up to laughter, by word or gesture, with passion or otherwise."[25]

Those who have wanted to save humor from such censorship have followed two general strategies. One is to retain the claim that laughter expresses feelings of superiority, but to find something of value in that. The other is to reject the Superiority Theory in favor of one in which laughter and humor are based on something that is not anti-social.

The first approach has been taken by defenders of comedy since Ben Jonson and Sir Philip Sidney in Shakespeare's time. Against the charge that comedy is steeped in drunkenness, lechery, lying, cowardice, etc., they argued that in comedy these vices are held up for ridicule, not for emulation. The moral force of comedy is to correct mistakes and short-comings, not to foster them. In Sidney's *Defense of Poesie*, the first work of literary criticism in English, he writes that, "Comedy is an imitation of the common errors of our life, which he [the dramatist] representeth in the most ridiculous and scornful sort that may be, so as it is impossible that any beholder can be content to be such a one."[26]

A modern proponent of the view that laughter, while based on superiority, serves as a social corrective, was Henri Bergson in *Laughter*. His ideas about laughter grew out of his opposition to the materialism and mechanism of his day. In his theory of "creative evolution," a non-material "vital force" (*élan vital*) drives biological and cultural evolution. We are aware of this force, Bergson says, in our own experience – not in our conceptual thinking but in our direct perception of things and events. There we realize that our life is a process of continuous becoming and not a succession of discrete states, as our rational intellect often represents it. Real duration, lived time, as opposed to static abstractions of time, is an irreversible flow of experience. Now Bergson admits that abstract knowledge is useful in science and engineering, but when we let it dominate our thinking, we handle our daily experience in a rigid, repetitive way, treating new events as mere instantiations of concepts. "What life and society require of each of us is a constantly alert attention that discerns the outlines of the present situation, together with a certain elasticity of mind and body to enable us to adapt ourselves."[27]

It is here that laughter comes into play. For Bergson, the essence of the ridiculous is "mechanical inelasticity" – someone acting in a rigid, repetitive way instead of a flexible, context-sensitive way. When we laugh at persons who are acting like machines, we do feel superior to them, and we are humiliating them, but that humiliation spurs them to think and act more flexibly, less like a machine. So, while laughter stings, it brings the ridiculed person back to acting like a human being.

Another way to save humor from being banned for undermining social order, as I said, is to reject the Superiority Theory of laughter. In the eighteenth century, this happened in two ways. First, Francis Hutcheson presented a systematic critique of the theory. Secondly, philosophers developed two alternative theories in which laughter was not anti social: the Incongruity Theory and the Relief Theory.

In "Reflections Upon Laughter," Hutcheson argued against Hobbes's claim that the essential feature of laughter is expressing feelings of superiority."[28] If Hobbes were right, he said, two conclusions would follow: (1) there can be no laughter where we do not compare ourselves with others or with some former state of ourselves; and (2) whenever we feel "sudden glory," we laugh. But neither of these is true. We sometimes laugh at an odd metaphor or simile, for example, without comparing ourselves to anyone. Hutcheson cites these lines about a sunrise:

> The sun, long since, had in the lap
> Of Thetis taken out his nap;
> And like a lobster boil'd, the morn
> From black to red began to turn.

Contemporary psychology offers support for Hutcheson's claim that we do not need to compare ourselves with anyone in order to laugh. In an experiment by Lambert Deckers, subjects were asked to lift a series of weights that looked identical. The first several did weigh the same, but then the unsuspecting subjects picked up one that was much heavier or lighter, whereupon they laughed. In laughing, they did not seem to compare themselves with anyone.[29]

Not only are feelings of superiority not necessary for amusement, Hutcheson argued, but they are not sufficient, either. We have feelings of superiority toward people we pity, for example, without laughing at them. If a well-dressed gentleman riding through London in a coach sees ragged beggars, the realization that he is much better off than they are is not likely to amuse him – "we are in greater danger of weeping than laughing."[30]

The Incongruity Theory: Humor as Irrational

After the Superiority Theory was shown to be faulty, two other accounts arose to compete with it, the Incongruity Theory and the Relief Theory. As with "Superiority Theory," these are terms of art and not names adopted by thinkers consciously participating in traditions. We'll discuss these accounts one at a time.

While the Superiority Theory says that what causes laughter is feeling superior to someone, the Incongruity Theory says that it is a perception of something incongruous.[31] This approach was taken by James Beattie, Immanuel Kant, Søren Kierkegaard, Arthur Schopenhauer, and many later philosophers and psychologists. It is now the dominant theory of humor in philosophy and psychology.

As Robert Latta and others have pointed out, the words "incongruous" and "incongruity" are used sloppily in many versions of the theory.[32] The dictionary says that incongruous things are "characterized by a lack of harmony, consistency, or compatibility with one another." *Congruere* in Latin means "to come together, to agree." In geometry, congruent triangles have the same shape and size; one fits exactly over the other. The prefix *in* means "not." So *incongruous* things "do not go together, match, or fit in some way," to use Latta's words.[33] He offers an example from the Roman poet Horace:

> If a painter chose to join a human head to the neck of a horse, and to spread feathers of many a hue over limbs picked up now here now there, so that what at the top is a lovely woman ends below in a black and ugly fish, could you, my friends, if favored with a private view, refrain from laughing?[34]

Applying the word "incongruity" to this painting fits the dictionary definition. But consider Paul McGhee's explanation of "incongruity" in which he says that he uses the term "interchangeably with absurdity, ridiculousness, and the ludicrous." These words, Latta points out, are *not* equivalent to "incongruity." To make matters worse, McGhee offers a second definition: "something unexpected, out of context, inappropriate, unreasonable, illogical, exaggerated, and so forth."[35] As Latta says, these words *do not* mean, "having parts that don't fit together."

Latta attacks several more theorists' uses of "incongruity" for straying from the dictionary. That can be justified, of course, if the extended meaning is determinate. And so I would like to present a core concept that is shared by most standard versions of the Incongruity Theory. Some of Latta's criticisms of incongruity theories may still have force, but at least the theory will have specifiable content.

The core concept in incongruity theories is based on the fact that human experience works with learned patterns. What we have experienced prepares us to deal with what we will experience. When we reach out to touch snow, we expect it to be cold. If a chipmunk is running toward us, we expect it to avoid us, not leap up and bite our jugular vein. If someone begins a story about George Washington, they may describe him as having faults, but we do not expect to hear that Washington plotted to murder all 56 signers of the Declaration of Independence.

Most of the time, most experiences of most people follow such mental patterns. The future turns out like the past. But sometimes we perceive or imagine a thing whose parts or features violate our mental patterns, as in the painting of a woman/fish that Horace imagined. Events, too, may not fit our mental patterns. It begins to rain heavily, but suddenly the clouds blow away and the sun shines brightly. A state attorney general establishes a reputation for being tough on prostitution; then as governor he is found to be a regular client of a call-girl agency.

The core meaning of "incongruity" in standard incongruity theories is that some thing or event we perceive or think about violates our normal mental patterns and normal expectations. Once we have experienced some thing incongruous, of course, we no longer expect *it* to fit our normal mental patterns. Nonetheless, it still violates our normal mental patterns and our normal expectations. That is how we can be amused by the same thing more than once.

Without using the word "incongruity," Aristotle hints at a connection between humor and this violation of mental patterns and expectations. In the *Rhetoric*, 3.2, he says that one way for a speaker to get a laugh is to set up an expectation in the audience and then violate it. He cites a line from a comedy: "And as he walked, beneath his feet were — chilblains [sores on the feet]." Similarly, Cicero, in *On the Orator*, says that, "The most common kind of joke is that in which we expect one thing and another is said; here our own disappointed expectation makes us laugh."[36]

Immanuel Kant's explanation of laughter is more complicated but also based on the violation of expectations:

> In everything that is to excite a lively convulsive laugh there must be something absurd (in which the understanding, therefore, can find no satisfaction). Laughter is an affection arising from the sudden transformation of a strained expectation into nothing. This transformation, which is certainly not enjoyable to the understanding, yet indirectly gives it very active enjoyment for a moment. Therefore its cause must consist in the influence of the representation upon the body, and the reflex effect of this upon the mind.[37]

For Kant, humorous amusement is primarily a physical pleasure arising from the "changing free play of sensations" that accompanies the play of thought.

The first philosopher to use the word "incongruity" to analyze humor was James Beattie, a contemporary of Kant. He sticks closest to the original meaning of incongruity when he says that laughter "seems to arise from the view of things incongruous united in the same assemblage."[38] The object of laughter is "two or more inconsistent, unsuitable, or incongruous parts or circumstances, considered as united in one complex object or assemblage."[39]

Schopenhauer has a more sophisticated version of the Incongruity Theory in which the cause of amusement is a discrepancy between our abstract concepts and our perceptions of things that are instantiations of those concepts. In organizing our sense experience, we ignore many differences between things that fall under one concept – as when we call both Chihuahuas and Great Danes "dogs." Amusement is being struck by the mismatch between a concept and a perception of the same thing, and enjoying the mental jolt that gives us. "The cause of laughter in every case is simply the sudden perception of the incongruity between a concept and the real objects which have been thought through it in some relation, and laughter itself is just the expression of this incongruity."[40] As an example, Schopenhauer tells of the prison guards who let a convict play cards with them, but when they catch him cheating, they kick him out. He comments, "They let themselves be led by the general conception, 'Bad companions are turned out,' and forget that he is also a prisoner, i.e., one whom they ought to hold fast."[41]

Kierkegaard uses the word "contradiction" much as others use "incongruity," for the violation of one's expectations. He cites the story of the baker who said to a poor woman, "No, mother, I cannot give you anything. There was another here recently whom I had to send away without giving anything, too: we cannot give to everybody."[42]

Except for Beattie, none of these thinkers wrote even an essay about laughter or humor: their comments arise in discussions of wider topics. Kierkegaard, for example, had a nuanced view in which humor is distinguished from irony, and both represent worldviews.[43] Furthermore, these "Incongruity Theorists" disagreed on several details about incongruity, disappointed expectation, absurdity, discrepancy, or contradiction, such as how they are related to laughter. So we have to be careful in talking about *the* Incongruity Theory. Nonetheless, the name has stuck and today, as mentioned, the Incongruity Theory is the most widely accepted account of humor in philosophy and empirical psychology.

In the late twentieth century, one serious flaw in several older versions of the theory came to light: they said or implied that the mere perception of incongruity is sufficient for humor. That is clearly false, since negative emotions like fear, disgust, and anger are also reactions to what violates our mental patterns and expectations. Coming home to find your family murdered, for example, is incongruous but not funny. Experiencing something incongruous can also evoke puzzlement or incredulity: we may go into a problem-solving mode to figure out how the stimulus might actually fit into our conceptual frameworks.

A recent attempt to carefully lay out necessary and sufficient conditions for humorous amusement is that of Michael Clarke. He sets out three defining features of humor:

1.   A person perceives (thinks, imagines) an object as being incongruous.
2.   The person enjoys perceiving (thinking, imagining) the object
3.   The person enjoys the perceived (thought, imagined) incongruity at least partly for itself, rather than solely for some ulterior reason.[44]

While this version of the Incongruity Theory is clearly an improvement on theories in which amusement consists simply in the perception of incongruity, it still seems not specific enough. As Mike Martin points out, we often enjoy incongruity in the arts without being amused.[45] In Sophocles' *Oedipus the King*, for example, Oedipus vows to do whatever it takes to bring the killer of King Laius to justice. Knowing that he is himself that killer, we in the audience may well enjoy the incongruity of such a self-threatening vow, but that isn't humor. Other aesthetic categories, too, involve a non-humorous enjoyment of some violation of our mental patterns and expectations: the grotesque, the macabre, the horrible, the bizarre, and the fantastic. In Chapter 4 we will discuss the enjoyment of incongruity in humor and contrast it with these other ways of enjoying incongruity.

Even assuming that the Incongruity Theory can be made specific enough concerning the enjoyment of incongruity, however, there is a more general problem with the very idea of enjoying incongruity. Put bluntly, how could anyone enjoy the violation of their conceptual patterns and expectations? Such enjoyment looks psychologically perverse or at least irrational. That is why, although the Incongruity Theory freed humor from the traditional stigma of being anti-social, it has not improved philosophers' assessments of humor much over the last three centuries. It answered some of the older objections to humor, but made way for a new one that may be more compelling for philosophers: the Irrationality Objection.

Kant came close to spelling out the Irrationality Objection in presenting his account of jokes. The punch line of a joke, he said, causes pleasure, but not gratification, for it cannot be gratifying to have one's expectations proved delusive and one's desire to understand frustrated.

The pleasure of humor is *in spite of* its frustrating our reason, and is based on the healthful effect that laughter has on our bodies:

> The jest must contain something that is capable of deceiving for a moment. Hence, when the illusion is dissipated, the mind turns back to try it once again, and thus through a rapidly alternating tension and relaxation it is jerked back and put into a state of oscillation. . . . If we admit that with all our thoughts is harmonically combined a movement in the organs of the body, we will easily comprehend how to this sudden transposition of the mind, now to one now to another standpoint in order to contemplate its object, may correspond an alternating tension and relaxation of the elastic portions of our intestines which communicates itself to the diaphragm.[46]

Now while Kant found the massage of the inner organs in laughter healthy, other philosophers have seen something perverse in human beings, the rational animals, engaging in joking, the whole point of which is to violate their conceptual patterns and frustrate their understanding. People who enjoy incongruity are like travelers who discover that they are headed in the wrong direction – and enjoy that discovery.

George Santayana, for example, went beyond the claim that enjoying incongruity is perverse, to say that it is impossible. The pleasure we take in humor, he said, must be in its physiological effects and in the "stimulation and shaking up of our wits," not in any enjoyment of incongruity per se:

> We have a prosaic background of common sense and everyday reality; upon this background an unexpected idea suddenly impinges. But the thing is a futility. The comic accident falsifies the nature before us, starts a wrong analogy in the mind, a suggestion that cannot be carried out. In a word, we are in the presence of an absurdity, and man, being a rational animal, can like absurdity no better than he can like hunger or cold.[47]

The view that as rational animals we always act to overcome incongruity has many parallels throughout Western thought. Consider, for example, the ancient principle called by eighteenth-century rationalists the Principle of Sufficient Reason. Held by Richard Taylor and others to be "almost a part of reason itself,"[48] it can be stated as follows: "For the existence of any being or the truth of any positive statement, there is something, known or unknown, which makes that thing exist or that statement true."

Everything, in short, is theoretically explainable. What seems puzzling or mysterious is not inherently so – it's just that the rational animals have not yet investigated it carefully enough. When they do, the mystery will evaporate. To an omniscient mind, everything would fit into rational patterns, so that nothing is more than *apparently* anomalous. There is nothing objectively incongruous or comic about the universe or the human condition, then, and so amusement is possible only for those who are ignorant or confused.

In Western science since the Enlightenment, it is an axiom that the world is rationally understandable. And so it is not surprising to find among scientists a commitment to Santayana's view that incongruity could not be enjoyable to human beings. "Anomaly is inherently disturbing," writes Barry Barnes, "and automatically generates pressure for its reduction."[49] In his influential book *A Theory of Cognitive Dissonance*, Leon Festinger uses the term "cognitive dissonance" for "nonfitting relations among cognitions," that is, for incongruity, and claims that cognitive dissonance, like hunger, automatically motivates us to reduce it and to "avoid situations and information which would likely increase the dissonance."[50]

Many psychologists who have theorized about humor have claimed that only young children are irrational enough to enjoy incongruity by itself. According to Thomas Schultz, for instance, after the age of seven, we require not just incongruity to be amused, but the resolution of that incongruity. Mature humor requires the fitting of the *apparently* anomalous element into some conceptual schema. Indeed, Schultz is unwilling to call unresolvable incongruity "humorous" – he calls it "nonsense."[51] The pleasure of humor in a mature person, according to this view, is not the enjoyment of incongruity, but the enjoyment of a kind of puzzle solving similar to what scientists do.

In Western philosophy and science, then, the dominant view concerning incongruity is that a rational adult should, or even can, face it in only one way, by trying to eliminate it. To appreciate incongruity would be immature, irrational, masochistic, or all three.

If we are to going to explain the value of humor, then, as well as its nature, we need to say much more than that we enjoy incongruity. That's what I will be doing in the chapters that follow, as I connect humor with play, and explore the social significance of humor and play, and their benefits to the species. Before that, however, we should look at the third traditional theory of laughter, the Relief Theory.

The Relief Theory: Humor as a Pressure Valve

In the eighteenth century, the Relief Theory arose alongside the Incongruity Theory to compete with the Superiority Theory. Its focus was on the physical phenomenon of laughter, especially its relation to the nervous system, something left unexplained by the Superiority and Incongruity Theories. In the medical science of the eighteenth century, it was known that nerves connect the brain, sense organs, and muscles. Nerves were thought to carry not electro-chemical impulses, but gases and liquids called "animal spirits." There was debate over their exact composition, but the animal spirits were thought to include blood and air. John Locke described them as "fluid and subtile Matter, passing through the Conduits of the Nerves."[52] So in the first versions of the Relief Theory, the nervous system was represented as a network of tubes inside which the animal spirits sometimes build up pressure, as in emotional excitement, that calls for release. A good analogy is the way excess steam builds up in a steam boiler. These boilers are fitted with relief valves to vent excess pressure, and, according to the Relief Theory, laughter serves a similar function in the nervous system.

The first published work to use "humor" with its modern meaning of funniness, Lord Shaftesbury's "The Freedom of Wit and Humour" (1711), was also the first sketch of the Relief Theory: "The natural free spirits of ingenious men, if imprisoned or controlled, will find out other ways of motion to relieve themselves in their constraint; and whether it be in burlesque, mimicry, or buffoonery, they will be glad at any rate to vent themselves, and be revenged upon their constrainers."[53] Over the next two centuries, thinkers such as Herbert Spencer and Sigmund Freud revised the biology behind this theory and added new elements of their own.

In his essay "On the Physiology of Laughter," Spencer says that in our bodies emotions take the form of nervous energy. "Nervous energy always tends to beget muscular motion, and when it rises to a certain intensity, always does beget it."[54] "Feeling passing a certain pitch habitually vents itself in bodily action."[55] In fear we make small movements that are a preparation for running away, and if the fear gets strong enough, that is what we do. When we're angry with someone, we make small aggressive movements such as moving closer to them and clenching our fists. If our nervous energy reaches a certain level, we do attack them. The larger movements of full-scale fear, anger, and other emotions vent the excess pressure much as the safety valve on the steam boiler vents excess steam pressure.

Laughter works in a similar way, only the muscular movements in laughter are not the early stages of any larger movements. Even if intense, laughter is not the beginning of fighting, fleeing, or any other action. Rather, laughter functions *only* as a release of excess nervous energy; other than that, Spencer says, the movements of laughter "have no object."[56]

The excess nervous energy that is relieved by laughter, according to Spencer, is the energy of emotions that have been found to be inappropriate. This energy is vented first through the muscles "which feeling most habitually stimulates," those connected with speech. If there is still more energy to be relieved, it spills over to the muscles connected with breathing, and perhaps finally to the arms, legs, and other muscle groups.[57]

To describe the mental side of this process, Spencer uses the language of the Incongruity Theory. "Laughter naturally results only when consciousness is unawares transferred from great things to small – only when there is what we call a descending incongruity."[58] Consider this poem by Harry Graham:

> I had written to Aunt Maud
> Who was on a trip abroad
> When I heard she'd died of cramp,
> Just too late to save the stamp.

Up until the last word, our feelings tend toward pity for the bereaved nephew writing the poem. But his last word makes us reinterpret everything, shifting our thoughts from a grieving nephew to an insensitive cheapskate. The nervous energy of our emotions for a grieving nephew is now pointless and is vented in laughter.

As presented by Spencer, or in the simpler form sketched by Shaftesbury, the Relief Theory doesn't have the stigmata attached to the Superiority Theory and the Incongruity Theory. Laughter, and by implication humor, are not anti-social or irrational, but simply a way of discharging nervous energy found to be unnecessary. As John Dewey put the idea, laughter "marks the ending . . . of a period of suspense, or expectation." It is a "sudden relaxation of strain, so far as occurring through the medium of the breathing and vocal apparatus . . . The laugh is thus a phenomenon of the same general kind as the sigh of relief."[59]

Reduced almost to the level of belching and farting in this way, laughter might be less interesting in the Relief Theory than it was in the other two, but at least it sounds innocuous. Few people who know about the Relief Theory, however, are familiar with Spencer's, Shaftesbury's, or Dewey's versions. By far the best-known version is that of Sigmund Freud in his *Jokes and Their Relation to the Unconscious*,[60] and his description of the relief function of laughter in jokes is not so innocent. It links laughter and humor not only to aggression but also to lust.

In that book, Freud distinguishes three laughter situations: joking, "the comic," and "humor." In all three, laughter releases energy that was summoned for a psychological task, but then became unnecessary when that task was abandoned. In joking that is the energy of repressing feelings; in the comic it is the energy of thinking; and in humor it is the energy of feeling emotions. We can say a word about each of these sources of laughter.

Freud's term for joking, *der Witz*, is not limited to "joke-telling," the recitation of prepared fictional narratives, but includes spontaneous witty comments, *bon mots*, and repartee as well. In all of these, he says, there is a release of psychic energy, not the energy of repressed feelings, but the energy that normally represses those feelings. Most summaries of Freud's theory overlook this point and simply describe laughter as a release of repressed energy.

According to Freud, most prepared jokes and witty remarks are about sex or hostility, because those are the big urges which society forces us to repress. In telling and listening to a sexual joke, or a joke that belittles an individual or group, we override our internal censor, expressing our repressed libido or hostility. The now superfluous energy summoned to repress those urges is then released in laughter.[61]

In those laughter situations which Freud calls "the comic," there is a similar release of energy that is summoned but then found unnecessary, only here it is the energy of thinking. As an example, he analyzes our laughter at a circus clown. In watching the clown stumble through actions that we would perform quickly and smoothly, there is a saving of the energy that we would expend to understand the clown's movements. According to Freud's theory of "mimetic representation," we expend a great amount of energy to understand something big and a small amount of energy to understand something small. So our mental representation of the clown's movements calls for more energy than the energy we would expend to understand our own movements in doing the same task. And that surplus energy is vented in laughter:

> These two possibilities in my imagination amount to a comparison between the observed movement and my own. If the other person's movement is exaggerated and inexpedient, my increased expenditure in order to understand it is inhibited *in statu nascendi*, as it were in the act of being mobilized; it is declared superfluous and is free for use elsewhere or perhaps for discharge by laughter.[62]

Freud's account of the third laughter situation, which he calls "humor," receives just a few pages at the end of his book, and is similar to Spencer's theory. Humor occurs "if there is a situation in which, according to our usual habits, we should be tempted to release a distressing affect and if motives then operate upon us which suppress that affect *in statu nascendi. . . .* The pleasure of humor . . . comes about . . . at the cost of a release of affect that does not occur: it arises from *an economy in the expenditure of affect.*"[63] Freud cites Mark Twain's story about his brother's working on building a road. One day the dynamite went off accidentally, blowing him high into the sky. When he came down far from the work site, he was docked half a day's pay for being "absent from his place of employment." Our laughter on hearing this story, Freud explains, is the release of energy that was summoned to feel sympathy for Twain's brother, but was then seen to be unnecessary. When we hear the unbelievable ending, we realize that pity would be inappropriate. "As a result of this understanding, the expenditure on the pity, which was already prepared, becomes unutilizable and we laugh it off."[64]

We have seen two versions of the Relief Theory, then, the simple one of Spencer, repeated in Freud's account of "humor," and the complex one in Freud's account of joking and "the comic." We'll comment on them separately.

Clearly there is a connection between at least some laughter and the expenditure of energy. Hearty laughter involves several areas of the brain and nervous system, and many muscle groups. People often describe a bout of heavy laughter as having a cathartic effect, much as exercise does. Dr. William Fry estimates that 20 seconds of hearty laughter gives the heart and lungs a workout equivalent to three minutes on a rowing machine.[65]

But acknowledging all this does not imply that in all humor emotional energy builds up and is released. There is energy expended in the act of laughing, of course; one study showed that 15 minutes of laughter can burn 40 calories.[66] But why say that the energy in laughter is the energy of emotions or thinking that have built up and now call for release?

Some humor stimuli may evoke emotions, but many seem not to. Single-frame cartoons picturing absurd situations, for example, seem able to make us laugh without feeling any emotions first. Consider the cartoon about the lion at the beginning of Chapter 3. Assuming that Freud would count this cartoon as humor, there must be pent-up emotional energy released when we laugh at it. That energy either was aroused by the cartoon itself, or had built up before we saw the cartoon. But neither seems necessary. What emotion might this cartoon arouse in us and then show to be inappropriate? Shock at a talking lion? Sympathy for the zebra and wilde-beest killed to make toppings for the pizza? If, on the other hand, Freud would say that the cartoon released emotions we had already built up before seeing the cartoon, what emotions might those be? Fear of lions? Sympathy for their prey? Again, it seems possible to be amused by this cartoon without feeling any of these emotions before seeing it.

Lots of playing with words also seems to be humor without relieving any pent-up emotions. Consider P. G. Wodehouse's line, "If it's feasible, let's fease it" or Ogden Nash's poem "Fleas":

> Fleas
> Adam
> Had'em.[67]

Not only is the simplest version of the Relief Theory problematic, but Spencer's version adds a detail, about what causes the energy to become superfluous, that is also problematic. He says that the humor stimulus must be a "descending incongruity," shifting us from thinking about something important to thinking about something unimportant. If the incongruity were to go the other way, we wouldn't laugh: "When after something very insignificant there arises without anticipation something very great, the emotion we call wonder results."[68] The problem with this claim is that sometimes we do laugh on shifting from the unimportant to the important. A friend of mine recently lost her mother. When she went to the office of the funeral director, she sat down and reached for her pack of cigarettes. "Mind if I smoke?" she asked. "Not at all," he said, "many of my clients smoked."

Robert Latta cites a similar example from a letter sent to the Dartmouth College Class of 1956 after their 25th Reunion:

DEAR CLASSMATES:
Our tremendously successful and never to be forgotten 25th Reunion marked another turning point for the Class of 1956. Having passed this memorable milestone, we are now eligible to participate in the Dartmouth Bequest and Estate Planning Program.[69]

Having commented on the simple version of the Relief Theory in Spencer's and in Freud's account of "humor," we can now turn to Freud's account of joking and "the comic." The basic problem here is that his hydraulic theory of emotions and thinking, as combined with his general psychoanalytic theory, does not seem plausible.

Freud says that the creation of jokes and witty comments is an unconscious process in which we let into our conscious minds thoughts and feelings that we normally repress. The trouble here is that many jokes and witty comments in speeches are created by professional writers, who approach the task with conscious strategies for generating set-ups and punch lines. Also, the mechanics of Freud's explanation of how the nervous energy is released in joke telling is problematic. We normally use psychic energy to repress hostile and sexual thoughts and feelings, he says, but when we joke, we "elude the censor" and bring those thoughts and feelings into consciousness. There is a saving of psychic energy – that is, the energy we normally summon for inhibiting these thoughts and feelings becomes unnecessary – and we vent that energy in laughter.

Many descriptions of Freud's account of joking skip these details and just say that in joking we express repressed feelings. But Freud explains the release of emotional energy in joking as the venting, not of the hostile and sexual energy, but of the energy normally expended to repress hostile and sexual thoughts and feelings. The problem here is that his claims about packets of psychic energy being summoned to repress thoughts and feelings, but *in statu nascendi* (in the process of being borne) being rendered superfluous, seem unverifiable, and so of no use in building a theory of humor.

Where we can draw conclusions from Freud's theory of joking and test them, at least some of the results go against Freud. For example, if he is right that the energy released in laughter is the energy normally used to repress hostile and sexual feelings, then it seems that those who laugh hardest at aggressive and sexual humor will be people who normally repress those feelings. But experiments by Hans Jurgen Eysenck showed the opposite: it is people who usually give free rein to their hostile and sexual feelings, not those who repress them, who enjoy aggressive and sexual humor more.[70]

Freud's account of his last laughter situation, "the comic," faces problems, too. Here the saving of energy is supposed to be with energy normally used for thinking, that is, for understanding something we perceive or think about, such as the antics of a clown. We summon a large packet of psychic energy to understand the clown's extravagant movements in, say, riding a bicycle across the circus ring. But as we are summoning it, we compare it with the small packet of energy required to understand our own simpler movements in doing the same thing. The difference between the two packets is surplus energy that we discharge in laughter.

Freud's ideas here about the "mimetic representation" of motion are idiosyncratic and have strange implications, such as that thinking about running a marathon takes far more energy than thinking about threading a needle. If Freud is talking about real energy that burns up calories, then dieters could quickly lose weight by thinking of running across the country, even thinking of someone else doing so.

The explanation of the venting of the "surplus psychic energy" in laughter is also problematic. Freud says that we use a large packet of energy to understand how the clown performs the task and a small packet of energy to think about how we would do the same thing. As the large packet is being summoned, it is compared with the small packet, and the difference is seen to be superfluous and so available for discharge in laughter. But if the energy here is energy used to think about the two movements, and we do in fact think about those movements, where is the *surplus* energy? The big packet was used to understand the clown's movements and the small packet was used to understand our own movements. Nothing is left over. If Freud were to respond that we do not actually go through with the process of thinking about the clown's movements, then how would we come to realize that those movements were too much for the task at hand, and how would we know what our own movements would be, to do the same thing?

Another problem for Freud here is accounting for the person who is comic because they reach their goals expending *less* energy than we would expend – Tom Sawyer getting the other boys to whitewash the fence, for example. Presented with such cases, Freud says that there is a difference here too, and the laughter depends on this difference "and not on which of the two the difference favors."[71] But then Freud has changed the mechanics of laughter significantly, and he owes us an explanation.

He also faced the apparent counterexample of the comic character who is stuck in a difficult situation and struggles to get out in much the same way any normal person would. Here Freud changes his story again, saying that the comparison in such cases is between the character's current difficult state and his former untroubled state.[72] Then he generalizes to what sounds like an incongruity theory:

> It is a necessary condition for generating the comic that we should be obliged, *simultaneously or in rapid succession*, to apply to one and the same act of ideation two different ideational methods, between which the "comparison" is then made and the comic difference emerges. Differences in expenditure of this kind arise between what belongs to someone else and oneself, between what is usual and what has been changed, between what is expected and what happens.[73]

Pursuing such examples further is justified only if Freud's ideas about "mimetic representation" and surplus psychic energy are reasonable, and, as I said, they aren't. My overall assessment of the Relief Theory in its simple and complex forms is that it is based on an outdated hydraulic theory of the mind.

The Minority Opinion of Aristotle and Thomas Aquinas: Humor as Playful Relaxation

While the overwhelming number of Western thinkers who commented on humor before the twentieth century criticized it, there were a few who appreciated its value. The most important were Aristotle and Thomas Aquinas, who treated humor as a virtue, under the right conditions. Aristotle discussed wittiness (*eutrapelia*, literally "turning well") in the *Nicomachean Ethics*, Book 4, alongside truthfulness and friendliness:

> Since life includes relaxation as well as activity, and in relaxation there is leisure and amusement, there seems to be here too the possibility of good taste in our social relations, and propriety in what we say and how we say it. And the same is true of listening. It will make a difference here what kind of people we are speaking or listening to. Clearly, here, too, it is possible to exceed or fall short of the mean. People who carry humor to excess are considered vulgar buffoons. They try to be funny at all costs, and their aim is more to raise a laugh than to speak with propriety and to avoid giving pain to the butt of their jokes. But those who cannot say anything funny themselves, and are offended by those who do, are thought to be boorish and dour. Those who joke in a tactful way are called witty (*eutrapelos*), which implies a quick versatility in their wits. For such sallies are thought to be movements of one's character, and, like bodies, characters are judged by their movements. The ridiculous side of things is always close at hand, however, and most people take more fun than they should in amusement and joking.[74]

As examples of impropriety and propriety in humor, Aristotle contrasts the Old Comedy of writers like Aristophanes, in which "the ridiculous element was obscenity," with the more sophisticated New Comedy of writers like Menander, who "tend toward innuendo."

Aristotle's comments on humor were neglected until medieval times, when Thomas Aquinas expanded upon them. In Question 168 of his *Summa Theologiae*[75] he discusses humor as a kind of play, in three articles: "Whether there can be virtue in actions done in play," "The sin of playing too much," and "The sin of playing too little." His view mirrors Aristotle's: humans need to rest occasionally from serious activity, and humor and other forms of play provide that rest.

As bodily tiredness is eased by resting the body, so psychological tiredness is eased by resting the soul. As we have explained in discussing the feelings, pleasure is rest for the soul. And therefore the remedy for weariness of soul lies in slackening the tension of mental study and taking some pleasure. In Cassian's Conferences it is related of blessed John the Evangelist that when people were scandalized at finding him at play with his disciples, he requested one of his questioners who carried a bow to shoot an arrow. When this had been done several times, the man, on being asked whether he could keep on doing so continuously, replied that the bow would break. Whereupon the blessed John pointed the moral that so, too, would the human spirit snap were it never unbent. Those words and deeds in which nothing is sought beyond the soul's pleasure are called playful or humorous, and it is necessary to make use of them at times for solace of soul.[76]

The person with the moral virtue associated with play and humor Aquinas calls "a *eutrapelos*, a pleasant person with a happy cast of mind who gives his words and deeds a cheerful turn."[77] Aquinas also judges the unwillingness to engage in humor a vice. To Aristotle's comment that the humorless person is crude, Aquinas adds that such a person is acting "against reason":

Anything conflicting with reason in human action is vicious. It is against reason for a man to be burdensome to others, by never showing himself agreeable to others or being a kill-joy or wet blanket on their enjoyment. And so Seneca says, "Bear yourself with wit, lest you be regarded as sour or despised as dull." Now those who lack playfulness are sinful, those who never say anything to make you smile, or are grumpy with those who do.[78]

In the other articles in Question 168, Aquinas shows his awareness of the traditional rejection of humor, by warning that humor and other play must include nothing obscene, injurious, or insolent, and that it must not make us neglect our moral responsibilities. But with those caveats, he presents humor, and play generally, as a valuable part of life.

Now these few comments hardly provide even a sketch of a philosophy of humor. But in light of the overwhelmingly negative assessments of humor from other philosophers, they are at least a start.

The Relaxation Theory of Robert Latta

One recent philosopher who has put relaxation at the center of his theory of humor is Robert Latta, whom we saw earlier as a critic of the Incongruity Theory.[79] Here is a condensed version of his Theory L:

The subject becomes unrelaxed . . . Then, in response to a stimulus event . . . he makes a rapid cognitive shift, as for instance in interpretation, orientation, expectation, or object of attention . . . which leaves initial-stage unrelaxation without object, point, ground, or function . . . Then he relaxes rapidly . . . through laughter . . . and experiences . . . the pleasure of humorous laughter, the fundamental pleasure of humor.[80]

Latta's idea of "initial-stage unrelaxation" is reminiscent of Spencer's and Freud's idea of built-up emotional energy. But Latta says that while unrelaxation may involve emotions, it doesn't have to. Small levels of "attentiveness, readiness, or effort" also involve unrelaxation – "even such comparatively relaxed behavior as taking part in everyday conversation just for the sake of talk, or doing easy reading, or idly surveying a familiar scene which promises nothing of unusual interest." In fact, Latta says, "Every normal person is at the initial stage most or all his waking hours."[81] While in this state of unrelaxation, according to Latta, the person experiences a cognitive shift which renders their attention, anticipation, or effort pointless, and they relax quickly through laughter.

Latta's book is a valuable contribution to humor theory, especially for the many ways it challenges incongruity theories. The idea of a *cognitive shift* captures something essential in the experience of amusement, and so in Chapter 3 I will incorporate that idea in my own theory. One kind of cognitive shift Latta mentions, furthermore, is "from engagement to detachment."[82] Here, too, there is overlap with my ideas about what I call "disengagement."

However, I don't think Latta has made a convincing case that relaxation is a defining feature of humor. While some humor involves relaxation, other humor does not. Many cultures have contests of humorous insults, for example. Ancient Germanic peoples called it *flyting*. In Elizabethan England, experts at comic insult were called "roarers"; Ben Jonson wrote a comedy, *The Roarer*. The ritual of comic insults in Trinidad is *picong*. Among African Americans, it is "the Dozens." In these rituals, there may be 40 or 50 funny lines spread over half an hour, with the audience laughing from the first to the last. But nobody relaxes. Their attention and anticipation increase, not decrease. As the participants come up with clever lines, the audience's appetite is whetted for even more clever lines. The funny insults are often based on exaggeration, such as "Yo' mama so fat, she have her own ZIP code." Such exaggerations produce cognitive shifts, as Latta says, but each cognitive shift does not render the audience's attention "without object, point, ground, or function." Instead it rewards and bolsters their attention, making them eager to hear greater and greater degrees of exaggeration. As they continue to laugh, they don't relax, but get more energized by the repartee, psychologically and even physically.

Here Latta might respond that there is relaxation eventually, *after the ritual is over.* Once the humor and laughter *have stopped*, the audience relaxes as they realize that thinking further about the fantastic insults they have heard is "without object, point, ground, or function." But if the insults were inventive, they are likely to stick in the audience's mind and even spur them to think of their own clever insults after the ritual is over. They might also imagine alternative twists to the repartee: "What he *should have* said then was '. . .'!" None of this is relaxation, as Latta understands that term.

While Latta's Theory L and the other theories we have looked at provide some insights into humor, then, none adequately explains the nature of humor, and the whole tradition of philosophy of humor hardly acknowledges, much less explains, the value of humor. In an attempt to do better, I have divided the rest of this book into separate chapters dealing with issues in psychology, aesthetics, and ethics. Then near the end I will return to the not-so-funny relationship between philosophers and humor.

Chapter 2

Fight or Flight – or Laughter

The Psychology of Humor

"*We're from the F.B.I., going from house to house
making sure that everyone is scared shitless.*"

Humor and Disengagement

Philosophers have been writing about laughter and humor since the time of Plato, but *humor* did not mean funniness until the end of the seventeenth century,[1] and only in the eighteenth century were *amusing, funny,* and *comic* used to mean *humorous.* So, through history, most discussions about what we now call humor have centered around laughter.

Before humorous amusement was distinguished from laughter, philosophers usually identified laughter with particular emotions – malice for Plato, self-glory for Hobbes, hatred or joy for Spinoza. After the distinction between amusement and laughter was made, several argued against identifying amusement with this or that emotion, but virtually all philosophers classified humorous amusement as some kind of emotion. I am one of the few to argue that amusement is so different from standard emotions that it is not useful to count it as an emotion at all. Here I will not present all of my arguments in detail,[2] but simply summarize the main ones. My purpose is to show what a unique phenomenon humor is, whether or not we continue to call amusement an emotion.

Emotions typically have four components: (1) *Beliefs and desires* cause (2) *physiological changes,* which together motivate (3) *adaptive actions.* The person's (4) *sensations of those physiological changes* are the "feelings" in emotions.[3]

Suppose that as I am walking past a fence, a Doberman Pinscher runs up to the fence, barking, snarling, and trying to climb over. Instant fear! I believe that the dog is about to attack me, and I desire to avoid being attacked. My belief and desire cause the secretion of epinephrine (adrenaline), and with it increased alertness and muscle tension, the release of blood sugar, faster heartbeat, shallower breathing, trembling limbs, the redistribution of blood away from the surface of my skin (which minimizes bleeding, if I am injured), the cessation of digestion (which saves energy), and other bodily changes. While I don't have sensations of all of these changes, I sense many of them, and my *feelings* of fear are those sensations.

My perception of danger and my desire to avoid it, and the resulting bodily changes, in turn, prompt "fight or flight" actions. With my heightened alertness, and increased energy and muscle tension, I quickly move back from the fence, pick up a stick or rock, and prepare to defend myself.

In anger, the other major "fight-or-flight" emotion, I believe that someone or something is threatening me or something I care about, and I desire to eliminate that threat. My belief and desire cause the release of the hormone norepinephrine, which triggers bodily changes that equip me to fight. I become narrowly focused on the offending person or thing, my breathing and heart rate increase, which brings more oxygen to my muscles, and I assume an aggressive stance. My angry appearance may be enough to get the offending party to back off, but if not, I am likely to attack.

Sometimes, even with fight-or-flight responses, we still get hurt or lose something we value. Then the typical emotion is sadness. The injury or loss has already occurred, so instead of fighting or fleeing, we slow down and withdraw from activity. Human sadness probably evolved from the self-protective reaction of lower animals to injury or sickness, in which the affected part of the body is immobilized and overall body movement is reduced. Withdrawing from activity reduces the chances of aggravating the injury, conserves energy, and so fosters healing and recovery. In humans and the higher animals, too, the negative feeling tone of sadness – the suffering – serves as negative reinforcement, motivating them to prevent similar suffering in the future.

In evolution, emotions promoted the survival of not just the individual, but the group and the species. The affiliative emotions of love and pity have been especially important. Sexual passion leads to mating and reproduction, and parental love motivates nurturing of the young. Pity motivates coming to the aid of group members who might otherwise die.

With this schematic understanding of emotions, we can now ask whether it is useful to classify humorous amusement as an emotion. Those who do so seldom give reasons, but the usual rationale seems to be that amusement has two of the elements mentioned above – physiological changes and sensations of those changes. In laughter, our diaphragms move in spasms, our facial muscles are contorted, our eyes tear, etc. We feel these changes, and, as in positive emotions, these feelings are pleasant.

But if we probe beneath the surface of these similarities, we find striking differences between amusement and standard emotions. In emotions, the bodily changes are caused by beliefs and desires, and those changes, along with the beliefs and desires, prompt adaptive actions. But none of these elements – beliefs, desires, or motivations for adaptive actions – are required in amusement.

At the market last week I found an eggplant with a protuberance in the middle that looked like Richard Nixon's nose. Seeing the eggplant as Nixon's head, I laughed. But I did not have to *believe* that the eggplant was Nixon's head, nor did I need any *desires* about the eggplant for it to amuse me. Fear and anger, by contrast, aren't triggered this easily. If the eggplant had looked like Osama bin Laden, seeing it that way would not have made me feel fear or anger toward it, because I would not have believed that it was threatening, and would not have desired to escape from it.

Several discussions in aesthetics have questioned the claim that emotions require beliefs in the reality of their objects.[4] We often speak of feeling fear, anger, and pity in reading novels, and in watching plays and movies with fictional characters. If these experiences really are emotions, then emotions don't seem to require belief in their objects. What is interesting about this objection in relation to humor is that while it is often raised about emotions in tragedy and melodrama, it is never raised about amusement in comedy. Dozens of articles have been published about whether we really pity Anna Karenina, or fear Dracula, but no one asks whether we are really amused by Falstaff or Daffy Duck. As Robert C. Roberts put it, "There is a presumption of belief-dependence in the case of emotions, which is lacking in the case of amusement."[5] Roger Scruton comments that, "This 'indifference to belief' is an important feature, and explains our reluctance to describe amusement as an emotion. Belief-independent fear – say, a phobia of black dogs – is deemed irrational, while belief-independent amusement is not."[6] In fact, while all standard emotions allow for irrationality, there is no such thing as irrational amusement.

My explanation for all these dissimilarities between amusement and standard emotions is that amusement is not, like emotions, a direct adaptation to dangers and opportunities, and so it does not involve the cognitive and practical engagement of beliefs, desires, and adaptive actions.

Since we need not believe that amusing objects are real, furthermore, we need not have desires about them, either. In negative emotions, the situation evoking the emotion matters to us, we care about it, it's important; and we want that situation to be different. We want the attacking dog to calm down, the bully to back off, the suffering person to recover. In positive emotions – say, joy at running into an old friend – the situation matters to us and we want it to continue. But countless jokes and cartoons feature fictional situations that do not matter to us and that we neither want to change nor want to maintain. Consider, for example, the cartoon about the lion ordering pizza at the beginning of Chapter 3.

Even when the object of amusement is real rather than fictional, no desires are required. To feel fear, anger, or love for people is to have positive or negative desires about them. Those I fear I want to stay away from me; those I love I want close to me. But I don't have to be attracted to or repelled by things I find funny.

If I'm taking a tour of Notre Dame Cathedral in Paris and see a chunk of cheese on a paper plate resting on the altar, I don't have to like or dislike the cheese in order to find its placement funny. We often have a disinterested attitude toward things that we laugh about. But you can't have a disinterested attitude toward the object of one of your emotions. It matters to you; you care about it.

Not only do many objects of amusement not evoke desires, but there is a tension between having desires about something and finding it funny. If a friend of mine is drunk and struggling to stand up, I won't find his awkward movements funny to the extent that I want him to get up smoothly and safely. To laugh at his movements, I have to suspend my practical concern for him. As Henri Bergson put it, humor requires a "momentary anaesthesia of the heart."

> Try, for a moment, to become interested in everything that is being said and done; act, in imagination, with those who act, and feel with those who feel; in a word, give your sympathy its widest expansion; as though at the touch of a fairy wand you will see the flimsiest of objects assume import-ance, and a gloomy hue spread over everything. Now step aside, look upon life as a disinterested spectator: many a drama will turn into a comedy.[7]

Here Bergson could have added the proverb *Qui sent, pleure; Qui pense, rit* (Who feels, cries; who thinks, laughs), or Horace Walpole's observa-tion that "this world is a comedy to those that think, a tragedy to those that feel."[8]

Because we need no beliefs or desires about objects of amusement, there is no need to do anything about them, either. While emotions prompt us to fight, flee, mate, nurture, or take other action in the face of danger or opportunity, amusement is idle. That is why, as Robert C. Roberts has pointed out, "we explain people's actions by referring to their anger, fear, and jealousy, but not by referring to their being amused."[9] This lack of motivation in humor is the basis of many ethical critiques of humor, as we'll see in Chapter 5.

Not only does amusement not motivate specific actions, but the more amused we are, the less capable we are of any action at all. Heavy laughter eliminates the rigidity of the torso, which is essential for gross motor skills. Our breathing is interfered with, our limbs shake, and we lose muscle tone and coordination. Wallace Chafe has even argued that the biological function of laughter is to disable, to incapacitate us.[10]

When afraid or angry, we are ready to run or attack – we're engaged. When we are amused, we may fall down and wet our pants – we're disengaged.

The pleasure of amusement, of course, can motivate us in one way – to keep the amusement going, or to repeat it, as by describing the funny experience to friends. But that motivation is quite different from the motivation in emotions to do something practical about the situation that evoked the emotion. In this respect, amusement is like the aesthetic enjoyment of music or fine art, which is a paradigm of disinterested pleasure. Emotions, by contrast, are paradigms of "interested" states.

So far, in discussing objects of amusement and objects of emotion, I have tried to keep the two logically parallel by referring mostly to persons, things, and situations. But we are amused by more than just those categories. *Bons mots* such as Oscar Wilde's "Work is the curse of the drinking classes," are neither persons, things, nor situations. Consider, too, Steven Wright's line, "I saw a sign that said, 'Twenty-four hour banking' – who's got time for *that?*" And Rita Rudner's "A friend of mine was in labor for 36 hours – I don't even want to do something that feels good *for 36 hours!*" Our amusement at comments like these is quite unlike the object-directed pleasure of an emotion such as love or joy. The words elicit an unexpected sequence of ideas and we enjoy the mental jolt, but there isn't a thing, person, or situation serving as an intentional object, as there is in standard emotions.

Indeed, humorous words don't even have to elicit funny ideas; their sounds alone may make us laugh. I once heard a lecture about the Berber people of North Africa. In the question-and-answer period, someone asked about the Berbers living in the larger towns and cities. The lecturer started her answer with the words, "Well, the *urban* Berbers . . ." The audience chuckled, not at the idea of Berbers in cities, but simply at the awkward *er* sounds.

Even in those cases we have described as having an object of amusement, it can be argued that it is not the thing or person that causes the laughter, but its relation to other things and to our expectations. If we laugh about the piece of cheese on the altar, for example, it is because our perception of its location is jarring.

Amusement and standard emotions, I conclude, involve different orientations to the world. Emotions involve cognitive and practical engagement with what is going on around us. We are serious, focused on dangers and opportunities, and prepared to act to further our interests. What is happening matters to us. The mental framework is Real/Here/Now/Me/Practical. Amusement, by contrast, involves cognitive and practical disengagement from what is going on around us. We are not serious, not concerned about dangers and opportunities, and not prepared to act. With much humor, such as Steven Wright's quip about the 24-hour banking, these aren't even possible.

Since emotions engage us with the situation we're in and amusement disengages us, they tend to suppress each other. I can't be afraid of you or angry at you – that is, feeling the emotions of fear or anger right now – and amused by you at the same time. I might get angry at my boss for micromanaging my work, say, and later, when I've calmed down, I could sit with friends at lunch satirizing the way he is always meddling. Then I might be amused. But this amusement is at the exaggerated satirical representation of the boss, not at the boss's action as it takes place, and my occurrent anger has passed. That's quite different from being amused by the boss's behavior itself at the same time as that behavior makes me angry.

Because of the natural opposition between amusement and negative emotions, we can joke with people to dispel their fear, as with a friend going into surgery. We can joke to calm people down from an angry argument, and to cheer them up when they are sad. And not just negative emotions suppress amusement. In sexual intercourse, for example, if one partner laughs about something, that shows a lack of passion; if they both crack up in laughter, the sex has been sidetracked. In Chapters 5 and 6, we'll see that the opposition between amusement and emotions is at the heart of the ethics of humor.

To repeat the disclaimer at the beginning of this chapter, nothing essential to my account of humor hangs on whether we continue calling amusement an emotion. As long as we understand the disengagement in amusement, we can call it whatever we want.

Humor as Play

We have been focusing on the two aspects of humor most often discussed by philosophers – laughter and amusement. But there is more to humor than *finding* things funny and laughing. Not only are we amused, but we amuse – we do and say things to make other people and ourselves laugh. Indeed, most humor is created by someone.

In amusing people, cognitive and practical disengagement are central. If you show up at your neighbors' door wearing a pirate costume, for example, you don't want them to think you are a real eighteenth-century brigand and wonder how you traveled through time. Nor should they recognize you but think that you've gone insane, and set about finding you professional help. You want them to be jolted by this unusual apparition, of course, but not treat it as a puzzle to be solved, or problem to be dealt with. You want them to simply enjoy it.

Another way of saying that in amusing people we are out for pleasure, and not to gain information or to accomplish anything, is that amusing people is a way of playing with them. In humans and animals alike, play usually occurs in the absence of urgent physiological needs, such as hunger, thirst, and escaping threats.[11] George Santayana defined play as spontaneous activity not carried out under pressure of external necessity or danger.[12] If under activity we include language and thought, we can say that play is disengaged activity. Pointless actions and fantasies are fine, as long as we enjoy them. As Thomas Aquinas said of *ludicra vel jocosa*, playful or joking matters, they are "words and deeds in which nothing is sought beyond the soul's pleasure."[13]

Now, sometimes humor and other kinds of play take the form of non-serious activities that would not be mistaken for serious activities, such as blowing bubbles and making up nonsense syllables. But more often, humor and play are modeled on serious activities. When boys play soldiers, for example, their movements look like aggressive activities, only they suspend the usual purposes, assumptions, and consequences of those activities. The boys aren't really enemies, nothing really explodes, and they only pretend to kill each other.

Similarly, in a conversation, when we joke about something we had just been discussing seriously, we don't switch to a new vocabulary and grammar, but use the same kinds of sentences with which we had been making assertions, asking for information, and doing other serious linguistic jobs. The difference in joking is that we use words in what Victor Raskin calls a *non-bona-fide* way.[14] We may exaggerate wildly, pose questions sarcastically, say the opposite of what we believe, express emotions we don't feel, make hostile remarks to friends, and break other linguistic conventions.

Joking is such a familiar activity that we can overlook how different it is from bona-fide uses of language. In Chapter 1, we saw how it violates Grice's Cooperative Principle and rules such as "Avoid ambiguity" and "Do not say what you believe to be false." It is also revealing to try to apply J. L. Austin's theory of speech acts to joking. Consider his distinction between locutionary acts, illocutionary acts, and perlocutionary acts.

A *locutionary* act is the physical act of uttering a meaningful sequence of words. If you have just asked to borrow my car, for example, and I utter the words "The gas tank is almost empty," I have performed a locutionary act. If I had said, "'Twas brillig, and the slithy toves did gyre and gimble in the wabe," I would not have performed a locutionary act. It is by means of locutionary acts that we convey information, ask questions, give commands, and do other things with words.

An *illocutionary* act is an act performed *in* performing a locutionary act. In saying that the gas tank is almost empty, I am performing the illocutionary act of *advising* you that you'll need to put fuel in the car.

A *perlocutionary* act is an act performed *by means of* performing an illocutionary act. By advising you that you'll need to fuel the car, I get you to fill the tank.

Austin's scheme works well with sincere, bona-fide uses of language, such as assertions, questions, commands, and performatives – promises, vows, apologies, verdicts, etc. But the scheme doesn't work with joking. Suppose that we're talking about how General Motors has recently closed several factories in order to cut costs, and you say, "Next they'll shut down *all* their plants, to really save some money." We can talk of a locutionary act here – your uttering a meaningful sentence. But there is no illocutionary act. In saying that General Motors is going to close down all their plants, you are not reporting, advising, or warning. If I took your utterance to be performing one of these illocutionary acts, and replied, "What a terrible decision! Shutting down all their plants will ruin them," I would show that I had misunderstood your quip.

A critic here might argue that there *is* an illocutionary act performed in saying, "Next they'll shut down *all* their plants, to really save some money." It is *joking* or *amusement*. That's the act you perform in uttering these words. I would answer that while in saying "The gas tank is almost empty," I am *advising you that* you need to put fuel in the car, when you make the quip about General Motors, you are not *joking me that* or *amusing me that* General Motors will close all their plants. Both of us know that GM is *not* closing all their plants, so that plant-closing is not an event you are amusing me about. The scenario is fantasy and is potentially funny precisely for its discrepancy with the facts. If I happen to enjoy that discrepancy, I am amused; if not, not. But amusing me or joking with me isn't an illocutionary act you perform in saying what you say.

When we assert something, give advice, and warn people, we use words in standard ways to bring about certain mental states in our listeners – believing, being concerned, etc. But when you joke about General Motors closing all their plants, you use the standard format of an assertion but without intending that I believe that assertion, or that I believe that you believe it. As we saw earlier, you suspend the guidelines of pragmatics like Grice's rules. If a joke like this confuses a listener, or makes them angry, there's the universal disclaimer – "I was only joking" – to tell them that this is a rogue use of language, so that they should not have expected the rules of language to be followed.

Another way to see how different joking is from uses of language that have illocutionary acts is to consider that when we're out to amuse people, there is a potentially infinite number of ways of doing so. If, as you were thinking up the quip about General Motors closing all their plants, you thought of a funnier one – about General Motors, or anything else – you might have uttered that other quip instead. All that counts is whether your words amuse me, and it doesn't much matter how that is done. Indeed, if silently making a funny face would be funnier yet, you might do that instead. We can see this latitude, and suspension of the pragmatics of ordinary language use, in the performances of stand-up comedians, who typically don't have a particular set of items to be presented. Instead they will say, or do, whatever seems likely to amuse the audience at any particular moment. That may be making wisecracks about the venue, jumping into a routine about the airlines, asking the couple in the third row if they're married, or doing something funny with the microphone. None of this freedom applies to bona-fide communication, of course. If my intention is to advise you that you'll need to put gas in the car, not just any words or actions will accomplish that.

Humorous uses of language often *look like* assertions, warnings, or advice, of course. Indeed, they often employ exactly the same words as a bona-fide use of language. But in humor the speaker is putting ideas into listeners' heads not to cause beliefs or actions, but for the pleasure that entertaining those ideas will bring. And listeners think about those ideas not to reach the truth about anything, or to figure out what to do, but just for the fun of it. Joking, I conclude, is a special play mode of using language in which we suspend ordinary rules of communication and give each other comic license to say anything, as long as the group enjoys it. As Thomas Aquinas said, there is but one criterion for successful joking and successful play – pleasure.

Laughter as a Play Signal

Analyzing humor as a kind of play helps us answer a question neglected by most philosophers studying humor: Why is amusement associated with that particular pattern of facial expressions, spasmodic vocalization, and other physiological events we call laughter? Couldn't amusement have been expressed in a wiggling of the toes or a trembling of the elbows? Or couldn't it have been an undetectable private state, like imagining Chinese red? A promising answer to such questions comes from ethologists studying play in animals. They suggest that laughter evolved as a play signal.

Because the quip about General Motors is absurd, few people would mistake it for a serious assertion. But in most humor and other play, what is said or done is closer to a serious utterance or action, and so there is a danger of misinterpretation. In social interactions, the non-serious is often interspersed with the serious, and we need to be able to distinguish them. One way we do this is through play signals. When saying or doing something non-seriously – as a joke, in jest, for fun, without meaning it, only fooling, just kidding – we often use words, facial expressions, and body language to tip off people about what we're up to. There are conventional markers for most forms of humor and play. If in conversation I say, "Have you heard the one about . . . ?" you know that I'm starting a joke and not a true story. If we're at a circus and three people in outlandish costumes ride into the ring on tiny bicycles, we know that whatever happens in the next few minutes is not to be taken seriously.

Without such cues, humor and other forms of play can easily be misunderstood. A good example is a routine done many times by Andy Kaufman (1949–84) in which he crowned himself the "Inter-Gender Wrestling Champion of the World," and bragged that he could "defeat any woman alive." Kaufman's fame as a comedian on *Saturday Night Live* was not enough of a play signal for many in his audiences, and so, in several cities, angry women came forward intent not just on pinning him for the $1,000 prize, but on hurting him. This stunt can be seen as a practical joke, like those on *Candid Camera*, that's missing the revelation that it's just for fun.

The lesson here is that when we switch from a serious to a play mode, we need a way of letting people know that what we are doing and saying is not serious. Otherwise, they may be offended and may even take violent action against us.

In the lower animals, the need for play signals is even more obvious, since most of their play takes the form of aggressive chasing, grabbing, and biting. Several ethologists believe that mock-aggression and defense were the earliest forms of play in animals, from which all other play developed.[15] Without a way to distinguish between being chased, grabbed, or bitten *playfully* and being attacked, they might turn play into deadly fighting. And so mother dogs, for example, initiate play with their puppies by rubbing faces with them, and gently biting or pawing at them. Howler monkeys start off rough-and-tumble play by making twittering squeaks to each other.

Ethologists, beginning with Jan van Hooff, have speculated that the first play signals in humans evolved from two facial displays in earlier primates. One was the "silent bared-teeth display," also called the "grin face" or "social grimace," which probably evolved into social smiling. The other was the "relaxed open-mouth display," or "play face," which probably evolved into laughter.[16]

In the silent bared-teeth display, the corners of the mouth and the lips are retracted, exposing the gums; the jaws are closed; there is no vocalization; body movement is inhibited; and the eyes are directed toward an interacting partner.[17] In most primates, this grin is similar to the aggressive, staring, *open-mouth* display evoked by threats, and it appears to have evolved from that aggressive face. The bared-teeth grin seems to have started both as a protective response (drawing back the lips is preparation for either biting or expelling something noxious from the mouth), and as a response to startling stimuli. Van Hooff speculated that in primate evolution, there was a progressive broadening of the meaning of baring the teeth. Originally defensive, over time it became a signal of submission and non-hostility. In species like ours, the silent bared-teeth display became "a reassuring and finally a friendly signal," the social smile.[18]

The second facial display van Hooff studied is the relaxed open-mouth face that primates show during playful chasing and mock-fighting. When one animal is really attacking another, the mouth is tense and prepared to bite hard. Playful biting, by contrast, is gentle and doesn't break the skin, so it is preceded by the relaxed open-mouth display, which, because it looks different, is not seen as threatening. The visual stimulus of the play face is usually accompanied by a sound stimulus – shallow, staccato breathing, similar to panting, which in chimpanzees is vocalized as "Ahh ahh ahh." Bonobos, gorillas, orangutans, baboons, and rhesus macaques make similar laugh-like sounds.[19] Together, the play face and the shallow staccato breathing send the message "This is just play, not real fighting." An easy way to elicit that face and laugh-like vocalization in apes is through the playful grabbing and poking we call tickling.[20] They also show that face and vocalization during rough-and-tumble play.

In human evolution, according to van Hooff and others, the friendly, silent, bared-teeth display became our social smile of appeasement.[21] The relaxed open-mouth display and its accompanying vocalization became laughter. As humans began walking upright, the front limbs were no longer used for walking and running, and so the muscles in the thorax no longer had to synchronize breathing with locomotion. That, combined with the lower position of the larynx (voice box) in the throat and the development of the pharynx, made it possible for humans to modulate their breathing and vocalize in more complex ways than the cries and calls of the lower primates.[22] They eventually would develop speech, but before that, they came to laugh in our uniquely human ways. Instead of the chimp vocalization "Ahh ahh ahh" on the in-breath, they produced "Ha ha ha" on the out-breath. And, with breathing decoupled from locomotion, they did not have to exhale once per step, as apes inhale once per step. While moving, their laughter could take many rhythms and forms – eventually, the guffaw, titter, chuckle, horse laugh, snicker, giggle, etc.

The hypothesis that laughter evolved as a play signal is appealing in several ways. Unlike the Superiority, Incongruity, and Relief Theories, it has a ready explanation for the stereotypical sound of laughter – as an easily recognized cue to the group that they could relax. It also explains why laughter, considered separately from humor, is overwhelmingly a social experience, as those theories do not. According to Robert Provine, who recorded 1,200 examples of laughter in conversations and had his students record the situations in which they laughed, we are 30 times more likely to laugh when we're with other people than when we're alone.[23]

The idea that laughter evolved as a play signal explains another feature of laughter revealed by Provine's research – that in conversation "most laughter is not a response to jokes or other formal attempts at humor."[24] Fewer than 20 percent of comments preceding laughter in Provine's sample were judged to be even remotely humorous.[25] These are typical of things people said before they laughed:

- Can I join you?
- I'll see you guys later.
- How are you?
- Does anyone have a rubber band?
- It was nice meeting you, too.
- Are you sure?
- I hope we all do well.
- Do you want one of mine?
- I think I'm done![26]

In conversation, there are times when laughter follows a witty comment or funny story, of course, but most of the time laughter seems to be simply a social gesture, signaling other people that we are friendly and they can relax with us.

Understanding laughter as evolving from a play signal is also promising as we turn now to ask how humor might have evolved.

Chapter 3

From Lucy to "I Love Lucy"

The Evolution of Humor

"Thin-crust, no onions, with extra zebra and wildebeest."

What Was First Funny?

Television programs about human evolution often dramatize how hominids began to walk upright, use tools, and harness fire, but we never see them laughing. Archaeologists can inspect the leg bone of a pre-human ancestor like Lucy, from 3 million years ago, to determine how she walked, but there is no funny bone to reveal if or how she laughed. And even with early *Homo sapiens*, there are no funny stone tools or cave paintings. In thinking about how early humans laughed and how humor evolved, then, we have to work with indirect evidence.

Jan van Hooff provided one useful clue, as we have seen. It is that chimpanzees, bonobos, gorillas, and orangutans have a laugh-like vocalization that accompanies a relaxed open-mouth play face, during tickling and rough-and-tumble play. Humans came from the same evolutionary line as these primates, having split off from chimpanzees 6 million years ago, and from the others before that. So it is reasonable to think of our laughter as evolving from a play signal we inherited from a distant ancestor we share with the great apes.[1]

This hypothesis looks more plausible when we consider that young children today laugh during the same activities in which chimps, gorillas, and orangutans show their laugh-like vocalization and play face. Babies first laugh during mock-aggressive activities like tickling, play-biting, and being tossed into the air and caught. Later they laugh in chasing games like "I'm going to catch you and eat you up!" All of these activities would seem dangerous to the child if they were not done in play. Biting, chasing, and grabbing are obviously aggressive. Tickling consists of grabbing and poking vulnerable areas like the stomach and ribs. Throwing a baby, non-playfully, is child abuse. With most babies, even seeing and hearing an adult laugh isn't enough for them to enjoy these aggressive activities, if they don't know the person. But when the mock aggression comes from someone familiar and trusted, who smiles and laughs, the baby usually joins in the play and laughs too.

Since young children laugh during the same activities as those in which apes show comparable play signals, and since the laughter of the earliest humans evolved from primate play signals, the development of humor in children today, from non-humorous stimuli like tickling, may well reveal how humor evolved in our species. To go beyond mere play to humor, early humans, like children today, had to engage in what Kant called "the play of thought" – "the sudden transposition of the mind, now to one now to another standpoint in order to contemplate its object."[2]

As many psychological studies have shown, the development of humor in children parallels their cognitive development.[3] While most infants don't laugh until four months, Jean Piaget describes a 2-month-old who would throw his head back to look at things from a different angle, bring his head back upright, and then throw it back again, laughing loudly as he swung between perspectives.[4] By eight months, peekaboo makes most babies laugh in a similar way.

As infants develop eye–hand coordination, they manipulate things to bring on these perceptual shifts, and they enjoy not only the shifts but their ability to produce them. Piaget cites the case of a 7-month-old who had learned to push aside obstacles to reach what he wanted:

> When several times in succession I put my hand or a piece of cardboard between him and the toy he desired, he reached the stage of momentarily forgetting the toy and pushed aside the obstacle, bursting into laughter. What had been intelligent adaptation had thus become play, through transfer of interest to the action itself, regardless of its aim.[5]

While these laughter-evoking play activities are enjoyable, there is nothing necessarily humorous in them. The stage of development where most theorists begin talking about humor is when young children enjoy exercising cognitive skills in a way they know to be somehow *inappropriate*, rather than just exhilarating. The fun here seems to be in violating a pattern that the child has learned.

Paul McGhee distinguishes four stages in the development of humor. The first, arising in the child's second year, he calls "Incongruous Actions toward Objects." Here the child knowingly does something inappropriate with an object, for fun. Jean Piaget reported that his daughter Lucien picked up a leaf and held it to her ear, talking as if the leaf were a telephone, and laughing.[6] At 18 months, his other daughter, Jacqueline, said "soap" and rubbed her hands together, but without any soap or water. Soon after that, she pretended to eat non-edible things such as paper, saying "Very nice."[7] Piaget accounts for such cases by saying that in treating one thing as if it were another thing, the young child is manipulating mental images, superimposing the schema of telephone, for example, onto the leaf.

The second stage of humor, according to McGhee, is the "Incongruous Labeling of Objects and Events." Once the child is comfortable with the names of things, actions, and events, she can play by misusing words. At 27 months, Piaget's daughter Jacqueline pointed to a rough stone and said, "It's a dog." Asked, "Where is its head?" she said, "There," pointing to a lump on the stone. "And its eyes?" "They've gone!" Three months earlier, Jacqueline "opened the window and shouted, laughing: 'Hi boy' (a boy she met on her walks and who was never in the garden). Then, still laughing, she added: 'Over there!'"[8]

The incongruous labeling of objects and events shades into McGhee's Stage 3, "Conceptual Incongruity." Once children have developed concepts for Mommy, Daddy, dog, cat, etc., which include their standard features, they can violate those concepts for fun. Dogs bark, for example, while cats meow. So when a child thinks of the reverse, that violates her concept and can amuse her. Kornei Chukovsky describes his daughter's first joke, at 23 months:

> My daughter came to me, looking mischievous and embarrassed at the same time – as if she were up to some intrigue. . . . She cried to me even when she was still at some distance from where I sat: "Daddy, oggie-miaow!" . . . And she burst out into somewhat encouraging, somewhat artificial laughter, inviting me, too, to laugh at this invention.[9]

Children in Stage 3 are highly visual, and so incongruous pictures amuse them, such as a drawing of an elephant in a tree.

McGhee's Stage 4 is "Multiple Meanings." At about age seven, children can appreciate riddles based on double meanings and phrases that sound the same, such as:

> Why won't you ever be hungry in the desert?
> Because of the sand which is there.

From age eight on, children's humor gradually becomes more grown-up, with cleverness, funny stories, and style in telling them becoming more important.

As children develop humor, then, they play in progressively more sophisticated ways with mental images, words, and concepts. They think in a way that is disengaged from conceptual and practical concerns – for fun rather than to orient themselves or to accomplish anything. They hold ideas in their heads, but in a way that makes no demands on them. The medium for most of this activity is language, especially language about what the child knows is not real. While make-believe is not necessary for humor, it is usually the easiest way to be sure that what is happening does not make cognitive or practical demands.

For early humans to develop humor, I suggest, they had to acquire this ability to play with thoughts. Playing requires security, as we have said, and life in the Pleistocene era was more dangerous than the lives of babies today. So I doubt that the first humor on Earth was in a game of make-believe like those of Piaget's daughters. A more likely candidate for the first humor would be a sudden reinterpretation of some perceptual experience, such as what the neuroscientist V. S. Ramachandran calls "False Alarm" laughter.[10] Like humorous make-believe in young children, it involves having a perception or idea without that perception or idea making cognitive or practical demands. To see what might have been involved in this disengaged mental processing, and how it might have benefited early humans, imagine the following scenario.

A band of early humans is walking across the savanna, when they spot a lion in the clearing ahead. They freeze in their tracks for a moment, but then they see that the lion is feasting on a zebra and doesn't even look up at them. With the sudden realization that the lion is not a threat, they laugh, signaling to each other "We're safe. We can enjoy this."

A more sophisticated kind of early humor might have looked like this. A group is sitting around a fire at night, when they see what looks like a horned monster coming through the tall grass. If it really is an invader, then they should be serious and emotionally engaged. Fear or rage would energize them to escape, or to conquer the monster. But what if "the monster" is actually their chief returning to camp carrying an antelope carcass on his head? Then their fear or rage not only will waste time and energy, but could easily lead to pointless killing. In that case, what they need is a quick way to block or to dispel fight-or-flight emotions. They need to disengage themselves and play with their perceptions and thoughts, rather than act on them.

They already have laughter as a play signal for potentially dangerous activities like rough-and-tumble play. Here they extend that play signal to a potentially dangerous experience: the horned-monster apparition. When someone in the group realizes that the monster is actually the chief, their cognitive shift evokes the play signal of laughter. That interferes with their breathing, lowers their muscular coordination, and eliminates the rigidity of the torso that is necessary for large motor activities.[11] So the laughing person is obviously no longer about to attack the chief – or even able to do so. The distinctive look and sound of their laughter signals "false alarm" to the others, telling them that they can relax too.[12] Among a group ready to attack or to flee, laughers would stand out for their lack of purposeful action and muscle control, and for their distinctive spasmodic vocal sounds.

The power of that "false alarm" signal shows today in laughter's contagiousness. It spreads quickly through a group, with each person's laughter tending to increase that of the others. That's why television sitcoms use "laugh tracks" and comedy nightclubs put the chairs and tables close together. Indeed, we don't even have to know what people are laughing about in order to "catch" their laughter. If you approach a group of friends laughing hysterically, you may begin to laugh before anyone explains what's funny.

False Alarm laughter is common today in both children and adults. In one psychology experiment, students are told that they will be handling rats. When they approach the cages and see toy stuffed rats, they usually laugh. V. S. Ramachandran tells of being in an upstairs bedroom when he heard a vase crashing downstairs. Thinking there was a burglar in the house, he steeled himself and walked to the top of the stairs, only to see his cat scurrying out of the living room. Instantly, he laughed.[13]

In False Alarm laughter situations, early humans did something more sophisticated than in tickling or mock-wrestling. They played with a cognitive shift, a rapid change in their perceptions and thoughts. The dangerous lion was suddenly a big cat enjoying its dinner. The monster suddenly became the chief. It was this ability to suddenly see things in new ways and enjoy the mental jolt, I suggest, that marked the transition from simple play to humor.

Once our distant ancestors had experienced the pleasure in False Alarm laughter repeatedly, they would have started creating similar situations for more fun. And here they would naturally get into make believe like that of children today. After the tribe laughed on discovering that the monster was their chief, someone may have re-enacted the funny event by putting animal horns on her own head and skulking through the grass. If that got laughs, she might have gotten a bigger set of horns or found a prop that made her look dangerous in a different way.

There are two possibilities with the re-enactment of the Attack of the Horned Monster. It could be done with everyone's knowledge, so that they all enjoyed the discrepancy between the horned monster and their clowning friend. That may have been the first comedy, indeed, the first drama of any kind. Secondly, the re-enactment could be done as a trick played on someone unaware of the pretending involved. At first that person would be scared, and then perhaps laugh on discovering there was no danger. The pranksters themselves would laugh not just at the horned monster that wasn't a monster, but at the tricked person's initial fear. Something like this was probably the first practical joke. The fun here may have led the laughing band to create other inappropriate-fear scenarios from scratch, such as by putting a dead snake on someone's food. Young children today laugh uproariously when they think they've tricked adults in ways like this.

Impersonating, mimicking, and pretending generally, of course, were central in the development of comedy. Make-believe *with* the audience's knowledge became stage comedy, clowning, mime, satire, parody, caricature, comic storytelling, joke telling, film comedy, and stand-up comedy. Kendall Walton has even argued that such make-believe is at the heart of all the representational arts.[14] Pretending *without* the audience's knowledge became practical jokes, spoofs, pulling someone's leg, *Candid Camera*, etc.

The big thing that allowed early humans to play with cognitive shifts, and so to engage in humor, was language. The easiest way to play with thoughts is to play with words. And the same change to an upright posture that made laughter possible made speech possible. As Robert Provine explains, "The evolution of bipedalism set the stage for the emergence of speech by freeing the thorax of the mechanical demands of quadripedal locomotion and loosening the coupling between breathing and vocalizing."[15] With speech, humans could recall past funny events like the Attack of the Horned Monster, just as families and friends today tell and retell funny stories from their shared past. They could add fictional details as they retold the stories, or create funny fantasies from scratch. Instead of manipulating things like animal carcasses to create humor, they could simply use words to describe funny situations.

Language also made possible two techniques that became central to comedy – the wild comparison and the wild exaggeration. If someone did something clumsy, someone else could compare them to a turkey or a dodo, and perhaps confer these as nicknames. Refined, that became wit. Exaggeration, perhaps the single most important comic technique, is easier in language and would have started early. Twenty thousand years ago, comments like "He was so scared that . . ." were probably among the top 10 funny lines.

Another source of pleasure made possible by language was playing with the sounds of words, and with multiple meanings, as in puns and double entendres.[16]

Humor eventually became part of all cultures and was institutionalized in dozens of ways, most notably comic storytelling. Hundreds of the world's myths are about trickster figures who play practical jokes and have tricks played on them. Many tricksters are animals, such as Coyote, Crow, and Rabbit in North America, and Reynard the Fox in Europe. The Winnebago, native to what is now Illinois and Wisconsin, had four dozen trickster tales, which other tribes adapted.[17] Here is "Trickster Loses His Meal" as told by the Anishinaabe:

One day Manabozho (Hare) killed a big moose. But as he was about to take a bite, a nearby tree made a loud creaking noise in the wind. Manabozho rebuked the tree for making noise, but as he turned back to his meal, the tree made the noise again. This time he climbed the tree to deal with the creaking branches, but the wind blew and he got trapped in the fork of the tree. Just then a pack of wolves came along. Manabozho yelled, "There's nothing over here. What are you looking for?" The wolves realized who it was and headed toward the voice. They found the moose and ate every last bit until nothing was left but the bones. The next day the wind shifted the tree branches again, and Manabozho got free. He thought to himself, "I shouldn't have worried about little things when I had something good in my grasp."

Monarchies from ancient Egypt and China to nineteenth-century Europe institutionalized humor in the form of the court jester, giving him permission to poke fun at the ruler and the court as no one else could.[18] Many religions celebrate a jester or fool figure. Islam has Nasreddin. Russian Orthodox Christianity has canonized three dozen Holy Fools. Dozens of North American native tribes have sacred clowns. The Ojibwa call them *windigokaan*; the Lakotah call them *heyokas*. They burlesque leaders and rituals, break rules, and ask questions no one else would. A basic gag is to reverse something, as by wearing clothes inside out or riding a horse backwards.

Many ancient religions ritualized anarchic comic behavior not just for priests but for everyone. Hinduism has Holi, a spring festival in which people play practical jokes, douse each other with water and paint, and in general act silly. Eastern Orthodox Christianity celebrates the week after Easter in a similar way, with people playing tricks on each other, as God tricked Satan with the resurrection of Jesus. In Bavaria in the fifteenth through eighteenth centuries, *Risus Paschalis* (Easter Laughter) involved sermons based on funny stories. Before that, medieval Christians had the Feast of Fools and the Feast of Asses, which, like Roman Saturnalia, held at the same time, let people mock authority and tradition, and in general, lighten up. That spirit survives today in Mardi Gras and Carnival.

In Greece in the fifth century BCE, behavior like this gave rise to "*komoidia*," comedy. The word originally meant "the song of the komos," a *komos* being a band of revelers worshipping Dionysus, god of "wine, women, and song." Often held in the spring, these festivals celebrated fertility, and often a huge phallus was carried on a pole or cart. As these events became more scripted, the performances of individual actors were added to the singing of the chorus, and dramatic comedy was born.

The early comedies of writers like Aristophanes, later called Old Comedy, abounded in sex, food, and drink, and often ended with revelry, as at a wedding banquet. Rites of Dionysus sometimes figured in the plot, and male characters wore large leather phalluses. In line with its origins in fertility rites, Old Comedy celebrated country life, and it mocked politicians, rich people, and other city-types. Political figures and institutions were challenged, as in *Lysistrata*, named after the comic heroine who leads the women of Greece in a sex strike to protest their men's constant warfare. The influence of Old Comedy on European literature shows up in writers like Rabelais, Cervantes, and Swift, and in contemporary buffoonery and political satire.

Greek New Comedy, discussed by Aristotle, began in the last part of the fourth century BCE. Its most famous writer was Menander. Though almost all the plays have been lost, they were imitated in the comedies of the Romans Plautus and Terence. Here the chorus has been eliminated, the style is more realistic, and the themes are more domestic and romantic than political and satirical. In place of mockery and fantastic situations are scenes from daily life with bragging soldiers, clever slaves, and young lovers trying to deal with stern fathers. That approach to comedy has been standard ever since, and can be seen in Shakespeare and Ben Jonson, and today in TV sitcoms and romantic comedies.

Given the centrality of language in the development of humor, both in our species and in children today, it's reasonable to think that if other primates developed language, they might develop humor too. In the last few decades, this hypothesis has been borne out by the gorillas, chimpanzees, bonobos, and orangutans who have learned various languages.[19] The most famous, Koko the gorilla, has over a thousand signs in American Sign Language. While gorillas in the wild have a laugh-like breathing pattern during tickling and rough-and-tumble play, they don't show evidence of the cognitive play of humor. But once Koko had a basic competence in using signs, she began to do what young children do when they have mastered words – she played with them. According to Francine "Penny" Patterson, Koko's trainer and friend, on December 10, 1985, Koko took a folder that she had been working with and put it on her head, signing "hat."[20] Similarly, Moja, a chimpanzee trained to sign by Roger Fouts, called a purse "shoe," and put the purse on her foot to wear.[21] Like Piaget's daughter pretending that the leaf was a telephone, this fits into McGhee's Stage 1 of humor development, "Incongruous Actions toward Objects."

McGhee's Stage 2, "Incongruous Labeling of Objects and Events," can be seen in this exchange between Koko and one of her keepers, Cathy:[22]

The dispute had begun when Cathy showed Koko a poster picture of Koko that had been used during a fund-raising benefit. Cathy had signed to Koko, *What's this?* by drawing her index finger across her palm and then pointing to the picture of Koko.

Gorilla, signed Koko.
Who gorilla? asked Cathy, pursuing the conversational line in typical fashion.
Bird, responded Koko.
You bird? asked Cathy, not about to let Koko reduce the session to chaos.
You, countered Koko, who by this age was frequently using the word bird as an insult.
Not me, you bird, retorted Cathy.
Me gorilla, Koko answered.
Who bird? asked Cathy.
You nut, replied Koko, resorting to another of her insults. (Koko switches bird and nut from descriptive to pejorative terms by changing the position in which the sign is made from the front to the side of her face.)
    After a little more name-calling Koko gave up the battle, signed, *Darn me good*, and walked away signing *Bad*.

Now sometimes Koko's incongruous labeling of things and people seems to arise simply from annoyance with her trainers, as when she calls them "dirty toilet,"[23] but other times it is accompanied by a play face, and she seems to enjoy misnaming things for its own sake. While she is no Lucille Ball, she seems to show a sense of humor that at least approaches that of kindergartners.

The Basic Pattern in Humor: The Playful Enjoyment of a Cognitive Shift Is Expressed in Laughter

If this account of the evolution of humor is on the right track, we are now in a position to offer a general account of humorous amusement. Today our humor is more sophisticated than that of early humans. We enjoy lots of complex fantasies, as in jokes, movies, and cartoons; contrast, for example, enjoying the lion cartoon at the beginning of this chapter, with early humans' enjoyment of the discovery that a real lion was no threat. Many of our comedies have three or four stories going on simultaneously. With books, television, and DVDs, we can experience amusement while we are alone. We also engage in clever repartee. Despite our sophistication, however, our humor has much in common with prehistoric humor. The basic pattern is that:

1. We experience a *cognitive shift* – a rapid change in our perceptions or thoughts.
2. We are in a *play mode* rather than a serious mode, disengaged from conceptual and practical concerns.
3. Instead of responding to the cognitive shift with shock, confusion, puzzlement, fear, anger, or other negative emotions, we *enjoy* it.
4. Our pleasure at the cognitive shift is expressed in *laughter*, which signals to others that they can relax and play too.

We can comment on these four aspects of amusement one at a time.

1. The cognitive shift

In the jargon of stand-up comedy, a cognitive shift involves a set-up and a punch. The set-up is our background pattern of thoughts and attitudes. The punch is what causes our thoughts and attitudes to change quickly. In some humor, especially jokes, the first part of the stimulus establishes the background, and the second part serves as the punch. In other humor, our mental background is already in place before the stimulus, and the whole stimulus serves as the punch. If, while taking a walk, we see identical twin adults dressed alike, we may chuckle because that perception conflicts, not with anything else on our walk, but with our assumption that each adult is an individual.

One simple technique in verbal humor is to shift the audience's attention from one thing to something very different, as in Woody Allen's "Not only is there no God, but try getting a plumber on weekends."[24] A more common technique is to make the audience suddenly change their interpretation of a word, phrase, or story to a very different interpretation. Most jokes work that way.

> **My boyfriend and I broke up. He wanted to get married. And I didn't want him to.** (Rita Rudner)

> **When I was a boy, I was told anyone could become President – I'm beginning to believe it.** (Clarence Darrow, while Warren G. Harding was President)

I love cats – they taste a lot like chicken.

Beauty is only skin deep – but ugly goes clear down to the bone.

It matters not whether you win or lose — what matters is whether *I* **win or lose.**

Such shifts of attention or interpretation usually fit the pattern Herbert Spencer called "descending incongruity" – they take us from what is "higher" to what is "lower." When McDonald's Restaurants began serving Egg McMuffins in the morning, Jay Leno said, "Great! Before, I could only eat *two* meals a day in my car." Here the shift is from advantage to disadvantage. Similarly, in his television feature "On the Road," about his travels around the USA, Charles Kurault said, "Thanks to the Interstate Highway System, it is now possible to drive from Maine to California and not see anything."

In humor generally, cognitive shifts tend to be toward what is less desirable, such as failure, mistakes, ignorance, and vices. On television programs featuring funny home videos, for example, the scenes are typically of someone falling down, crashing a bicycle, or sneakily taking the last piece of cake. Comic characters, as Aristotle noted, are worse than average.[25] For all the enjoyment that humor brings, humor is typically not *about* enjoyment, but about problems. Hence Mark Twain's quip that "There is no laughter in heaven."[26]

In general, the greater the contrast between the two states in the cognitive shift, the greater the possible amusement. Woody Allen's jump from asserting atheism to complaining about plumbers takes us from the cosmic to the trivial. But suppose he had written, "Not only is there no God, but innocent people often suffer greatly" or "Not only are doctors' house calls a thing of the past, but try getting a plumber on weekends." Both of those involve transitions, but they are too small and easy to make to have much promise as humor.

Victor Raskin has shown that jokes maximize the difference in the cognitive shift by moving from one *script*, or set of background assumptions, to an *opposed* script – from decent to obscene, for example, or wise to foolish.[27] In Mae West's quip, "Marriage is a great institution – but I'm not ready for an institution," the first phrase makes us think of time-honored traditions, while the second phrase makes us think of being committed to a psychiatric hospital.

In funny real-life experiences, the shift does not have to be between opposites, but it usually involves a significant difference between the mental states. We hear a knock at the door and we approach it thinking someone is going to be on the other side wanting to speak to us. In our heads the script is Answering the Door. If we open it to find two Girl Scouts selling cookies, our second mental state follows the first smoothly; everything is normal. We are still Answering the Door. But if we open the door to discover our dog whapping her tail against it, we undergo a cognitive shift. We reinterpret the sound from a person's knocking to a dog's tail-wagging, and drop our expectation that we will be speaking with someone. No longer Answering the Door, we are Letting the Dog In. Those are not opposite scripts, but they are different enough to jolt us. If we enjoy that jolt, that's amusement. A less drastic cognitive change would be less likely to amuse us. Suppose that we opened the door to find a new telephone book that had just been dropped on the porch. This isn't exactly what we expected – no one wanted to speak to us – but it's close. A human being had knocked on the door to alert us to something. So there is much less possibility for humor here.

Most of what I've said about the cognitive shift in humor is familiar to those who know the Incongruity Theory. What I'm doing can be seen as describing what experiencing incongruity is like, without using that often vague term.

2. The play mode

There is nothing automatic about enjoying cognitive shifts. Our perceptions, thoughts, and attitudes are the guidance system for our lives, and any rapid change in them threatens our control over what we are doing and what is happening to us. To a lesser or greater degree, when we experience a cognitive shift, we don't know what might happen next or how to proceed. Here the dictionary definition of *puzzled* is illuminating: "to be at a loss what to do." At the minimum, we may be momentarily disoriented; at the maximum, we may see our lives as in danger. So cognitive shifts are potentially disturbing. What biologists call the "orienting reflex" is essential in keeping animals alive, and fight-or-flight emotions equip them to handle surprises when immediate action is called for. So it's perfectly understandable that seriousness is the default mode for us and all other animals. The non-serious play mode is a luxury.

Sometimes the potential disturbance in humor is nothing more than temporary mild confusion, as in listening to non-tendentious word play, and then it is easy to go into the play mode. But most humor, today as in the Pleistocene era, is a reaction to cognitive shifts that could be more threatening, such as facing danger, failing, misunderstanding other people, quarreling with neighbors, etc. Most humor, as we said, has always been about problems.

We have several ways of taking a playful attitude toward problems rather than reacting with cognitive or practical concern. The most obvious is by fictionalizing them. When we tell a joke, draw a cartoon, or produce a film about a fictional situation, we allow our audience the luxury of dropping the concerns they ordinarily have about comparable real situations. Cartoons like those of Charles Addams and Gary Larsen, for example, are full of situations in which someone is about to get hurt or killed. But knowing that those situations are not real, we can treat them playfully. Sympathy doesn't arise to block our enjoyment of the potentially disturbing scene. The more obviously fictional the character is, the easier the play mode is to achieve. Many people are disturbed rather than amused, for instance, by the way the Three Stooges hurt each other with hammers and saws. But I've never heard anyone make similar complaints about the way Roadrunner drops anvils and dynamite on Wile E. Coyote.

Even real problems can be treated playfully under the right circumstances. Distance may be enough to do the trick. Last night my wife and I laughed watching a TV news story about two elephants that had escaped from a circus in Toronto. In the video they were ambling down a residential street, defecating on lawns. Had we been two of those Torontonians cowering behind their curtains, however, it's unlikely that we would have been in the play mode to laugh.

The passage of time also permits us to play with what is potentially disturbing. What puzzled, scared, or angered us last year, or even yesterday, may now be the stuff of funny stories. When old friends reminisce, indeed, many of the events they laugh hardest about were crises at the time. As Steve Allen put it, tragedy plus time equals comedy.

Another factor in comic disengagement is one's role – or better, one's lack of role – in the potentially disturbing situation. If at lunch you spill a blob of ketchup on your shirt that looks like a bullet hole, that might strike me as funny. But I'm less likely to be amused by ketchup on my own shirt. As Will Rogers put it, "Everything is funny if it happens to the other guy." For Mel Brooks, "Tragedy is me cutting my finger, comedy is you falling down a manhole and dying."

These and other psychological phenomena disengage us from situations that would otherwise be disturbing. They "aestheticize" problems so that the mental jolt they give us brings pleasure rather than negative emotions.

While I have been distinguishing cases of amusement from cases of negative emotions, there are times when we seem to experience both. On

March 18, 1999, for instance, the evening news in Britain featured a story about the comedian Rod Hull, who had died falling off his roof while adjusting his TV aerial during a soccer match. Many viewers laughed but then felt awful for doing so. There is also the category of "black humor," where the same story can evoke amusement, shock, disgust, and even horror. In the simple examples of such cases, I suggest, we experience pleasure and negative emotions sequentially, or we oscillate between them. Some of those who laughed about Hull's death initially enjoyed the odd story, but then stopped enjoying it as they felt guilt over their insensitivity. But things can get more complicated. It seems possible for us to enjoy something and *simultaneously* be disturbed by our ability to enjoy it – "guilty pleasure," we call it. Notice here, though, that the object of pleasure and the object of displeasure are different. Consider those who were amused by the news of Hull's death, and *at the same time* felt guilty. They were disengaged enough from the suffering of Hull and his family to enjoy *the odd way he died*. And, while still enjoying that, they experienced negative emotions about *their own ability to enjoy such a thing*.

3. The enjoyment

We all know that it feels good to laugh and most philosophical analyses of amusement include pleasure as an essential element. But few philosophers have said much about that pleasure. I want to say three things about the pleasure in humor – it is social, exhilarating, and liberating.

First, the natural setting for humor, as for play generally, is a group, not an individual. Kierkegaard asked a friend, "Answer me honestly . . . do you really laugh when you are alone?" He concluded that you have to be "a little more than queer" if you do.[28] According to Henri Bergson, "You would hardly appreciate the comic if you felt yourself isolated from others. Laughter appears to stand in need of an echo."[29]

It's hard to get into the play mode by oneself. Often when I experience events alone, especially those involving setbacks, I don't see the humor in them until I am later describing them to other people. And even if I experience an event as funny while I'm by myself, it's unlikely that I'll enjoy it *as much* as when I later share it in conversation.

A few years ago I spent two weeks by myself building a house on a lake, far from the nearest neighbors, and without a telephone. The work went well and was satisfying. I made some goofy mistakes and had a few lucky surprises. A flying squirrel nesting under the eaves made odd noises at night. A flock of wild turkeys made even stranger sounds as they ran across the path outside the kitchen window. Had I been with someone,

I would have found humor in most of these events. But being alone, I found almost nothing funny.

When we are alone, of course, we can read funny books and watch funny programs on television. But these recent forms of humor are built upon our abilities to communicate and interact with other people. For 98 percent of human history there was no writing and all funny stories were social performances. Even with the invention of writing, most reading was public recitation to a group, until the popularization of printing just five centuries ago. Even when people began to read printed books privately, they usually thought of themselves as in communication with the author, like people listening to a storyteller. A standard format for novels well into the nineteenth century was one person telling another person a story, as if they were together. Here, for example, is a passage from the beginning of Charlotte Bronte's *Shirley*:

> Yet even in those days of scarcity there were curates: the precious plant was rare, but it might be found. A certain favoured district in the West Riding of Yorkshire could boast three rods of Aaron blossoming within a circuit of twenty miles. You shall see them, reader. Step into this neat garden-house on the skirts of Whinbury, walk forward into the little parlour – they are at dinner. Allow me to introduce them to you: – Mr. Donee, curate of Whinbury; Mr. Malone, curate of Briarfield; Mr. Sweeting, curate of Nunally.

Watching humor on television is even stronger evidence that humor is essentially a social pleasure. Programs with a studio audience, such as the late-night talk shows, game shows, and the ones showing funny home videos try to make "our viewers at home" feel as if they are part of a large group. We see and hear other people laughing, and we laugh. Many sitcoms are recorded in front of an audience, and though we don't see them, we hear their laughter, again to make the experience social. Even sitcoms that are not recorded in front of an audience usually add a "laugh track" to create the same social feeling.

Part of the pleasure of laughing with other people is enjoying their company, of course, and this pleasure can be distinguished from amusement per se. So there is no necessary correlation between the amount of laughter and the degree of amusement. Nonetheless, it seems that things are more likely to amuse us, *and* more likely to make us laugh, when we are with other people.

A second aspect of the pleasure in humor is that it is lively, or as the psychologist Willibald Ruch says, exhilarating.[30] Kant described joking as the "play of thought" and compared it to the "play of tone" in music and to the "play of fortune" in games of chance. In all three, he said, our changing ideas are accompanied by a "changing free play of sensations . . . which furthers the feeling of health" by stimulating the intestines and the diaphragm.[31] In joking,

> the play begins with the thoughts which together occupy the body, so far as they admit of sensible expression; and as the understanding stops suddenly short at this presentiment, in which it does not find what it expected, we feel the effect of this slackening in the body by the oscillation of the organs, which promotes the restoration of equilibrium and has a favorable influence upon health.[32]

Whatever we may think about Kant's grasp of physiology here, he understands that amusement is not a sedate pleasure, like looking at a lovely sunset, but a lively delight involving mental gymnastics. Aristotle said that witty people have "a quick versatility in their wits."[33] He spoke of "sallies" of witty remarks, comparing lines in conversations to sudden military attacks. As in an exciting battle, in the best humor we're not sure what might happen next.

My third observation about the pleasure in humor is that it is liberating.[34] In the comic mode, people think, say, and sometimes do all kinds of things that are normally forbidden. Extreme examples are the Roman Saturnalia, the medieval Christian Feast of Fools, and Mardi Gras and Carnival. But even the tamer humor of polite joking challenges authority figures and traditional ways of thinking and acting. It gets us out of mental ruts. As Milton Berle said, "Laughter is an instant vacation." In Greek comedy, even the gods were lampooned, and there is an old saying among Hasidic Jews: If God lived on earth, people would break his windows.

In humor we can poke fun at not just civic and religious authorities, but the whole serious approach to life, including what Robert Mankoff, Cartoon Editor of *The New Yorker* magazine, calls "the hegemony of reason." Ever since Aristophanes' *The Clouds* ridiculed Socrates, the pedant and the absent-minded professor have been the butts of jokes. In Chapter 7, we will see how Buddhism incorporates humor into its philosophic method in order to throw a monkey wrench into our ordinary logical thinking. Schopenhauer recognized the liberating pleasure here when he said that, "It must therefore be diverting to us to see that strict, untiring, troublesome governess, the reason, for once convicted of insufficiency."[35]

In the humorous frame of mind, we can challenge any standard belief, value, or convention. Dave Barry is typical of gentle humorists who poke fun at society in a way that doesn't stray far from normal thought patterns. Here are his comments on the jogging craze:

> Running is the ideal form of exercise for people who sincerely wish to become middle-class urban professionals. Whereas the lower classes don't run except when their kerosene heaters explode, today's upwardly mobile urban professionals feel that running keeps them in the peak form they must be in if they are to handle the responsibilities of their chosen urban professions, which include reading things, signing things, talking on the telephone, and in cases of extreme upward mobility, going to lunch.[36]

But humorists can jolt our mental patterns in deeper ways. Consider the value system implied in this stand-up bit by Rita Rudner:

I love to sleep. It really is the best of both worlds. You get to be alive *and* unconscious.

In humor, we also get to challenge the hegemony of reason by giving free reign to imagination. In his essay "Humor,"[37] Freud said that humor does for adults what make-believe play does for children – it allows our thoughts to proceed according to the "pleasure principle" rather than "the reality principle." Like children in fantasy play, adults amusing each other permit any sequence of ideas at all, as long as it brings them pleasure. Consider, for example, the titles of three books by Richard Brautigan: *Sombrero Fallout: A Japanese Novel*, *Revenge of the Lawn*, and *Loading Mercury with a Pitchfork*. Here's a passage from *Sombrero Fallout*:

> He wished he had that avocado now. He would put some lemon juice on it and his hunger would be taken care of. Then he would have something else to worry about. He could return to thinking about his love for the lost Japanese woman or he could occupy his mind with some chicken shit thing of no significance. He never lacked things to worry about. They followed him around like millions of trained white mice and he was their master. If he taught all his worries to sing, they would have made the Mormon Tabernacle Choir sound like a potato.[38]

The pleasure of humor, then, goes far beyond Woody Allen's comment that it's the most fun you can have with your clothes on. Humor gives our minds a workout at the same time it liberates them. Enid Welsford's comment about the traditional comic fool applies to humor generally: it has "the power of melting the solidity of the world."[39] It aestheticizes our experience so that what would otherwise be puzzling, shocking, scary, disgusting, enraging, or saddening becomes the stuff of fun.

4. The laughter

The last element in this analysis of humorous amusement is the most familiar – laughter. People who have never heard of a "cognitive shift" or the "play mode," or even "humor" and "amusement," know about laughter. Before the late seventeenth century, when "humor" and "amuse" acquired their current meanings, there was only the word "laughter" for what are now called "humor," "amusement," and "laughter." Some languages still do not distinguish amusement as mental from laughter as physical. Of those that do, many have simply imported the English word "humor." Lin Yutang, for example, introduced it into Chinese in 1923, and it is now transliterated as "youmo."[40]

The new concept of amusement was based on laughter. *Amuse* meant "to make someone laugh or smile with pleasure"; *amusement* meant "the state of being caused to laugh or smile with pleasure." And there was no active verb for "to be amused" except "to laugh." As Jerrold Levinson says, "The propensity of the state of amusement to issue in laughter is arguably what is essential to its identity, and underpins the widespread intuition that humor and laughter, though not coextensive, are nevertheless intimately related."[41] That is why Levinson puts the tendency of amusement to issue in laughter at the center of his theory of humor.[42]

When we enjoy a cognitive shift, there is a natural tendency to laugh. We don't learn it any more than we learn the disposition to cry; both emerge in normal brain development. In all cultures, babies begin to smile between 2 and 4 months of age, and to laugh shortly after that. Even babies born blind and deaf smile and laugh. In a normal mother–child relationship, the baby's laughter evokes her own, and a virtuous cycle ensues, each one's pleasure and laughter increasing the pleasure and laughter of the other. That shared pleasure increases the mother's affection for the baby and the baby's attachment to her. Later, as the child interacts with other people, sharing laughter establishes a social bond with them. All this fits well with the idea that laughter is a play signal. Between parent and child; between child and sibling; between friends, lovers, colleagues, etc., laughter sends the message, "We are safe. I enjoy this – you enjoy it, too."

If amusement is a kind of pleasure that naturally tends to issue in laughter, it follows that if someone feels no inclination to laugh about something, it does not amuse them. They may understand why other people laugh about it; if it is a joke, they "get" it. But if they feel no inclination to laugh, then it does not give them the kind of pleasure involved in amusement.

Because humor is fundamentally a social experience, someone's failure to share amusement is often a matter of concern. If at a party a friend of ours doesn't laugh once in three hours, we're likely to think that someone offended them or that they are depressed. When something makes us laugh out loud but our friend doesn't even smile, we are likely to ask, "What's wrong?" If someone tries to amuse us with a quip or a joke, but we aren't amused, the polite thing to do is fake a laugh, so that they will think they have succeeded. Fake laughs are physiologically different from the real thing, but the motive here is noble: as in receiving a gift, if someone is trying to please you, you should appear pleased.

Another way to see the linkage of amusement and laughter is to contrast amusement with other ways of enjoying a cognitive shift. In discussing the Incongruity Theory in Chapter 1, we mentioned that the audience at *Oedipus the King* may take pleasure in the mental jolt they get from the ironic lines, such as Oedipus's vow to pursue the murderer of Laius. But that pleasure is not amusement, at least for ordinary audiences of tragedy. The easiest way to distinguish such non-comic pleasure from amusement is to ask: "Is there an inclination to laugh?" We will go into more detail in Chapter 4, but here is an example to test the intuition that the distinguishing feature of amusement as a kind of enjoyment is the disposition to laugh.

The 1960s television program *The Twilight Zone* had an episode called "To Serve Man" that begins with a man named Chambers lying on a table in a spaceship. He gives us a flashback to explain how he got there. One spring day a fleet of alien spacecraft had landed on Earth. The aliens called themselves Kanamits. At the United Nations, they explained that they had come as friends. They offered the delegates new technology, an end to famine, and an invitation to visit their planet. Chambers tells us that, as a decoding expert, he was put on a team assigned to translate a book brought by the Kanamits, whose title had been deciphered as "To Serve Man." The people of Earth soon accepted the Kanamits and their technology. Deserts bloomed and armies were disbanded. In the penultimate scene, people are standing in line, eager to board spaceships headed for the Kanamits' planet, and Chambers is among them. As he is walking up the steps to the ship, his assistant, Pat, who had continued working on translating the Kanamit book, comes rushing toward him. She is held back by the Kanamits, but yells out, "Don't get on the ship. The book – *To Serve Man* – it's a *cookbook*!" Chambers struggles, but is forced aboard the ship. Brought back to the present,

Chambers looks directly at the camera and tells us that it doesn't matter whether we are on the ship with him, or back on Earth: we will all be eaten by the Kanamits.

The plot structure in this drama is like that in thousands of jokes. At the beginning we interpret "To Serve Man" one way, and at the end we shift to an opposite interpretation. Enjoying this shift from Philanthropy to Cannibalism is the basic pleasure in this story. But almost no one laughs at the line "The book – *To Serve Man* – it's a *cookbook!*" I would say that is because this line wasn't meant to be amusing and didn't amuse. And if someone did laugh at it, a natural response of others in the room would be a puzzled or disgusted, "You think that's *funny*?!"

For a simpler test case, try reading to a group of philosophers this sentence attributed to Nietzsche:

The world is beautiful, but it has a disease called man.

Some may not enjoy this statement at all. Others may enjoy it but not be amused by it, perhaps as an insight into European culture. Still others may be amused by it. How can you tell the third group from the other two? By their tendency to laugh.

To summarize, the pleasure in humor has a natural disposition to issue in laughter. That laughter serves as a contagious social signal: "We are safe. I enjoy this – you enjoy it too." And laughter is itself enjoyable. When we think that someone should be amused by something, we expect to see at least the beginning stages of laughter. And when we think that someone should not be amused by something, we do not expect to them to laugh.

However plausible this linking of laughter to amusement might be, it has its critics. The most prominent is Noël Carroll, who offers several counterexamples to what he calls the Dispositional Theory of Humor of Jerrold Levinson (in Levinson's article "Humour" in the *Routledge Encyclopedia of Philosophy*). Thinking over Carroll's arguments, I think, will give us even more insight into the relation of laughter to humor:

> According to Levinson, something is humorous just in case it has the disposition to elicit, through the mere cognition of it, and not for ulterior reasons, a certain kind of pleasurable reaction in appropriate subjects . . . where this pleasurable reaction (amusement, mirth) is identified by its own disposition to induce, at moderate or higher degrees, a further phenomenon, namely, laughter. Thus, for Levinson, humor cannot be detached from all felt inclination, however faint, towards the convulsive bodily expression of laughter.[43]

Carroll argues that while "laughter is a regularly recurring concomitant of humor among standard issue human beings," "I do not think that our concept of humor necessarily requires an inclination towards laughter."[44] As counterexamples to Levinson's Dispositional Theory, he offers "telepathically communicating brains in vats, disembodied gods, and aliens without the biological accoutrements to support laughter or even smiling."[45] Then he adds a fourth counterexample:

> Imagine a community of humans who, as a result of grave cervical cord injuries, lack the ability to move air owing to the inhibition of the muscles in their diaphragm, thorax, chest, and belly. These people cannot laugh, since they do not possess the necessary motor control to respirate, or even to feel any of the pressures that dispose "normals" towards laughter. . . . But surely they, like the gods, could create, exchange, and enjoy in-jokes. . . . Would we say that this society lacked humor?[46]

What can we say about these counterexamples? Do they show that the linkage between amusement and an inclination to laugh is a mere accident of human evolution, and nothing stronger, like a conceptual connection? With concepts as new and as culturally variable as *humor* and *amusement*, it is hard to mount an airtight argument about necessary connections, but I don't think that these counterexamples show that the inclination to laugh is *not* part of our concept of amusement.

(1)   First, the community of "telepathically communicating brains in vats" raises many questions. If there is a community, then these brains perceive other brains as in relation to themselves. Is that done through perceptions of virtual bodies – their own and those of others? If they do have perceptions of virtual bodies, do they have "sensations" of torsos, mouths, and breathing – their own and those of others? If so, don't they have proprioceptive "sensations" of laughing, and visual and auditory perceptions of other virtual bodies laughing? If not, I'm not inclined to say that these brains are amused. Whatever pleasure they have seems like a different pleasure.

If, on the other hand, these brains do not have perceptions of virtual bodies, then what does their experience of persons and things consist in? And what could constitute "societies" here? Until such questions are answered, I don't know whether there is even a concept of persons here, much less a concept of persons who "have humor as a feature of their societies."

(2)   Carroll's second counterexample is also unclear:

> Suppose a community of disembodied gods enjoyed incongruities but neither laughed nor felt sensations of levity, because they lacked the physical equipment. Would we say there was no humor there, even though they create, exchange, and enjoy things that look like jokes . . . Remember that these jokes give them pleasure.

While some theologians have written about persons who never had bodies, there is no clear concept here. The Bible certainly does not describe any god that is non-physical or without a body. Yahweh has a face and hands and resides above the earth. In Psalm 2 it even says that he laughs. What would a person be who did not take up space and was not located in space? How would such a being do anything or experience anything, much less experience incongruities and "create, exchange, and enjoy things that look like jokes." And how could we speak of a "community" of whatever these are? What is there to count? And what is pleasure for something non-physical?

(3)   The third counterexample is more plausible: "communities of . . . aliens without the biological accoutrements to support laughter or even smiling" who nonetheless "have humor as a feature of their societies." We have a well-established genre of science fiction about persons who do not have human biology, and, Carroll argues, "we would not charge a science fiction writer with conceptual incoherency if she imagined an alien society of the sort just mentioned and also described it as possessing humor."[47] Here I would ask for details about what counts as humor in such a society. Suppose that Carroll responds that these aliens "create, exchange, and enjoy things that look like jokes." What is it about their behavior that makes us say their interchanges are *joking*? How can we tell that there is *non-bona-fide* communication going on? How do we know that they are *enjoying* their activities? Do they have typical ways of showing pleasure? Is their pleasure contagious? Part of what humans enjoy in humor is the physical experience of laughing: amusement is not mere pleasure "in the mind" triggering physical manifestations, while laughter is "in the body." And the pleasure and laughter in humor are contagious – one person's pleasure and laughter boost other people's, in a virtuous cycle. Do the aliens have anything comparable?

Maybe we could get enough details here to see strong similarities between what the aliens do, and ourselves engaging in humor. Perhaps the wiggling of their antennae seems to function in their psychology as laughter functions in ours. Then we might say that antenna-wiggling "is their laughter." I am not averse to extending concepts like laughter or amusement; after all, that's how *amuse* and *humor* came to have their current meanings. And if we extend the concept of laughter to the aliens' antenna-wiggling, then perhaps we can ascribe humor to them.

But if the aliens do not have something functionally equivalent to laughter, my intuition, set against Carroll's, is that whatever pleasure they experience is not the same as amusement. Carroll is right that "there are pleasures, such as certain aesthetic and/or intellectual pleasures, that do not require any distinctive bodily sensations."[48] But I don't count amusement among them. Amusement went by the name of "laughter" for millennia, and still does in many cultures, because the inclination to laugh is part of the phenomenon. There is only one kind of person we have experienced – *Homo sapiens* – and in that kind of person, a kind of pleasure evolved along with the play signal laughter.

(4) Carroll's last case is the clearest of the four because it involves human beings with normal brains. Although their severed nerves have left them incapable of laughing, or even breathing on their own, he says that surely they could "create, exchange, and enjoy in-jokes." I agree, but would say that these people are not as badly off as they sound at first. While they cannot laugh, presumably they can smile, and smiling can be a warm-up for laughter. So they have a kind of incipient laughter issuing from their pleasure and signaling that pleasure to other people. Secondly, before their spinal cord injuries, presumably they did laugh when they were amused, and they still have motor impulses to laugh, though these nerve signals never arrive at the muscles in their torsos. If Carroll rejects these two assumptions and narrows his example to people with grave cervical cord injuries *and* paralyzed faces *and* brains that no longer send motor signals to laugh, then it's much harder to imagine his "society" of "injured jokesters." The contagion of laughter and smiling would be missing; whatever pleasure these people experience, it wouldn't spread as amusement does with us. There would be no play signals in their faces, either, so that it would be hard to tell when they were joking. Part of the pleasure of humor, too, is in the physical experience of laughing. They're missing that, as well.

Carroll might respond here that these people still have humor, but humor in a reduced form. At that point, he and I would simply be butting intuitions. As disagreements like this show, "humor" and "amusement" are not old, well-defined terms, but words given several new meanings just three centuries ago. There simply is no single concept of humor and no single concept of amusement for which we can list necessary and sufficient conditions. Often "humor" has been distinguished from "wit," for instance, while many people count wit as a kind of humor. For some people, "humor" includes a kindly attitude toward human foibles; others talk of cynical, misanthropic humor. Theorists like Thomas Schultz don't count the laughter of 4-year-olds at nonsense as humor, saving the term for cases in which incongruity is resolved. Others like Paul McGhee count children's enjoyment of nonsense as humor. Even the *kind* of phenomenon that amusement is has not been agreed upon. Most philosophers count it as an emotion, as we've seen, while Roger Scruton, Robert C. Roberts, and I contrast it with emotion.

We could get around some of these difficulties by stipulating that we will use "humor" in the broadest sense that anyone reputable has used it, so that wit and misanthropic wisecracks will count. That is how most scholars use the term, as in the title of the journal *Humor*. But there would still be marginal cases that no one has made a persuasive case for including in or excluding from the denotation of "humor" and "amusement." Is children's laughter at peekaboo an early stage of humor, for example, or is it not yet humor? If I get a phone call saying that I've won the state lottery and I laugh, is that amusement or just joy? What if I get the call on my cell phone at the courthouse during my bankruptcy hearing? If I'm enjoying a magic act in which a young woman gets into a trunk, and after a tap of the magician's wand, a tiger emerges from the trunk, does my laughter express amusement or just astonishment? How about if the young woman turns into an old man?

In the face of questions like these, I think the best we can do is to explain the ways that "humor" and "amusement" have been used, and analyze paradigm cases that fit under most standard usages of these terms. A search for necessary and sufficient conditions would be futile.

The Worth of Mirth

Although humor, as a kind of play, is for pleasure and not for cognitive or practical gain, it has had many cognitive and practical benefits for the human race, just as play in general has benefited us and other animals.[49] So when I say that humor is not practical, and when I talk about its practical disengagement, I am referring to the attitude of the participants – their lack of practical goals – and am not saying that humor has no benefits.

A parallel with humor here is our enjoyment of music, which we typically listen to not to reach a goal but just because we like the experience. That non-practical motivation is compatible with music's having benefits, such as relaxing us and strengthening social bonds.

Another disclaimer is in order. While humor and other kinds of play are sometimes beneficial, they are not always beneficial, as we will see in Chapter 6.

In exploring the benefits of humor, we can start with the benefits of play in general. The most often mentioned is that in playing, young animals learn skills they will need as adults. In carnivores, for example, play consists largely of the movements of hunting. Young lions stalk, chase, gently bite, and bring each other to the ground, all of which are hunting skills. Similarly, men have been hunting with rocks and spears for millennia, and so boys around the world play by throwing things at targets. Men have also fought with each other from time immemorial, and so boys wrestle and play soldiers.

Studies with rats and with humans have shown how important mock-fighting is in psychological development. Rats deprived of such play grow up unable to judge when and how to defend themselves, and so they swing between excesses of aggression and passivity.[50] A study of sociopathic murderers in Texas revealed no common factor among them *except* a deprivation of childhood play in 90 percent of them.[51]

In playing, animals do not simply go through the stereotypical motions of adult skills, but move in exaggerated ways. Colts at play don't just run, but make split-second turns at high speeds. Young monkeys play by leaping not just from branch to branch, but from trees into rivers. Children at play not only run, but skip, dance, do cartwheels, and stand on their heads. Adolescent boys at play are well known for pushing dangerous actions as far as they can, leading to thousands of deaths a year. Marek Spinka has suggested that in such play, young animals test the limits of their speed, balance, and coordination, and so learn to cope with un-expected situations, such as being chased by a new kind of predator.[52]

What motivates them to play is not anticipation of future benefit, as we said, but the pleasure of the activities themselves. As Michael Lewis put it, "The importance and meaning of play, at least for humans, would appear to be its affective function; in a word, play is fun."[53] The activities that humans and other animals seem to find the most fun are those in which they exercise their abilities in unusual and extreme ways, but in a relatively safe setting. That's a big part of the appeal of sports, for example.

This account of play helps explain the cognitive and practical benefits of humor. We can start with the cognitive benefits. In humor the abilities we exercise in unusual and extreme ways are those of thinking. That is reflected in the original meaning of *wit* – all our intellectual and perceptive powers. Kant, as we said, described wit as "the play of thought." We engage in mental operations such as imagination and putting things into categories, "although nothing is learnt thereby," Kant says. The pleasure comes simply from "the change of representations in the judgment . . . no thought that brings an interest with it is produced, but yet the mind is animated thereby."[54]

In playing with thoughts, we develop our rationality, part of which is processing our perceptions, memories, and imagined ideas in a way that is free from our here and now, and our individual perspective.[55] In the lower animals, mental processing is based on present experience and present needs, and so they react to excessively novel or strange stimuli with practical concern. That concern evokes negative emotions like fear, anger, and sadness, which motivate animals to do something, such as run away in fear, attack in anger, or withdraw from activity in sadness. Humans, by contrast, can think about their experiences abstractly and objectively, and so react to anomalies in non-practical ways such as scientific curiosity, artistic imagination, and humorous amusement.[56]

To become rational, early humans needed a mental mode in which they could be surprised, especially by failure, without going into fight-or-flight emotions such as fear and anger, which inhibit abstract, objective thinking. Humorous amusement is just such a mode. In finding a situation funny, we can transcend practical concern and enjoy its surprising features. Instead of running away or fighting, we can think calmly and playfully about what we have experienced. So humor helps people cope with difficult situations, as psychological studies show.[57] Max Eastman suggested that "we come into the world endowed with an instinctive tendency to laugh and have this feeling in response to pains presented playfully."[58]

The contrast between amusement and negative emotions is found even in their physiology: emotions are centered in the brain's limbic system, while humor is centered in the more rational cerebral cortex. Humorous laughter reduces heart rate, blood pressure, muscle tension, and stress chemicals (epinephrine, norepinephrine, cortisol, DOPAC) in the blood, which increase in fear and anger. And while negative emotions suppress the activity of the immune system, humorous laughter enhances it.[59]

Most of the practical benefits of humor hinge on its emotional disengagement. As mentioned earlier, in emotions we are focused on what can be gained or lost, and we are motivated to take action. We are serious. The perspective is Real/Here/Now/Me/Practical. What is happening matters. In humor, by contrast, we are disengaged from what is happening, not calculating dangers and opportunities, and not preparing for action. We aren't serious.

In early humans, whose lives were similar to those of apes, emotions were usually adaptive. Fear got them out of danger, anger helped them overcome obstacles and enemies, jealousy prompted them to protect their mates. But the more human ways of life diverged from those of apes, the more the Real/Here/Now/Me/Practical perspective of emotions was too narrow to be adaptive. In modern life, fight-or-flight emotions are usually counterproductive. When was the last time you faced a problem for which the ideal solution was running away or attacking someone? Indeed, fear and anger are the dominant emotions in the contemporary epidemic we call "stress."

Humor is an excellent way to disengage ourselves from negative emotions. Consider road rage. Most of the time, I'm a reasonable person. But behind the wheel of a car, I become sensitive to the smallest mistakes of other drivers. Years ago, I heard a routine by George Carlin that I now repeat aloud at the first signs of road rage:

Did you ever notice on the highway that everybody going faster than you is a maniac, and everyone going slower than you is a moron?

In laughing at this quip, I automatically rise out of my Real/Here/Now/Me/Practical perspective to see other drivers, and myself, more objectively.

Even disasters can be handled with humor. During the Blitzkrieg over England in 1940, one London shop was heavily damaged. The owner placed a sign in the window, "OPEN AS USUAL." When a second night of bombing destroyed the roof, he replaced that sign with another: "MORE OPEN THAN USUAL."

In Santa Barbara, California in 1994, after several hundred houses were burned to the ground, one family put up a sign: "OUR CHIMNEY'S BIGGER THAN YOURS."

Such joking would not be adaptive, of course, if it blocked necessary practical action, but in these cases the sign painters had already done what they could to respond to the destruction. Steeping themselves in negative emotions would have hindered their psychological and physical recovery, and so joking was a healthy alternative.

Nothing – not even death – is beyond the bounds of comic disengagement. After writing *I Want to Grow Hair, I Want to Grow Up, I Want to Go to Boise*, a poignant book about children fighting cancer, Erma

Bombeck was herself diagnosed with breast cancer, which required a mastectomy. She reacted this way:

> The humor that has been such an important part of my life kicked in automatically. I thought of the thousands of luncheons and dinners I had attended where they slapped a name tag on my left bosom. I always smiled and said, "Now, what shall we name the other one?" That would no longer be a problem. Nor did I give a thought to dying. I subscribe to George Burns' philosophy, "I can't die yet. I'm booked."[60]

People like Bombeck who step back from problems to laugh experience less stress and are more resilient in the face of what are crises to other people. Many psychological studies, as mentioned earlier, have shown that humor serves as a buffer against stress, and that people with a good sense of humor go through fewer and less pronounced emotional swings.[61] In Chapter 6 we will look at still more benefits of humor.

Though humor is a form of play, then, it is far from unimportant. In that way, it is like drama, music, and the other arts. Indeed, one group of the arts – comedy in the widest sense – is devoted to making us laugh. In the next chapter, we'll go into more detail as we consider the aesthetics of humor. But before leaving its psychology, we can summarize.

Humorous amusement is a psychological process that we usually experience with other people. It evolved in early human groups as a kind of play in which they were disengaged from concerns that were not beneficial, as when a threat turned out to be only apparent. Instead of being disturbed by the cognitive shifts they were experiencing, they enjoyed them. The physiological changes in this pleasurable state were directly opposed to those in negative emotions. Blood pressure, heart rate, and muscle tension were reduced instead of increased, and immune system activity was enhanced rather than suppressed. In contrast to negative emotions, which trigger action, laughter was disabling. The distinctive visual and auditory features of laughter, moreover, made it effective as a play signal, expressing well-being and pleasure, and so laughter was contagious. Like other pleasurable experiences, too, laughing was something humans wanted to repeat, and so they created situations to evoke it. Today laughter still expresses well-being and pleasure, and a major group of the fine arts is devoted to it.

Chapter 4

That Mona Lisa Smile
The Aesthetics of Humor

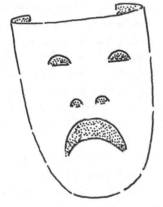

"I don't get it."

"You never get it."

Humor as Aesthetic Experience

In *Lives of the Artists*, the first European art history book, Vasari described how the young Leonardo started off by making statues of laughing women. That early interest is obvious in his *Mona Lisa*. Countless other artists, from the vase painters of ancient Greece to the contemporary group Guerrilla Girls, have incorporated humor into their work, but art historians have said little about it. As E. H. Gombrich commented, "We have become intolerably earnest. . . . The idea of fun is even more unpopular among us than the notion of beauty."[1] Until recently, the story was much the same in philosophical aesthetics, but in the last 20 years that has begun to change.

A central idea in aesthetics is aesthetic experience. While philosophers have characterized it in different ways, there is general agreement that it is a kind of appreciation in which we perceive or contemplate something for the satisfaction of the experience itself, not in order to achieve something else. Starting in the early eighteenth century, with Anthony Ashley Cooper, the Earl of Shaftesbury; Francis Hutcheson; and Joseph Addison, the lack of self-concern and personal advantage in aesthetic experience was called "disinterestedness." Kant's *Critique of Judgment* (1790) is the best-known account of it.

Having an aesthetic interest in something is contrasted with having a practical interest or cognitive interest in it. A collector might enjoy looking at an Etruscan sculpture she owns because she's thinking about the large bids it will draw in the Sotheby's auction next week. An historian might take pleasure in examining the work for what he learns about funeral practices of the period. But someone enjoying the sculpture aesthetically attends to the way it looks and feels, rather than to any practical or cognitive gain it promises.

This idea of attending to something for the pleasure of the experience, rather than to gain knowledge or reach a goal, applies to humorous amusement, too. We are not amused in order to achieve anything. Without cognitive and practical concerns, we simply enjoy the looking, listening, and thinking. Theorists of both humor and art have spoken of "distance" in the way I have spoken of disengagement.

An object of amusement, too, like objects of aesthetic experience, may be something in the natural world, such as an oddly shaped rock or cloud; something made or done for appreciation, such as a movie; or something utilitarian that happens to have interesting features, such as a bottle-capping machine in a brewery.

Humor and aesthetic experience are also similar in their emphasis on imagination and surprise. In both, we often see things from unusual perspectives, find unexpected similarities, and think creatively. Both artists and humorists are commonly praised for their cleverness and for the novelty of the fantasies they create.

With their emphasis on imagination and surprise, and their enjoyment of experience for its own sake, humor and aesthetic experience can be understood as kinds of play. Aquinas's comment that "Those words and deeds in which nothing is sought beyond the soul's pleasure are called playful or humorous" applies also to aesthetic experience. In play, ordinary conventions about what may be said and done are suspended, and so we give humorists, novelists, and dramatists considerable freedom from linguistic rules about sincerity and truth, rules of etiquette, and societal mores. That license often leads to moral questions about humor and art.

Strengthening the link between humor and aesthetic experience are the literary and performing arts that are designed to evoke amusement. We can call them "comedy" in the broadest sense. They include stage and film comedy; comic operas; cartooning; and comic storytelling, essays, novels, and poetry. Enjoying a performance of *A Midsummer Night's Dream* or reading Mark Twain is a paradigm of aesthetic experience.

Like other aesthetic realms, comedy can be distinguished into genres: satire, parody, lampoon, burlesque, caricature, farce, slapstick, limerick, etc.

Many works of art can be thought of as jokes. In 1960 Jean Tinguely exhibited *Homage to New York* for the first and last time. It consisted of a large moving contraption that destroyed itself. Patrons laughed and cheered. The title of Marcel Duchamp's adaptation of the Mona Lisa, *L.H.O.O.Q.*, is a pun. It is pronounced the same as "Elle a chaud au queue" – "She has a hot ass." Duane Hansen's hyper-realistic life-size sculptures of people beg to be used as practical jokes. His *Museum Security Guard* has sometimes been placed in galleries, where patrons at first mistake it for a real man but then discover the trick, only to laugh.

Despite such examples of humor which are art, other instances of humor lack the disinterestedness of aesthetic experience. Male joking, for instance, often involves competition, humiliation, and the enjoyment of others' suffering, as first noted by Plato and Aristotle.[2] At least in extreme cases, amusement at such humor does not seem aesthetic. Several years ago near Tallahassee, Florida, two workers for the power company were digging a ditch. One found a vine that looked like a snake and, as a joke, tossed it high in the air to come down on the other man's head, yelling "Snake!" His partner had a heart attack and died. There seems to be little that qualifies as aesthetic here. Even if the victim of the joke had not suffered the heart attack, the joker's pleasure in scaring him seems more like sadism or what Hobbes called "self-glory" than aesthetic pleasure.

Another kind of humor that seems non-aesthetic is the sexual joke told to shock or embarrass, rather than to amuse the listener. Almost a century before this kind of joking was discussed as "sexual harassment," Freud analyzed it as a substitute for seduction.[3]

What distinguishes aesthetic from non-aesthetic humor, then, is the person's motivation. In aesthetic experience, we are not out for sexual gratification, enhanced self-esteem, or other self-interested emotions, but are enjoying the experience of the object itself. Here there is a parallel between funny objects and aesthetic objects in general. Any work of art, or any natural object, can be enjoyed in non-aesthetic as well as in aesthetic ways. A general could enjoy a sunset for its promise of clear weather for his dawn attack. Someone could masturbate looking at the Venus de Milo. Similarly, the director of a film comedy could take pleasure in watching its funniest scenes because those promise big profits. And a politician could delight in an editorial cartoon because it is costing his opponent votes. There are non-aesthetic as well as aesthetic ways of enjoying anything, humorous or not.

Another way to approach the issue of when humor is an aesthetic experience is to return to our description of amusement as the playful enjoyment of a cognitive shift that naturally leads to laughter. Sometimes when we enjoy a cognitive shift, our pleasure is mixed with the enjoyment of something else, such as a state of affairs signaled by the shift. To that extent, it is less playful. If my pretentious neighbor, wearing an expensive silk suit, is showing off his new swimming pool to guests, and accidentally falls in, I might enjoy the cognitive shift, *and* take Hobbesian delight in his humiliation. That second kind of glee is neither necessary nor sufficient for humor, but it can accompany the enjoyment of the cognitive shift. Such non-playful emotions as Hobbesian self-glory tend to make the enjoyment non-aesthetic. Indeed, if the enjoyment of such self-centered emotions is all that is involved, I would argue that there isn't even humor. If I am playing a game with my arch-rival and win handsomely, my gloating laughter does not express amusement.

Humor tends to be aesthetic, then, to the extent that the cognitive shift is enjoyed for its own sake, playfully, and not for any boon that it signals. Humor is aesthetic to the extent that it is not mixed with self-interested pleasures.[4]

A corollary of these claims is that if Hobbes and Freud were right that personal motives like aggression and sexual desire are essential to humor, then humor would never be disinterested enough to be an aesthetic experience.

Humor and Other Ways of Enjoying Cognitive Shifts: The Funny, Tragic, Grotesque, Macabre, Horrible, Bizarre, and Fantastic

In linking humor and aesthetic experience, I noted that they both emphasize surprise and unusual perspectives. And so the enjoyment of cognitive shifts occurs not just in comedy but in the arts generally. Mike Martin cites as an example Grant Wood's painting *American Gothic*. A woman and a man are standing in a rigid formal pose. Her hair is neatly combed and pulled back tight. And yet there is a prominent wisp of hair curling loosely downward.[5] That out-of-placeness, that incongruity, strikes some as funny, but others appreciate it without finding it funny. Martin also cites the ironies in the plot of *Oedipus Rex* and the disjointed bodies in Picasso's *Guernica* as incongruities that no one finds funny.

It is not enough to say that humor is the enjoyment of incongruity, then, because humor is only one of the modes in which we enjoy cognitive shifts. The aesthetic categories of the tragic, grotesque, macabre, horrible, bizarre, and fantastic are six others.

Two things distinguish humorous amusement from these six: playfulness and the tendency to laugh. We do not laugh every time we are amused – we may be alone, or attending a funeral – but laughter is the natural accompaniment of amusement. That's why for the two millennia between Plato and Shaftesbury, before anyone used "humor" or "amusement" as we do now, the word "laughter" did the job of "humor" and "amusement."

In the other six categories above, the cognitive shift does not evoke laughter. The tragic, grotesque, macabre, and horrible also lack the playfulness of amusement, in that they are emotionally engaged responses. The cognitive shift evokes a negative emotional state, which, though somewhat unpleasant, also brings a kind of satisfaction. In tragedy, Aristotle said, we feel pity and fear. He could have added admiration for the hero. In the grotesque, the macabre, and the horrible, we feel fear or disgust.[6] The puzzle called the Paradox of Tragedy, which asks how we can enjoy negative emotions in art that we do not enjoy in real life, can be generalized to these other modes as well. Just as we want to see *Oedipus Rex* but wouldn't want to trade lives with King Oedipus, we enjoy reading Stephen King's horror novels and watching movies based on them, but wouldn't want to live through the grotesque, macabre, and horrible events in them. Indeed, our experience of these events is disturbing and unpleasant *within* our experience of the book or movie. At some emotional level, we *don't want* to see the severed head of the dog crawling with maggots, and we *don't want* the babysitter to get clawed to death. It can even be argued that in the tragic, grotesque, macabre, and horrible, what we enjoy is not the negative emotions, but something accompanying them, such as admiration for the tragic hero, titillation, or relief from boredom.

Humorous amusement, by contrast, is by itself a positive state with no negative emotions. That is why there is no Paradox of Comedy. In response to the Paradox of Tragedy, some have denied that we actually feel emotions in response to fictions. Others such as Noël Carroll have claimed that we experience special emotions like "art-horror."[7] But no one claims that we are not actually amused by fictions, or that there is a special kind of "art-amusement."

The last two aesthetic modes involving mental jolts – the bizarre and the fantastic – lack the tendency to laugh found in amusement, but may accommodate a certain emotional disengagement and playfulness. In this way, they can be closer to amusement than the tragic, grotesque, macabre, and horrible are. The bizarre and the fantastic elicit what psychologists call the "orienting reflex," our natural desire to make sense of what we experience. Here there is a negative state but it need not be emotional, unless we count disorientation and confusion as emotions. In the bizarre, the emphasis is on the recalcitrance of the phenomenon to fit our conceptual patterns – "This is just too weird," we might say of a Dali painting of melting watches or a burning giraffe. In the fantastic, the emphasis is on imagination, that of the creator of the incongruous phenomenon, and our own in recreating it in our minds and trying to make sense of it.

Of all these six aesthetic modes, the fantastic seems the most similar to humor. It seldom involves thoughts of harm, at least to ourselves, and there is more room for emotional disengagement and playfulness than in the other five modes. One school of fantastic art, Surrealism, was especially playful and close to humor. *The Encyclopedia of Philosophy*'s definition of Surrealism is, in part, "belief . . . in the disinterested play of thought."

André Breton described the appeal of Surrealist images: "It is the marvelous faculty of attaining two widely separated realities without departing from the realm of our experience, of bringing them together, and drawing a spark from their contact."[8] Like a joke, in which we switch interpretations at the punch line, several Surrealist images can be viewed under two aspects, as in Salvador Dali's *Slave Market with Disappearing Bust of Voltaire* – a group of figures forming a pattern of light and dark that looks like Voltaire. Dali also played with titles, as in *Fast Moving Still Life*.

René Magritte was similarly playful in eliciting cognitive shifts. *Chateau in the Pyrenees* is a realistic depiction of a castle in the mountains, but both castle and mountains are inexplicably suspended in the sky. *Anniversary* is a painting of a boulder – that almost completely fills a room. *Mysteries of the Horizon* is a conventional representation of a quiet neighborhood at nightfall, except that there are three crescent moons in the sky. As one critic wrote of Magritte's work, "Everything seems proper. And then abruptly the rape of common sense occurs, usually in broad daylight."[9]

It would have been easy for Magritte to design his works to make viewers laugh, but he didn't. Explaining how he got first got interested in painting, he said, "My interest lay entirely in provoking an emotional shock."[10] I think that what Magritte was going for was *cognitive* shocks – not *emotional* shocks, which seem incompatible with "the disinterested play of thought." In any case, for the vast majority of viewers, his paintings are fantastic or bizarre rather than humorous.

Tragedy vs. Comedy: Is Heavy Better than Light?

Having contrasted humor with other aesthetic modes, we can now turn to its value. Here traditional discussions have centered on created humor rather than found humor, and especially on dramatic comedy. Since ancient times, evaluations of comedy have compared it with tragedy, and tragedy is usually deemed superior, at least by intellectuals. Comedy is often counted as "light" and inconsequential, while tragedy is thought "heavy" and important. Those who accept this view seldom ask why comedy has been created in profusion by nearly all cultures, while only European culture has produced tragedy – and then only a few examples during a few historical periods.

In defense of comedy, I will sketch several contrasts between it and tragedy.[11] Though I focus on dramatic comedy, most of my comments apply to other kinds of created humor as well.

The overarching difference is that comedies are designed to evoke amusement, while tragedies are designed to evoke emotions – primarily fear, pity, and admiration for the hero. Comedies and tragedies foster these responses not only to events on stage and in books, but to similar events in real life. Like other literature, they shape our attitudes toward experience generally, which is why we speak of the tragic vision of *life* and the comic vision of *life*, not simply the tragic and comic visions of *literature*.

We saw in Chapter 2 how amusement and emotions involve different orientations to experience. In emotions, we are engaged with the Real/Here/Now/Me/Practical, while in amusement we are disengaged and play with what we experience. Since tragedy fosters an attitude toward life based on negative emotions, and comedy fosters a non-emotional, playful attitude, one way to evaluate tragedy and comedy is by comparing the value of these attitudes. This may seem like a non-aesthetic approach, more suited to ethics, but, as Noël Carroll has pointed out, except for certain modern schools of aesthetics that tried to make art independent of life, critics since Aristotle have been evaluating works of literature by considering the attitudes they evoke.[12] A work that fosters attitudes that harm the audience and motivate them to harm others seems, to that extent, inferior to a work that fosters attitudes beneficial to the audience and people around them. Consider "snuff movies" – films for which unknown actors are hired to make ordinary pornography, but then during the filming are bound, tortured, and killed. Viewers pay hundreds of dollars for the pleasure of seeing real torture and real murder. This entire genre, I contend, is flawed for the sadism it promotes.

In evaluating tragedy and comedy, then, I assume something that was considered obvious until a century ago – that artworks fostering attitudes conducive to human flourishing are better, *ceteris paribus*, than artworks that promote harm to humans.

What is helpful and harmful to humans has changed over the million years we've been on the planet. Our natural cravings for sugar and fat, for example, served early hunter-gatherers well, when these nutrients were hard to come by. Today in the United States, where sweet, fatty foods are readily available, these cravings have led to obesity in almost 30 percent of the population. Similarly, anger energized our distant ancestors to scare off or overcome predators and enemies, while today outbursts of anger usually don't solve problems, but create new ones.

As mentioned in Chapter 2, anger, along with fear, equipped early humans to handle physical threats, by motivating them to either overcome or escape them, hence the term "fight-or-flight" emotions. When threats got the better of them, and they were injured or lost someone or something important, then sadness immobilized them, allowing them to heal physically and psychologically. It also motivated them to avoid similar situations in the future. Sympathetic sadness – pity – motivated them to help group members in need.

Today these emotions can still benefit us in the same ways, but often they do not. The modern phenomenon called stress, a major contributor to heart disease, cancer, and other leading causes of death, is a combination of fear and anger. In stress, our bodies and brains react as if we were physically threatened, as by a predator. The hormones epinephrine, norepinephrine, and cortisol are pumped into the bloodstream, increasing heart rate and blood pressure. Muscles tense in preparation for fighting or fleeing. The immune system is suppressed. But there is no predator, so the muscle tension, nervous energy, and hormones are not dissipated. As this physiological arousal is repeated several times a day, our bodies, especially our hearts and immune systems, are damaged. Stress is now at epidemic proportions in the industrialized world, costing American employers an estimated $200 billion a year.

Another epidemic in the U.S. – depression – involves the third and fourth emotions above, sadness and pity. Modern life brings countless bad experiences to us and others. If we react to all or most of them emotionally, we can become immobilized in clinical depression.

In asking about the value of tragedy and comedy, then, we need to pay attention to what benefited whom when. To make the best case for tragedy, we should look at the ancient Greek world where it began. There, three tragic emotions – fear of unforeseen calamity, pity for group members who needed help, and admiration for heroic leaders – were generally beneficial.

The ancient world was tribal. Most people depended on kin to stay alive. Group hunting and tribal warfare were common, and both required leaders. So obedience to military leaders was prized. Different levels of leadership created hierarchies of who had to defer to whom. A good soldier was willing to kill or die on command and did not challenge authority or tradition. Related virtues were loyalty to comrades, a sense of honor, courage in battle, and steadfastness in the face of suffering. Because military and political positions were held by men, too, domination of women by men was natural in these cultures.

Two artistic genres promoted military virtues. The first, epic, was found in almost all ancient cultures. The Greeks had the *Iliad* and *Odyssey*, the Romans the *Aeneid*, and the Hebrews the book of *Joshua*. The second genre, tragedy, was much rarer. But both inculcated emotions and attitudes in audiences by presenting as role models heroic figures with high degrees of military virtues.

Over the course of history, things have changed considerably. Militaristic tribalism in its modern form – nationalism – has annihilated hundreds of millions of people and threatened to destroy the planet in a nuclear conflagration. The wars of the twentieth century can be viewed as a *reductio ad absurdum* of militaristic tribalism. Male domination of females has also proved harmful in many ways, to men as well as women. While the emotions promoted by tragedy and epic were helpful in keeping ancient societies going, then, many of those emotions are now dangerous to the human race.

Even in ancient Greece, some people questioned militaristic tribalism and the emotions that supported it. One way was by counterbalancing tragedies with comedies. The great dramatists wrote both. To submit a tragic trilogy for a festival, in fact, they had to include a satyr play to be performed at the end for comic relief. These burlesque dramas starred legendary heroes, often taken from the accompanying tragedies. The chorus was eleven wisecracking satyrs – creatures part human, part goat, and part horse, with a reputation for lechery, drunkenness, and cowardice.

Aristophanes, the master of Old Comedy, developed many of the techniques we enjoy in comedy today.[13] His plays have dialogue that starts with tragic meter and diction, but then shifts. In *Lysistrata*, where Greek women hold a sex strike to end the fighting between the city-states, the chorus, sounding like the chorus in *Oedipus Rex*, asks Lysistrata why she is upset:

CHORUS: What is't that troubles thee? Speak to thy friends.
LYSISTRATA: "'Tis shame to say, yet grievous to conceal.
CHORUS: Then do not hide from me the ill we suffer.
LYSISTRATA: In brief the tale to tell – we need a fuck.

Instead of the emotions evoked by tragedy and epic, and the military attitudes they fostered, comedy offered a non-emotional, playful approach to life, portraying it not as a series of battles, but as a series of adventures in which we play as well as work. The problems in comedy were much the same as in tragedy, but they didn't evoke pity and fear in the audience. Nor did the lead characters indulge in "Woe is me" self-pity. As Edward Galligan has written, "Comedy may deal with all sorts of dark, disquieting material but finally it explores and celebrates the image of play."[14]

The non-emotional, playful attitude of comedy made it different in many ways from tragedy. One is that it promoted mental flexibility while tragedy promoted mental rigidity.[15] By celebrating a narrow range of emotional responses to problems, tragedy fostered formulaic patterns of thought and action. By celebrating disengaged, spontaneous responses to problems, comedy fostered adaptive, more rational thought and action. If we consider this contrast carefully, we can see that the traditional assessment of comedy as trivial is – well – laughable.

In the brain, emotions are mediated in the limbic system, an evolutionarily ancient part that lies below the cerebral cortex. The limbic system is not as simple or mechanical as the brain stem, the "reptilian brain" lying below it. But its function is similar – to react quickly and automatically to dangers and opportunities. The best-known reactions are "fight or flight." Gripped by fear or anger, we act in the same ways billions of animals have acted before us, going all the way back to early mammals. We don't think carefully, critically, or imaginatively: we may not think at all. And so, in an outburst of anger at our children, say, we may automatically yell the same words we yelled the last time they angered us.

Tragic heroes are role models for the mental rigidity of emotions. They often face problems with simplistic, standard conceptual schemes that divide the world into good and bad, honorable and dishonorable, etc. Sophocles' Antigone, for instance, thinks that she must either obey Creon's order not to bury her brother, and thereby dishonor her family – or bury her brother, and be executed as a traitor. But any comedy writer would tell you that's a false dilemma. In the same predicament, Lucille Ball would get someone else to remove the body at night, or stage a chariot crash as a diversion, snatching the body away in the confusion. The world of tragedy is full of problems that would be quickly solved in comedy, with a little imagination.

Humorous amusement is based not in the limbic system but in the cerebral cortex. Unlike emotions, which we share with other mammals, humorous amusement involves higher-order thinking, especially seeing things from multiple perspectives. To get even simple jokes requires that we have two interpretations for a phrase in mind at the same time.

Comedies also work with more complex conceptual schemes than tragedies. They usually have more characters and more types of characters, and often several simultaneous plots.

Unlike tragedies, too, where actions have inevitable consequences, comedies emphasize the contingency of events – the way that any event could be followed by quite different alternatives.

While tragic heroes have a low tolerance for novelty and disorder, comic protagonists thrive on both. In tragedies, unfamiliar people and experiences are dangerous, while comic protagonists treat novelty as opportunity. As Edward Galligan says, comedy embodies the "conviction that the unknown will turn out to be at least as good as the known, that we will, somehow, land right side up."[16]

Tragic heroes show mental rigidity not only in their lack of imagination but in their stubbornness. Negative emotions have a momentum of their own, largely because their hormones linger in the bloodstream. That's why if we become enraged with someone we mistakenly think has done us wrong, our anger doesn't disappear as soon as we discover our error. In fact, we may unconsciously search for another motive to be angry, so as to not waste the emotion.

The inevitability in tragedy is often due as much to the hero's stubbornness as to fate. Consider what happens, and why, in Shakespeare's *Romeo and Juliet*, Melville's *Moby Dick*, and Hemingway's *Old Man and the Sea*. As Walter Kerr pointed out, already by the time of Sophocles, the Greeks had perfected "the tragedy of the locked will" – most famous in Oedipus's obsession with finding the murderer of Laius, and in Antigone's and Creon's refusal to meet each other halfway. In tragedy, of course, it's not called stubbornness but honor, determination, patriotism, devotion to duty, idealism, virtue, etc.

The stubbornness of tragic heroes shows in their concern with vengeance and their unwillingness to forgive. As Aristotle said, in comedy enemies often become friends, but in tragedy they never do.

If a person with a locked will or an obsession appears in a comedy, by contrast, it's not as a hero to be admired, but as the butt of joking. Characters with *idées fixes*, as Bergson called them, include the laughable miser, the pedant, and the hypochondriac. What's valued in comedy is not "staying the course," to use George W. Bush's phrase, but adapting thought and behavior to what's happening. Like tragic heroes, comic protagonists face big problems, but they think rather than feel their way through them. Instead of chaining themselves to a principle or a tradition and dying in the process, they find a new way to look at things, wriggle out of the difficulty, and live to tell the tale.

The mental rigidity of tragic heroes is reinforced by their militarist attitudes. As Conrad Hyers points out, in the culture in which tragedy was born, the most highly praised virtues were those of a good commander or good soldier.[17] Then, as now, military leaders had to give orders, often with little information or time to think. Soldiers had to obey them without questioning, as in Tennyson's line, "Ours not to reason why, ours but to do and die." If commanders had more time to think, they might issue different orders, but once they give their orders, everyone has to treat them as the right thing to do. If each soldier thought for himself, there could be no armies.

Commanders, too, have a good reason – or better, a good motive – to stick to any decision they make. If, even occasionally, they issued orders and then reversed them, they would be admitting fallibility and undermining the confidence of their troops. So it's natural for them to be "iron-willed," that is, stubborn.

All this mental rigidity makes some sense on the battlefield, but as an attitude to life generally, it is folly. So at the same time they were developing tragedy, the Greeks developed comedy, the first institution to challenge militarism and the heroic ethos. Satyr plays satirized mythic heroes. Aristophanes' *Lysistrata* mocked tribal militarism and patriarchy. In early film, many of Charlie Chaplin's comedies ridiculed war as a way to solve problems. Later came *Dr. Strangelove: Or How I Learned to Stop Worrying and Love the Bomb; How I Won the War*, starring John Lennon; and *M*A*S*H*. The 2003 invasion of Iraq brought us Michael Moore's *Fahrenheit 9/11*, along with the wisecracks of Molly Ivins, Bill Mahar, and Jon Stewart.

The comic critics of militarism often take on its inherent sexism, too, as in *Lysistrata*, the first feminist play. While men dominate in tragedy and epic, comedy features women in leading roles, and female characters are more varied and interesting.

Comedies also mock hierarchies and elitism. Tragedy concentrates on upper-class heroes of noble birth like Oedipus and Hamlet; comedy celebrates what we now call diversity, where each person counts for one. Since ancient Greek and Roman comedy, for example, servants have bested their masters. In the 1956 film *The Court Jester*, the rightful king is a baby, the comic protagonist (Danny Kaye) is a circus entertainer who takes orders from Captain Jean (Glynis Johns), and those who save the day are midget acrobats.

What, then, can we conclude about the relative value of tragedy and comedy? However valuable the attitudes fostered by tragedy were in past centuries, they are now largely obsolete, and some of them dangerous to the survival of the species. Comedy fosters a more rational, critical, creative attitude that is more adaptive. It grew out of fertility rites and ever since has emphasized the basics in human life – food, sex, and getting along with family, friends, and even enemies.

Treating life as a series of battles is now a source of harmful stress. The playful, imaginative attitude fostered by comedy not only feels better, but makes us healthier psychologically and physically. As mentioned in the last chapter, after hearty laughter, the stress chemicals epinephrine, norepinephrine, cortisol, and DOPAC are reduced, along with muscle tension, blood pressure, and heart rate. And while the immune system is suppressed in negative emotions, it is enhanced in laughter. Physicians and nurses themselves have long had their own kind of humor, usually too "dark" for public consumption, that allows them to keep their cool instead of succumbing to disgust, fear, anger, and sadness. In hospitals, "code brown" means a bowel movement deposited in an inappropriate spot, such as under a bed; to "poot" or to "crump" is to take an irreversible turn for the worse. Critics with little medical experience might call such humor callous, but those who spend their lives in hospitals know that it expresses a refusal to let potentially tragic events be tragic. An encouraging sign here is that over a hundred American hospitals now have "comedy carts" or whole "humor rooms" or "play rooms" for patients and their families.

This is not to say that tragic emotions are never beneficial in modern life. Compassion for those who need help is still important. But pity can easily become a feeling valued for itself rather than as a goad to helpful action, as it is in many people addicted to soap operas. Comedy rejects not pity but sentimentality. As Jane Austen's character Emma Woodhouse says to her sentimental friend Harriet, "If we feel for the wretched, enough to do all we can for them, the rest is empty sympathy, only distressing ourselves."

In responding to life's problems, what comedy recommends is not emotions but thinking – and rethinking. In this way, comedy is like Buddhism, with its insistence that the way we look at things is more important than things-in-themselves, if there even are such things. Like Buddhism, too, comedy rejects the self-centeredness that attends emotional attachment. While a tragedy focuses on an individual, the basic unit in a comedy is a group, such as a family, a village, or a bunch of co-workers. And the good of the group trumps the good of the individual. In the 1998 Irish comedy *Waking Ned Devine*, an older man dies of a heart attack on learning that he has won the national lottery. Such an event could easily fit into a tragedy, but here the rest of the village comes up with a scheme to keep Ned's death secret and have another villager impersonate him to claim the huge jackpot. If the ruse works, everyone will split the winnings. As the government agent comes to the village to arrange payment of the prize, Lizzie Quinn, an irritable, unsociable woman, threatens to reveal the plan unless she gets half the money. The other villagers refuse to give her more than anyone else will get. On her way to make the phone call that will put the whole village in prison, Lizzie's wheelchair accidentally rolls over a cliff into the ocean. Despite her disability and awful death, theater audiences cheer, because she was thinking only of herself. In the last scene of the film, the now prosperous villagers toast Ned Devine.

In comedy, as in tragedy, there are misfortunes and death, but because the characters are "all in this together," the experience is much easier to get through. Mishaps that would be painful and depressing if endured alone are often fun when shared. Even Ned's and Lizzie's deaths are not tragic, since they bring prosperity to the village.

Enough with the Jokes: Spontaneous vs. Prepared Humor

Having defended humor in literature and film, let me close this chapter by stepping down to a humbler kind, humor in conversation. We may go weeks or years without seeing a Shakespeare play, but we seldom go a day without humor in conversation. Indeed, for most of us, it's our most common aesthetic experience.

A major source for the low opinion many people have of humor is one kind of humor in conversation – jokes. When Kant, Schopenhauer, and Freud analyzed humor, they used fictional jokes as their prime examples, and in recent scholarship about humor, joke telling takes center stage. The philosopher Ted Cohen's book *Jokes* makes it sound as though joke telling is essential for creating intimacy and building community. I would point out, however, that the telling of prepared fictional jokes is a culturally specific, historically late phenomenon that has been on the wane for at least 30 years.[18] More importantly, I would argue that joke telling does not build intimacy or community as well as another kind of humor – spontaneous humor in conversation.

Many years ago I did an hour-long interview on CBC radio to plug a book about humor. The host of the show had read it carefully and we had a lively discussion about the value of humor in relation to imagination, aesthetic sensitivity, friendship, and mental health. All of the funny examples we discussed were from real life. Then he "opened up the phone lines." For the next half-hour, every call consisted of someone asking me what I thought of one or more jokes. One man wanted me to rank-order three jokes, presumably so that he could tell the funniest one more often. I politely told the first few callers that I don't tell jokes when I'm with friends and I haven't much interest in listening to them or analyzing them. But subsequent callers rattled off their jokes anyway, apparently unable or unwilling to accept the distinction between humor and joke telling.

Academic research on humor has suffered from the same concentration on jokes and other prepared "texts," to the neglect of spontaneous, real-life humor. In the social sciences this preference is methodologically understandable, since jokes are repeatable, created for a wide audience, and so easy to use in experiments. But if we think about the humor we create and enjoy in our daily lives, most of it is not prepared fictional texts but stories and observations about real-life experiences.

Funny anecdotes and spontaneous humor, whether natural or created, are more situation-dependent than prepared humor, less accessible to a wide audience, and so less suitable for analysis in the social sciences. "You had to be there," as we often say when someone doesn't laugh at our description of something that cracked us up at the time. Nonetheless, there is a satisfaction we take in anecdotes and spontaneous humor that is lacking in even the best-prepared jokes.

For convenience, I will call prepared fictional humor in conversation "jokes," and I won't refer to funny anecdotes and observations as jokes. The person who presents prepared fictional humor I'll call the "joke teller." Contrasted with jokes will be anecdotes and spontaneous comments. The person presenting this material I'll call the "wit."

I use the "prepared" and "spontaneous" in order to have shorthand terms to work with, but they actually cover at least three distinctions, as we'll see:

- humor that arises on the spot vs. humor that is prepared and later performed from memory or from a written text;
- humor that arises from real-life experiences vs. humorous fictional narratives; and
- humorous stories that arise from the experience and imagination of their tellers vs. humorous stories that one person creates and another person tells.

To make my case for the superiority of funny anecdotes and comments over jokes, I want to examine three differences between the joke teller and the wit:

1. The joke teller is a performer but not a creator of humor, while the wit both creates and performs humor.
2. The joke teller is limited to the jokes they can remember, while the wit is potentially unlimited in the humor they can create.
3. The joke teller interrupts the conversation, while the wit keeps it going.

We can expand these points one at a time.

1. While both the joke teller and the wit perform humor, the wit creates it as well. Certainly we can admire the skillful telling of a joke, if

only because most people lack that skill. But even so, the impact that a joke can have in a conversation always seems potentially less than that of a well-told, real-life story, or a funny comment made about something said or done in the conversation. One reason for this impact is that we admire what is done spontaneously over what is prepared, especially when what is prepared was created by someone other than the performer. For all the applause we give a musician performing another person's composition, for example, we give greater applause, other things being equal, to the person performing his or her own composition; and greater applause still to the person improvising music on the spot. There is a thrill to live jazz with its loose, improvised turn taking, that fully scored music does not evoke.

A good part of our appreciation of the improvised performance is in response to the skill involved. While it is hard to play a virtuoso piano piece or to tell a joke perfectly, it is much harder not only to perform but to create the music or the humor, and still harder to create it on the spot. B. F. Skinner observed that admiring people is in part marveling at them or wondering at them, and we marvel and wonder at what we cannot explain. "It is therefore not surprising that we are likely to admire behavior more as we understand it less."[19] Almost anybody, with enough practice, can tell a joke successfully. The person who can come up with funny comments on the spot, however, is much rarer, and so more highly admired.

If we marvel most at the utterly spontaneously wit – the person like Robin Williams who can create humor from scratch on the spot – we also admire the person who can work a good anecdote into our conversation, even if we know that person has used versions of the story before. What we appreciate here is partly the skill in adapting the material to this occasion. But we also appreciate the provenance of the anecdote – the relation between what the speaker is relating, on the one hand, and their experience and way of looking at the world, on the other.

I propose a general principle, the Authenticity Principle, that applies not just to humor but to anything in conversation: Other things being equal, it is more interesting to hear people speaking from their own experience and knowledge, and from their own viewpoints, that it is to hear them deliver texts composed by someone else. That's a big part, I think, of why most political speeches today don't grab people. They don't proceed from the mind and heart of the speaker, but are purchased from speechwriters.

There is another value to the real-life anecdote: it is based on real events. Here I propose a second principle, the Reality Principle. Other things being equal, we are more able to get interested in, and be moved – to laughter, to tears, in every way – by real events than by fictional events. That's why the marketing for so many books and movies says, "Based on a true story."

One place to see the natural advantage of the person telling about some funny event that really happened to them, over the teller of prepared jokes, is in contemporary stand-up comedy. This is not the same as conversation, of course, but the most successful stand-up comics talk to their audiences in as conversational a way as possible. When they use a funny story, they tell it as having really happened, and to themselves, rather than telling it as a fictional story, or as having happened to just anybody. "I ran out of change for the parking meter yesterday" is always preferred to "One day this guy ran out of change for a parking meter."

We in the audience are usually willing to go along with the premise that the story is true and from the comic's experience, just because this will enhance the effect of the story on us. That's part of the artistic license we give the comic. In conversation we do not always grant such license to people telling funny stories. We sometimes resent the person telling a story – funny or not – who pretends to have been part of the events described but who we know was not even there. Especially troublesome in conversation is the person who appropriates other people's anecdotes and presents them as their own experiences. Having a number of funny experiences that have happened to you and that you have crafted into great stories is a mark of accomplishment. The stories you can tell are part of your life and mark out your uniqueness as a person. A good share of what we appreciate about the stories a person tells is what they show us about that person – their life and way of looking at the world. Enjoying someone's stories is enjoying the person. It's bad form to simply steal such stories from other people – a kind of identity theft!

2.   The second difference between the joke teller and the wit mentioned above is that the joke teller is limited to the jokes they can remember on any particular occasion, while the wit is potentially unlimited. We all probably know someone who has a good memory for jokes, but cannot create humor. Even when the jokes are well performed, there is something different between listening to such a person and listening to a wit. For we all know what the joke teller is going to do. They have memorized a few jokes and now they are going to present them to us. After that the humor will be over. The witty person, on the other hand, can process almost any material – events of the week, stories that have already been told in the conversation, or whatever – through a humor filter, and amuse

us with their comments. Part of the pleasure of listening to the wit is knowing that the humor is being created on the spot, but part of it, too, is knowing that there's a lot more where that came from.

3. The third difference between the joke teller and the wit lies in their relation to the conversation itself. The telling of a joke is a performance which interrupts a conversation, while telling funny anecdotes and making humorous comments on what is being said in a conversation contribute to the flow of that conversation.

The essence of conversation, I suggest, is that two or more people relate their experiences to one another, exchange information they have gathered from various sources, and exchange their evaluations and attitudes about what they have experienced and learned. Let me call these activities exchanging experiences, exchanging information, and exchanging views. The participants in a conversation may have said some of what they are saying in previous conversations, but the sequence of comments is unrehearsed, and participants are free to react to what has been said by presenting experiences, information, and views of their own. If someone merely wants others to listen to them, and does not allow them to discuss what they say, we euphemistically call that "monopolizing the conversation," but it is really *interrupting* or *ending* the conversation.

Now different conversations have different proportions of experiences, information, and views, and some may not have all three. But exchanging these constitutes a conversation. If something else occurs in a conversation, such as one person's performing something for another's appreciation, that interrupts the conversation. If we are sitting in my living room talking, and I ask if you want to hear my new bagpipes, then while I am playing the bagpipes the conversation has halted. Not only are we no longer talking, but we are no longer interacting: I have become the performer and you the audience. When I have finished my performance, the conversation may pick up where it left off, and perhaps the bagpiping will be a topic of conversation; but while I am playing and you are listening, our conversation has stopped.

Joke telling interrupts a conversation in much the same way as bagpiping, though not usually to as great an extent. Jokes, after all, are linguistic – the same form as conversation – and so the transition from conversation to joke telling is not as big a jump as from conversation to bagpiping. More importantly, jokes are often told in a setting that invites the audience to tell jokes of their own. This is akin to the turn-taking of conversation. But still, joke telling is interruptive of conversation in several ways.

For one, a joke is not a recounting of an experience of the person telling it, nor is it information they have learned, nor is it their views on anything. It is a fictional text created by someone outside the conversation – who knows who? – that is performed pretty much as rehearsed. It has none of the flexibility of spontaneous conversation.

Not only is the joke not proceeding from the person telling it, as moves in a conversation do, but the joke does not allow listeners to respond with experiences, information, or views of their own. All they can do is laugh or not laugh. They may use the occasion to then tell a joke of their own, but that is just to turn everyone else, including the previous joke teller, into the audience for another performance. It is much like your responding to my bagpiping by getting out your clarinet. It is quite unlike the turn-taking of conversation, in which the comments of the participants build on each other organically or dialectically.

In contrast to the interruption of a conversation by joke telling, consider how the contribution of the wit keeps the conversation going. Suppose we are talking about running out of gas on the highway, and my friend tells about running out of gas the first time he drove his first car – a little Renault whose equipment was totally foreign to him. He walked back to a gas station he had passed and returned to his car with a can of gasoline. He looked in the back for a gas cap but found none. He looked along the sides of the car and found no cap. Finally he looked under the hood, found an appropriate-looking cap, and poured in the gas. He got back in the car and tried to start it, but all he heard was the cranking of the engine. When the tow truck arrived, he learned that not only was he still out of gas, but he now had a gallon of gas in his radiator.

Now this event took place 40 years ago, and Ted has talked about it many times. Some of the wording has been polished. But whenever he tells the story, it is still a move in a conversation. He still lets the others in the group ask questions and make comments as he goes along. And he still gets all kinds of responses to the end of his story. People do not merely laugh or not laugh. They connect the story to Ted's lack of mechanical aptitude, they relate it to their own experiences with the small foreign cars of the 1960s, and they tell their own funny stories of automotive mishaps. What Ted has done is very different from telling a joke, even a joke about a guy running out of gas. (Notice that this story would never make it as a joke.) Ted has shared a bit of his life with us, indeed a bit that shows us quite a bit about himself. He has not stopped the conversation but has participated in it and kept it going.

Spontaneous humor, I conclude, is not only more common than joke telling, but more important in bringing people together and allowing them to exchange experiences, information, beliefs, and attitudes. This may make conversational humor sound like an unqualified boon to the human race. But, as we'll see in the next chapter, it isn't, because spontaneous humor, like joke telling, can have harmful consequences.

Chapter 5

Laughing at the Wrong Time
The Negative Ethics of Humor

"Have a good day, God bless, and for heaven's sake, lighten up."

In exploring traditional accounts of humor in Chapter 1, we touched on several moral objections to it. In this chapter, we will examine those objections systematically and suggest a way to handle the morality of humor in general. Then in Chapter 6 we'll explore the positive ethics of humor. In both chapters I follow the lead of traditional philosophers and religious thinkers in focusing on the harmful or beneficial effects that laughter and humor have on people. Some of these thinkers spoke of vices and virtues associated with humor, but those vices are considered bad and those virtues good because of how they affect persons – those with the traits and people they interact with. Plato and Hobbes, for example, said that ridicule can make us more mean-spirited, so that we treat other people badly. Aristotle and Thomas Aquinas spoke of ready-wittedness as a virtue because it helps us relax and enjoy each other's company.

Today in ethical discussions, it is common to distinguish "consequentialist" theories such as utilitarianism from virtue ethics, deontological ethics, natural law ethics, etc. Consequentialist ethics, it is sometimes said, sees the value in virtues merely instrumentally, while virtue ethics thinks of virtues as intrinsically valuable. But until a few decades ago, writers on the morality of laughter and humor didn't advocate single meta-ethical positions like these. They simply looked at what indulging in humor did to people, whether for ill or good. And that included fostering vices and virtues, which were themselves considered bad or good for the effects they had on people. This traditional approach will be my approach.

I'll begin with eight common moral objections to humor, and then develop my own ethical assessment based on the playful disengagement in humor. In this chapter that will cover ways in which humor can be harmful, and in the next chapter, we'll look at ways it can be beneficial.

The ethics of humor has received considerable attention over the last 30 years, but one topic has gotten almost all the attention – racist and sexist jokes. While clearly important, consideration of these jokes is a small part of the ethics of humor that was not even mentioned in ethical writings about humor until the late twentieth century. We will be discussing racist and sexist jokes, but within a wider account of the ethics of humor that covers both its negative features, in this chapter, and its positive features, in the next.

Eight Traditional Moral Objections

As mentioned in Chapter 1, through history the vast majority of moral evaluations of humor have been negative. And most of those were condemnations of laughter, since humor was not distinguished from laughter until the eighteenth century. There are eight basic charges, several of which we have already cited:

1.   Humor is insincere.
2.   Humor is idle.
3.   Humor is irresponsible.
4.   Humor is hedonistic.
5.   Humor diminishes self-control.
6.   Humor is hostile.
7.   Humor fosters anarchy.
8.   Humor is foolish.

The general pattern in these objections is to link humor with morally objectionable effects, such as violence and sexual promiscuity. Since, presumably, we oppose those effects, we should oppose humor, too. The problem with this approach is that it does not make a moral case against *all* humor, or even against humor per se. For any activity that we could think of, some instances could be associated with something objectionable. Consider the volunteers who bring hot meals to old people in their homes. Some of them may be confidence men lining up victims. But such a possibility doesn't provide a moral objection to bringing hot meals to old people, because there is no essential connection between doing that and bilking people out of their life savings. Similarly, the eight objections above don't show an essential connection between humor and something objectionable. We can consider them one at a time.

1. Humor is insincere

This objection is based on the non-bona-fide communication and action in much humor. Good people mean what they say and do, but jokers don't. They are "only fooling." Such speech and behavior can be dangerous, as we saw with the ditch-digger's pretending that the vine was a snake. That's the point of the warning cited from the Bible: "A man who deceives another and then says, 'It was only a joke,' is like a madman shooting at random his deadly darts and arrows" (Proverbs 26:18–19). And even when insincerity is not physically dangerous, it can upset social relationships. As an Arab saying goes, "Laughter cancels the deal."

Now, while this objection applies to some humor, it is not a general objection to humor because not all humor involves pretending and insincerity. When old friends reminisce about a funny incident from 40 years ago, for example, no one need be insincere. And when I experience humor while alone, such as laughing at a silly mistake I made, non-bona-fide communication or action isn't even possible.

Some humor does involve pretending, of course, but even here there need be nothing objectionable. Actors devote their careers to pretending to be other people, but no one complains about insincerity. Nor would anyone complain if a new biography of Robert Frost revealed that he had never in fact stopped by woods on a snowy evening. Even in a practical joke, where someone is fooled by the pretense, there may be nothing objectionable if they can join in the fun.

2. Humor is idle

As a form of disengaged play, humor does not accomplish anything. Early Christian leaders objected to it for that reason. The fourth-century bishop John Chrysostom condemned laughter as "a moment of indifference."[1] His contemporary Gregory of Nyssa said that, "Laughter is our enemy because it is neither a word nor an action ordered to any possible goal."[2] In the seventh century, John Climacus said that the mother of laughter is insensibility.[3] In the twentieth century, Anthony Ludovici contrasted laughing about a problem with solving it:

> Humor is, therefore, the lazier principle to adopt in approaching all questions, and that is why the muddle is increasing everywhere. Because the humorous mind shirks the heavy task of solving thorny problems and prefers to make people laugh about them. . . . Truth to tell, there is in every inspired and passionate innovator a haughty energy which is incompatible with the cowardice and indolence of humor.[4]

This charge of not accomplishing anything applies to much humor, but not to all. While humor does involve a disengaged attitude, that attitude itself may have benefits, and so indirectly accomplish something. When Winston Churchill announced that Mussolini had declared war on Great Britain, for example, he did it with a joke: "Today, the Italians have announced that they are joining the war on the side of the Germans. I think that's only fair – we had to take them last time." With this joke, Churchill reduced the anxiety of the British people and thus allowed them to get through the long fight ahead. Medical research shows that laughter not only reduces anxiety but also reduces pain and boosts the activity of the immune system. Again, the disengagement in humor may have indirect benefits. And even when humor does not achieve any further benefit, it need not be objectionable. Some things are valuable in themselves rather than instrumentally. Listening to music, watching the sun set, making love – these "idle" activities can be fulfilling in themselves, and so can humor.

3. Humor is irresponsible

This objection, too, is based on the disengagement in humor. When we are disengaged from what is happening around us, in laughter or other forms of play, we are not attending to our duties. Worse, laughter is often at wrongdoing. From the beginning of comedy in ancient Greece, the liar, the lecher, the adulterer, the glutton, and the drunk have been stock characters. When we enjoy them on stage, or are amused by their counterparts in real life, we suspend moral concern. Laughing at a friend who is too drunk to stand up, for example, we're not trying to help that person. And when we laugh at drunks in movies, this critique says, we are inuring ourselves to the problem of alcoholism in our culture. A morally responsible attitude toward people with vices includes the desire to reform them and rules out enjoyment of their vices.

The pamphlet cited earlier by the Puritan William Prynne put the case this way: comedies evoke laughter at some "obscene, lascivious, sinful passage, gesture, speech or jest (the common object of men's hellish mirth) which should rather provoke the Actors, the Spectators to penitent sobs, than wanton smiles; to brinish tears than carnal solace."[5]

A reasonable response to this objection is to admit that it applies to many cases of humor. Later in this chapter, we will explore several. When our amusement displaces or blocks concern and action that are called for, as with the drunk friend, then it is objectionable. But not all humorous situations call for concern or action. If I see a basset hound whose face reminds me of my grandfather, and I chuckle, there is nothing that I should be doing about that coincidence instead. And so the humor here is not irresponsible.

Even in practical situations, moreover, humor can be a psychologically healthy way to respond to setbacks. If in rushing to prepare a meal, I drop a ripe tomato on my shoe, laughing and getting on with the cooking is more productive than getting upset and stewing in self-blame. In the very practical profession of medicine, people engage in humor to keep emotionally cool and so in command of their skills.

Humor can also be responsible when it focuses attention on something that should be corrected. Since the days of Ben Jonson, satirists have justified their trade by saying that satire corrects the shortcomings being laughed at. While that is not always true, and while direct moral censure might sometimes be more effective, certainly some satirists have gotten their audiences to pay attention to incompetence, hypocrisy, and deception. Bill Mahar and Jon Stewart's television comedy about the presidency of George W. Bush, for example, served as political education for millions of Americans.

4. Humor is hedonistic

Humor and other forms of play are pursued for pleasure. We are acting not out of obligation, but just for fun. If someone were always joking, they would never act out of obligation. Such hedonists would be at least amoral, and probably immoral.

This tension between morality and pleasure is emphasized in traditions that teach soul/body dualism and associate pleasure with the body. In these traditions, the moral life requires curbing desires for pleasure rather than indulging them.

An intense form of pleasure is sex, and women's laughter has been thought to be a sexual stimulant to men, so laughter has often been associated with sexual license. In East Asian countries even today, a woman who laughs with her mouth open is thought to be promiscuous. In Western culture, comedy has been linked to licentiousness from the beginning. On the Greek stage, comic characters wore large phalli and many jokes were sexual double entendres. The whole ritual honored Dionysus, the god of wine and sexual frenzy.

The Church Fathers Jerome, Ambrose, and John Chrysostom warned that laughter could lead to illicit sexual activity. According to John Climacus, "Impurity is touching the body, laughing, and talking without restraint." People without temperance, he said, "have a shameless gaze and laugh immoderately."[6]

Unlike the other objections we're discussing, this one *is* based on an essential feature of humor – that it is a kind of enjoyment. Nonetheless, it does not establish an essential connection between enjoyment and wrongdoing. While any pleasure may whet our appetite for more, not all pleasure pushes us into hedonism. We can enjoy fine food, music, and art, for example, without doing anything wrong. Similarly, we can enjoy humor.

To the charge that humor fosters sexual license, the answer is that much humor is unrelated to sex. And even humor that is *about* objectionable sexual behavior need not *promote* such behavior. Amusement and laughter tend to diminish sexual passion, as we said earlier.

5. *Humor diminishes self-control*

Self-control is a universal ideal found in both religious and secular moral codes. But laughter involves a loss of muscle tone and coordination, and in a silly mood we are more likely to do things we would ordinarily avoid. Among the ancient Greeks, and among the early Christians influenced by them, this loss of self-control provided a major objection to laughter, as we saw in Chapter 1.

But while much humor involves a loss of self-control, not all does. Churchill's joke about the Italians *increased* his fellow Britons' self-control by reducing their negative emotions. Similarly, people in stressful occupations like medicine and police work often engage in humor in a way that reduces the stress and increases their self-control.

Even laughter which does reduce self-control is not necessarily objectionable, as long as that reduction does not lead to doing something objectionable or failing to do something required. As Thomas Aquinas said, enjoying a hearty laugh can be an innocent and welcome release from tension and negative emotions.

6. *Humor is hostile*

Many moralists who warned of the loss of self-control in humor said that while laughing, it is natural to release violent urges. As noted in Chapter 1, Plato warned that the young Guardians of the ideal state should avoid laughter, and the Church Fathers discouraged it.

Here again we have a charge against only some humor. What's more, as we'll see in the next chapter, humor often serves as a social lubricant to reduce conflict and promote cooperation.

7. *Humor fosters anarchy*

According to traditional critiques, the cumulative effect of the vices associated with laughter and humor is a breakdown of the social order. From Aristophanes on, comedians have mocked political, intellectual, and religious leaders and institutions. While tragedy, along with epic, celebrated the heroic, patriarchal tradition of warrior leaders, comedy challenged that tradition. In Aristophanes' *Lysistrata*, for example, women brought the whole military and political system of the Greek city-states to its knees, making the men look foolish. In his comedy *The Acharnians*, the demigod Amphitheus is sent to earth but finds himself short of cash. So he has to borrow from humans. In *The Frogs*, the god Dionysus, travelling to Hades across the infernal lake, must pay for his passage and even has to help row the boat, which makes his backside sore. At Pluto's gate, he gets scared and soils himself. Then, in a challenge to his claim of divinity, he is whipped to see if he cries (real gods don't cry). All such mockery in comedy, Plato complained, is a threat to religion and to social order in general.

My twofold response to the charge that humor fosters anarchy is that much humor does not, and the humor that does challenge the status quo is sometimes beneficial. Aristophanes' *Lysistrata* called attention to the absurdity of the constant warfare between the Greek city-states, and to values neglected by centuries of patriarchy. In ancient Athens, comedy and democracy grew up side by side, and the critical spirit of comedy seems an important part of modern democracies. In Germany in the 1920s, cabaret comics were the first public figures to question the rise of Hitler. In the 1960s and 1970s, stand-up comedians like Godfrey Cambridge and Lili Tomlin helped raise people's consciousness about racial and gender discrimination.

8. Humor is foolish

This last of the traditional objections can be seen as an amalgamation of several other objections we have considered. To call laughing persons fools is to charge them with being intellectually, emotionally, or morally defective. In the Bible, the opposite of the fool is the wise person. "The wise man has eyes in his head, but the fool walks in the dark," says Ecclesiastes 2:14. While foolishness is expressed in laughter, wisdom is associated with sadness, as in Ecclesiastes 7:3–4: "Sorrow is better than laughter, for by sadness of countenance the heart is made glad. The heart of the wise is in the house of mourning; but the heart of fools is in the house of mirth."

In Christianity there is a tradition recommending sadness to counteract foolishness and to give one's life sober wisdom. The Epistle of James (4:9) encourages Christians to "Lament and mourn and weep. Let your laughter be turned into mourning and your joy into dejection." John Climacus had similar advice: "In your heart, be like an emperor . . . commanding laughter: 'Go,' and it goes; and sweet weeping: 'Come,' and it comes."[7]

Like the other objections to humor, of which this is an amalgamation, this one does not apply to all humor and does not present an objection to humor per se.

None of the traditional global objections to humor, I conclude, is reasonable. And so if there are morally objectionable kinds of humor – and it seems there are – then we need a more sophisticated analysis to pick them out and show what is wrong in them. Such an analysis should also tell us when humor is morally praiseworthy and why – something we'll do in the next chapter.

The Shortcomings in the Contemporary Ethics of Humor

There are a few philosophers today writing in a broad way about the ethics of humor – e.g., Robert C. Roberts, John Lippitt, Laurence Goldstein, and Nickolas Pappas. But the simplistic analysis of a few limited examples characteristic of traditional ethical assessments of humor is still widespread. Most contemporary ethical writings on humor, for example, center around what Ronald de Sousa calls the *phthonic* element – the malicious beliefs and attitudes – in racist and sexist jokes. Even if this approach yielded a correct analysis of racist and sexist jokes, it would have explained only a small part of the ethics of humor. But worse, this approach is usually naïve even for the jokes it tries to explain.

The most common kind of ethnic joke, for example, is a story in which one or more members of an ethnic group do or say something that shows stupidity, laziness, sexual immorality, or some other shortcoming. Most philosophers have simply assumed that these jokes are expressions of hostility toward the "target" group. Michael Philips's often-cited article "Racist Acts and Racist Humor" begins: "Racist jokes are often funny. And part of this has to do with their racism. Many Polish jokes, for example, may easily be converted into moron jokes but are not at all funny when delivered as such."[8]

Philips's classification of Polish jokes as racist flies in the face of what social scientists have learned about ethnic jokes in the past three decades. From studying thousands of jokes around the world, anthropologist Christie Davies discovered that the same "stupid" jokes told about Poles in the US are told about the Belgians in France, the Sikhs in India, and the Tasmanians in Australia. Similarly, jokes attributing cowardice and other vices to ethnic groups are found in dozens of countries. And everywhere, Davies shows, the social pattern is the same. People tell ethnic jokes not about a group they despise, but about a familiar group, much like themselves, who live at the margin of their culture.[9] Joke tellers usually do not believe the characterizations in the jokes to be true. Poles are not believed to be generally stupid, Greek males are not believed to be all homosexuals, and Italians are not believed to be cowards. What the joke tellers are laughing at is a slightly different version of themselves, Davies says, and their laughter is typically not hostile or malicious. When one group hates another, they express their feelings in more direct and damaging ways than by telling jokes.

"Stupid" jokes became popular over the last two centuries, according to Davies, because of people's anxiety about staying abreast of current knowledge and skills, especially in the workplace. The heyday of Polish jokes in the United States a few decades ago was not a time when Americans felt hostile to Poles or discriminated against them; Polish people had already been well integrated into American culture. But this was a time when Americans wondered about science education in the US. Consider the joke about the Polish astronaut who announced that he was planning to fly his rocket to the sun. When asked how he could withstand the sun's heat, he said, "Don't worry, I'll go at night." According to Davies, this joke did not express Americans' contempt for Poles as stupid, but their fears about their own scientific and technological ignorance.

Philosophers aren't the only ones who jump to conclusions in calling jokes "racist." In 2002 British MP Ann Winterton was forced to resign from Parliament for telling the following joke at a dinner:

> There were an Englishman, a Cuban, a Japanese man, and a Pakistani on a train. The Cuban throws a cigar out the window, saying they are ten-a-penny in his country. The Japanese man throws a Nikon camera out, saying they are ten-a-penny in his country. Then the Englishman throws the Pakistani out the window.

The punch line here implies that the Englishman was about to say that Pakistanis were ten-a-penny in his country. Does this punch line put down Pakistanis? If it does, what negative trait does it ascribe to them? It seems more plausible to say that the butt of this joke is racist English people, who treat Pakistanis and other former colonials unfairly. The Pakistani in this joke doesn't do anything, and isn't even described. It is the Englishman who acts, by murdering him. If the target of the joke is English racism, of course, the joke isn't an expression of prejudice and hostility toward Pakistanis.

It may not be possible to decide on one interpretation of this joke, or any joke, as *the correct* interpretation. Different people tell the same joke in different ways and are amused for different reasons. A racist who hates Pakistanis may enjoy the joke above because it involves the murder of a Pakistani. Someone else may laugh at the clever way the punch line preserves the narrative's rhythm of throwing something out the window, with a shocking result. A third person, perhaps Pakistani, may laugh at the irrational way the Englishman thought that the occasion of discarding readily available things justified his murdering the Pakistani. In light of all their discussions about indeterminacy and meaning, philosophers should be especially sensitive to the different ways jokes can be interpreted, but most articles in philosophy journals provide one interpretation per joke as *the* interpretation, and then confidently tell us what that interpretation implies.

One of the most widely discussed jokes in the ethics of humor comes from Ronald de Sousa's "When Is It Wrong to Laugh?"

> Margaret Trudeau [former wife of Canadian Prime Minister Pierre Trudeau] goes to visit the hockey team. When she emerges she complains that she has been gang-raped. Wishful thinking.[10]

De Sousa describes a conversation with a university student who claimed to have written this joke. He told the student that "the joke seems to imply certain beliefs. One is the belief that all women secretly want to be raped."[11] The student protested that what the joke was really about was the common knowledge that Margaret Trudeau was promiscuous. De Sousa agreed that this is an assumption of the joke, but commented that,

> Embedded in the very use of the word "promiscuous" in this context are something like the following propositions: that rape is just a variant form of sexual intercourse; that women's sexual desires are indiscriminate; and that there is something intrinsically objectionable or evil about a woman who wants or gets a lot of sex. These are sexist assumptions.[12]

I agree with de Sousa that those three propositions are sexist and that calling a woman "promiscuous" implies a negative assessment of women's getting a lot of sex. But I don't see a good reason to accept his claim that someone telling the Margaret Trudeau joke assumes that the sexual desires of all women are indiscriminate, or assumes that all women secretly want to be raped. Why can't the joke simply mock *Margaret Trudeau* – not all women – for having indiscriminate sexual desires? Doesn't calling a woman "promiscuous" compare *her* sexual desires with those of *normal* women, that is, women who are *not* promiscuous?

Answering such questions is difficult because the joke itself is structured so poorly that the punch line seems to make the text incoherent.

If Margaret Trudeau *complained* that she had been gang-raped, then why attribute *wishful thinking* to her? If she is engaged in wishful thinking, then she *wasn't* gang-raped? But then why did she complain that she was? Was she, perhaps, lying in order to bring a pleasing fantasy before her imagination? De Sousa doesn't even ask such questions. In the belief that "all rape jokes are variants of the same basic joke,"[13] he simply offers his analysis of this joke as the correct one.

A More Comprehensive Approach: The Ethics of Disengagement

I will be discussing racist and sexist jokes, but as part of a general ethics of humor. And in these moral reflections, I want to pay attention to the special psychological and linguistic features of humor, instead of, for example, treating jokes as if they were assertions, as many philosophers do. The central feature here is the playful disengagement of non-bona-fide language and actions.

This non-practical, non-cognitive orientation is something humor shares with play in general and with aesthetic experience. In all three, we are for the moment not concerned with gaining knowledge or achieving practical gain.[14] We are disengaged, idle, "distanced." While joking with friends, for example, nothing is urgent, no action is called for. We are not attending to anyone's needs, but are like art lovers strolling through a gallery or music lovers listening to a concert. That is why Ludovici spoke of the "indolence of humor"[15] and Hobbes said, "They that are intent on great designs have not time to laugh."[16]

The practical disengagement of humor, as we have seen, helps explain the opposition between amusement and negative emotions. To have practical concern about a situation is to be emotionally involved with it. A situation that does not meet with our approval naturally elicits fear, anger, or hatred, if we are focused on ourselves; and compassion, if someone else is suffering the setback. As Henri Bergson said, "Laughter is incompatible with emotion. Depict some fault, however trifling, in such a way as to arouse sympathy, fear, or pity; the mischief is done, it is impossible for us to laugh."[17]

When we want to evoke anger or outrage about some problem, we don't present it in a humorous way, precisely because of the practical disengagement of humor. Satire is not a weapon of revolutionaries.

Humor involves cognitive as well as practical disengagement. While something is making us laugh, we are for the moment not concerned with whether it is real or fictional. As we have said, the creator of humor puts ideas into our heads not to communicate information, but for the delight those ideas will bring. And so we grant comic license to people telling funny anecdotes, letting them exaggerate the absurdity of real situations, and create extra details. Indeed, someone listening to a funny story who tried to correct the teller – "No, she didn't spill her drink on the mayor *and* the governor, just on the mayor" – will probably be hushed up by the other listeners.

As in play and in aesthetic experience, the practical and cognitive disengagement in humor can have harmful effects. I will focus on three. First, the disengagement can be irresponsible, as we neglect actions that are called for, and do things that should not be done. Secondly, it can block compassion. And thirdly, it can promote prejudice.

First Harmful Effect: Irresponsibility

Humor can disengage us from what we are doing or failing to do. To follow the parallel with play and aesthetic experience, there is nothing intrinsically wrong with playing music, but when Nero played as Rome burned, that was objectionable. There is nothing intrinsically wrong with creating *bons mots*. But when Marie Antoinette responded to reports of famine by saying "Let them eat cake," that was objectionable because, as queen, she was supposed to care about her people.

In our daily lives, we sometimes "laugh off" a problem or criticism instead of taking appropriate action. If my doctor puts me on a special diabetic diet, warning me of blindness or early death if I don't follow it, then I may discount her advice with a quip like "She's fatter than I am" and ignore the diet. Or if my friend needs my help in controlling his alcoholism, and the next time he gets drunk I laugh at his antics instead of helping him restore self-discipline, then my humor is also irresponsible.

In Stanley Milgram's famous experiments with obedience to authority figures, where subjects were ordered to give potentially fatal electric shocks to people simply for not remembering word associations, 14 of 40 subjects burst out laughing and then administered the shock.[18] Here laughter seems like whistling in the dark, a way to suppress legitimate concern.

In laughing off some problem, we treat it as trivial. It is unimportant, "no big deal," and thus doesn't call for our attention. An extreme case of humor supporting irresponsibility is the "total cynic" who laughs at everything and assumes no responsibility for anything. The MTV program *Beavis and Butt-Head* is based on such characters.

This disengagement fostered by humor is often deliberately used by politicians to deflect criticism. During their famous debates, as Abraham Lincoln began waffling on an important issue, Stephen Douglas accused him of being "two-faced." Lincoln responded, "Ladies and gentlemen, I leave it to you. If I had two faces, would I be wearing this one?" When John Kennedy was criticized for using his father's massive wealth to finance his bid for the Presidency, he staged an event at a fund-raising dinner. Pretending to open a telegram, Kennedy said, "I have just received a telegram from my generous daddy: 'Dear Jack, Don't spend a dollar more than is necessary. I'll be damned if I'll pay for a landslide.'" In his first televised debate with Walter Mondale before the 1984 election, incumbent Ronald Reagan sounded uninformed and confused. Critics said that as the oldest presidential candidate in history, he was simply not up to the job. For the next TV debate, therefore, Reagan's handlers prepared a funny line for him to memorize. As soon as a reporter asked about the "age issue," Reagan said, "I am not going to make age an issue in this campaign. I am not going to exploit for political gain my opponent's youth and inexperience." The audience laughed, the age issue evaporated, and Reagan went on to win by one of the greatest margins in history. He was probably in the early stages of Alzheimer's disease, as we now know, but this joke made it impossible for anyone to bring up such a possibility.

Second Harmful Effect: Blocking Compassion

Another way the disengagement in humor can cause harm is by blocking compassion for those who need help. In such cases, humor can harm in two ways – by displacing action, and by insulting those who are suffering, thus increasing their suffering. Suppose that I am walking along an icy sidewalk and see someone awkwardly slip and fall into a puddle, breaking his wrist. If I stand back and laugh, then not only have I not helped him, but my treating his accident as mere material for my amusement has demeaned him, belittled him, made him feel that he doesn't matter. From the way I am laughing, it seems that his suffering is no more important than the pain of Wile E. Coyote in Roadrunner cartoons. As Peter Jones put it, "The victim of laughter is confronted by the reaction of a mere spectator."[19]

In cases of mild suffering, we call such humor insensitive or callous; in more serious cases we call it cruel. Consider the cover of the July 1974 "Dessert Issue" of *National Lampoon* magazine. In 1971 George Harrison and others had done a charity concert to benefit victims of a famine in Bangladesh. That was made into the record album *Concert for Bangladesh*, whose cover was a photograph of a starving child. The cover of *National Lampoon's* "Dessert Issue" looked almost identical to that photograph, only it was of a *chocolate sculpture* of a starving child, with part of the head bitten off.

A good deal of humor in past centuries was similarly cruel. Laughing at dwarves and people with deformities, and at the mentally retarded and the insane, was common. In ancient Roman slave markets, deformed and idiotic children often brought high prices because buyers found them amusing. Cruelty also grew into sadism, as people caused the suffering that they enjoyed. The Roman emperor Trajan celebrated a military victory in 106 CE by having 5,000 pairs of gladiators fight to the death. In fifteenth-century Paris, burning cats was a form of home entertainment. Before the French Revolution, members of the nobility would visit insane asylums to taunt the inmates, by clanking their canes across the bars, for example. In Britain, bear-baiting was popular until the nineteenth century. For a special royal festival attended by Elizabeth I in 1575, 13 chained bears were torn to death by dogs. Idi Amin is said to have cut off the limbs of one of his wives and sewn them onto the opposite sides of her body, for his own amusement. A more recent example of sadistic humor is the humiliation of prisoners by Americans in Abu Ghraib prison in Iraq. When asked why they made the men pile on top of one another naked, soldiers said that it was a joke, "just for fun."

Even when such fun does not involve the suffering of someone present, so that it does not directly humiliate people and increase their suffering, humor can promote insensitivity, callousness, or cruelty toward those being laughed about. The *National Lampoon* cover was probably not seen by starving children in Bangladesh or their parents, but still, it tended to inure readers of the magazine to their suffering, the suffering of other famine victims, and, generally, human beings needing help.

Such desensitization can be objectionable even when the humorous situation is fictional. In the best-selling video game "Grand Theft Auto," players stealing cars score extra points for hitting pedestrians, who scream and bleed on the screen. The debate over the last several decades about the effects of watching violence on television is relevant here. While it has not been proven to everyone's satisfaction that watching television violence motivates viewers to act violently, it does seem clear that watching thousands of violent acts on television each year makes viewers less upset by real violence and less compassionate toward its victims. Similarly, laughing at fictional suffering can make us less sensitive to real suffering.

Perhaps the most widely accepted moral rule is to not cause unnecessary suffering. From that it follows that we should not laugh at someone's problem when compassion is called for.

Third Harmful Effect: Promoting Prejudice

The two harmful effects of humor we have seen so far – blocking action and blocking compassion – are based on the way humor disengages us *practically* from what we are laughing about. A third harmful effect is based on the way it disengages us *cognitively* from the object of amusement. Here we will finally get to what is wrong with racist and sexist jokes. But we need to be careful in pinpointing what's wrong here. Many ethical analyses of sexist and racist jokes treat them as if they were assertions intended to create or reinforce prejudicial beliefs in listeners. For example, Michael Philips introduces the question "Is truth a defense against the charge of racism?" in this way: "What if members of that group really have or statistically tend to have an unflattering characteristic a joke attributes to them? Surely we are allowed to notice this and to communicate this information to one another."[20]

Ronald de Sousa traces the evil in sexist and racist jokes to the sexist and racist beliefs that they imply, typically beliefs about undesirable traits in the target group. The joke about Margaret Trudeau, according to de Sousa, is based on the belief that all women secretly want to be raped, and so listeners can't find it funny unless they have that belief. Merrie Bergmann, agreeing with this "anhypothetical" analysis of sexist humor, says that "Sexist humor does not just incidentally incorporate sexist beliefs – it depends upon those beliefs for the fun . . . the story about Trudeau is funny only if rape is desirable to women."[21]

While de Sousa and Bergmann are right that the tellers of sexist and racist jokes promote prejudice, their understanding of how this occurs is simplistic. Like most ethicists analyzing sexist and racist jokes, they overlook the fact that sexist and racist jokes, like jokes in general, are known to be fictional by tellers and audience alike. We often introduce jokes with play signals such as, "Have you heard the one about . . . ?" and we use the present instead of the past tense to indicate that what we are saying is not a report of a real event.

Adding to this unreality, what characters in jokes say and do is unlike what real people say and do. When these characters are stupid, lazy, or sexually promiscuous, the degree of those shortcomings is usually exaggerated far beyond what they are in any real human being. In the Polish astronaut joke, the man's belief that flying to the sun at night would keep him cool isn't just stupid, but more stupid than any real person's beliefs.

This fantastic exaggeration found in so much humor is ignored by virtually all ethicists writing about ethnic jokes, who treat those jokes as if they were assertions that Poles are stupid, black people are lazy, etc. Such bald assertions, however, are not funny and are easy to falsify. When people are communicating information, listeners often think that what a speaker is saying or implying is false, and so they question or contradict that person. But we don't question or contradict joke tellers. No one hearing the joke above would say, "There *are* no Polish astronauts," or "Most Poles *are not* stupid." Neither those telling this joke nor their listeners are committed to a belief in the existence of Polish astronauts, or to a belief that Poles in general are stupid.

Indeed, we could enjoy this joke even though we had no beliefs at all about Poles. The first time I heard a version of this joke, at a humor conference in the Netherlands, it was told about a *Frisian* astronaut. I had no idea who Frisians were, but I still enjoyed the picture of the astronaut saying that traveling at night would solve the problem of the sun's heat. The next day when I learned that the Frisians are an ethnic group living in the northern part of the Netherlands, I still did not *believe* that Frisians are stupid, any more than I *believe* that Poles are stupid when I laugh at Polish jokes.

The stupidity of the character in this joke, I suggest, is not a piece of information being communicated, but a fantastic idea being presented for playful enjoyment. What most people enjoy in hearing this joke is not a belief that they are superior to Poles or Frisians, but the mental gymnastics they go through in making sense of the line "I'll go at night" – all the while knowing that no real person would say such a thing in earnest.

Whatever might be objectionable about telling standard sexist and racist jokes, then, it is not that they *assert* or *imply* that certain groups of people have preposterous degrees of stupidity, sexual promiscuity, etc. But that does not let the tellers of such jokes off the moral hook, for there are other ways to promote prejudice. Those who circulate racist and sexist jokes do it, I suggest, not by making truth-claims but by being *indifferent* to the truth. They are disengaged cognitively and practically from the stereotypes in what they are saying, and they don't care about the harm that circulating those stereotypes may cause.

What usually makes these jokes harmful is that they present characters with exaggerated degrees of undesirable traits who represent groups that some people believe actually have those traits. Indeed, we sort such jokes into genres largely by naming the ethnic or gender group and the shortcoming, that is, the stereotype being exaggerated. There is the Dumb Blonde joke, the Flighty Fag joke, the Dishonest Greek joke, etc. To write a new joke of one of these types, you create a story about members of the target group that attributes an exaggerated degree of the short-coming to those characters.

The fun in these jokes is based on stretching negative stereotypes. Whether the tellers of sexist and racist jokes accept those stereotypes or not, their playing with them through exaggeration converts morally objectionable ideas into palatable ones. Putting a "play frame" around stereotypes in a joke aestheticizes them, removing them, at least tempor-arily, from moral scrutiny. As listeners enjoy sexist and racist jokes, they let harmful stereotypes in under their moral radar. A straightforward assertion might quickly draw criticism, but an exaggerated version of a stereotype presented in a clever way will probably be simply enjoyed.

Humor's play frame allows prejudicial ideas to be slipped into people's heads without being evaluated. It even allows for the creation of stereo-types that any reasonable person would reject out of hand were they asserted. In the 2006 comedy *Borat: Cultural Learnings of America for Make Benefit Glorious Nation of Kazakhstan*, Sacha Baron Cohen plays a Kazakh journalist who is a crude, boorish, incestuous, anti-Semitic, racist, Gypsy-hating, sexist boor, as are the other Kazakhs in this fake doc-umentary. Borat introduces the "town rapist" and boasts that his sister is the "Number Four prostitute in our country."

In reality, no Kazakhs appear in the film: Cohen based his new stereo-type on people he met in southern Russia. The village shown and its inhab-itants are Rumanian. Real Kazakhs are not Slavic but a mix of Turkic and Mongolian, and they don't look like Cohen or the people in the film. In the nineteenth century the Kazakhs were invaded by Russia; thousands died resisting colonization and conscription into the Russian army. Under Stalin and Khruschev, huge tracts of their grazing land were con-verted to agriculture to feed Russians. For resisting, a million and a half Kazakhs died, along with 80 percent of their livestock. Russian settlers were brought in to displace Kazakhs, until by the 1970s Kazakhstan was the only Soviet republic in which the native people were in the minority.

In creating his new fictitious stereotype of Kazakhs, with negative features often attributed to Russians, Cohen insulted Kazakhs twice. He portrayed them as having vices they don't have: anti-Semitism was never widespread in Kazakhstan, nor was the persecution of Gypsies; women have rights equal to men's. And secondly, the vices he attributes to Kazakhs he took from stereotypes of their Russian oppressors. The deep offense here was obvious in a four-page advertisement taken out by the government of Kazakhstan in the *New York Times* before the release of the film, to counteract the stereotype Cohen had created. A simple question asked by critics was why Cohen had not thought up a fictitious country to go with his fictitious stereotype.

Racist and sexist jokes are not alone in their power to convert objectionable stereotypes into aesthetic objects. Some antique dealers, for example, specialize in items from the racist American culture of the nineteenth and twentieth centuries, such as lawn ornaments of "house niggers" and commercial packages featuring images like Aunt Jemima – an obese "mammy" with fat lips and a stupid expression. If challenged about trading in such items, dealers typically say that they do not endorse the racism, but are simply collecting Americana. While there are legitimate historical reasons for preserving such objects, it is important to be aware of the way they have promoted racism in the past and can do so today.

What is objectionable about sexist and racist stereotypes, of course, is that they categorize all members of a group as being interchangeable and as having certain shortcomings. Instead of respecting group members as individual persons, those who think in stereotypes tend to write them all off as inferior. They belittle, demean, dismiss them. To use the archaic verb from which we get "contempt," they contemn the whole group – they treat its members as low, worthless, beneath notice. As Richard Mohr has said of anti-gay jokes, "The individual as distinctive is erased, dissolved into a prejudged type which determines in society's eyes all of his or her significant characteristics. The jokes . . . presume that a gay person is nothing but his sexual orientation and its efflorescences."[22]

Pace de Sousa and Bergmann, nothing as cognitively sophisticated as belief is required for such jokes to do harm. Mere repeated thinking of groups in negative stereotypes is enough to prompt us to treat real individuals not according to their actual merits and shortcomings, and so justly, but as automatically inferior because they belong to those groups. In milder cases, this mistreatment may involve only condescension, but in other cases, as under Jim Crow, South African apartheid, and homophobia, it involves malicious distrust, hatred, oppression, and even murder. That's why groups who have suffered from such mistreatment often show resentment for the humor that stereotyped them – American blacks for Jim Crow humor, women for sexist jokes, and gays for "fag jokes."[23]

The objectionableness of jokes based on stereotypes, I suggest, is not all-or-nothing, but is proportional to the harm those stereotypes are likely to cause. Where a stereotype leads to little or no harm, a joke based on it may even be acceptable to the target group as a badge of their identity. Comedian Jeff Foxworthy has built a huge career in stand-up comedy and publishing on telling "redneck jokes" to "rednecks." Handsome, well dressed, and articulate, Foxworthy doesn't exhibit the features of the rednecks in his jokes. But Dan Whitney, who performs as "Larry the Cable Guy," dresses and acts slovenly, vulgar, and stupid, and in doing so has endeared himself even more to redneck audiences. Whitney is currently the most successful comedian in the United States, making $250,000 per performance.

Another group stereotyped in jokes who seem to like the stereotype is lawyers:

> Two lawyers on a fishing trip in Alaska awake one morning to see a grizzly bear running toward their tent. One hurriedly starts putting on his running shoes.
>
> "Don't be a fool," the other lawyer says. "You can't outrun a grizzly bear."
>
> "I don't have to outrun *him*," the first lawyer says, "I only have to out-run *you*."

This joke is based on the image of lawyers as tough-minded and un-caring, and retelling it helps keep that stereotype alive. But does the joke or the stereotype lead to the mistreatment of lawyers? Do people act condescendingly toward lawyers, insult them, or deny them jobs because of that stereotype? Hardly. Lawyers are a powerful and respected group in our society, and the stereotype of the tough-minded, unsentimental lawyer enhances rather than threatens their power and position. In fact, lawyers even put that stereotype to work in TV commercials and Yellow Pages advertising for law firms.

Another group enjoying considerable power and prestige in our cul-ture is physicians. There are hundreds of doctor jokes based on stereo-types, particularly of doctors as egotistical and irritable. Speaking at a conference of physicians recently, I tested out this joke from the *Journal of Nursing Jocularity*:

> Why do nurses *like* PMS?
> Because once a month they get to act like doctors.

Only half of the doctors laughed. Maybe that's because being stereotyped as temperamental and irrational is more insulting to doctors than the stereotype of lawyers in the bear joke is to lawyers. But still, doctors continue to enjoy great prestige and respect in our society, and do not have their civil rights denied them.

All this contrasts sharply with the harm black people, women, and homosexuals have endured because of the stereotypes circulated about them. Not only have they been insulted, but they have suffered discrimination in voting, in buying real estate, and in the courts. Racist and sexist stereotypes cost them money, respect, status, and power. That is precisely why so many people object to sexist and racist jokes, while not objecting to lawyer and doctor jokes. A good example is the outrage prompted by radio talk show host Don Imus in April 2007 when he referred to the mostly black women's basketball team of Rutgers University, who had lost the NCAA finals game a day earlier, as "nappy headed hos." That comment got him fired by CBS.

The stereotypes perpetuated by jokes are more objectionable, then, when they are about people who lack social status and power, and when those stereotypes are part of the social system that marginalizes them and "keeps them in their place." Here we can rightly criticize what Joseph Boskin calls "the complicity of humor."[24]

From considering the cognitive and practical disengagements in humor, and the irresponsibility, cruelty, and other forms of harm that can result from them, we can propose a general ethical principle, along the lines of "Don't play with fire": Do not promote a lack of concern for something about which people should be concerned.

Chapter 6

Having a Good Laugh
The Positive Ethics of Humor

"But, seriously . . ."

While the disengagement in humor can be harmful in several ways, as we've seen, it can also be beneficial. This chapter will further examine humor's benefits, to build a positive ethics of humor. My approach is that of Aristotle, who coined the term *eutrapelia*, and Thomas Aquinas, who defined *eutrapelos* as "a pleasant person with a happy cast of mind who gives his words and deeds a cheerful turn."[1] Both considered humor, under the right circumstances, a virtue, that is, a habit that was an *areté*, an excellence.

Aristotle distinguished two kinds of virtue, intellectual and moral. With humor, we will see, these are closely related, since the way we perceive and think has a lot to do with the way we act and treat other people. The basic value of amusement is that it allows us to transcend narrowly focused, emotional responses to situations, so that we think and act more rationally. As we saw in Chapter 2, humor involves the ability to process our perceptions, memories, and imagined ideas in a way that rises above what is real, here, now, personal, and practical. That ability is not found in the lower animals, but evolved in humans as part of our rationality.

Brian Boyd has suggested that the evolution of humor was in part a way of preparing early humans for novel and surprising experiences.[2] The ability to enjoy surprises made them more flexible and adaptable in the many new environments into which they ventured.

Intellectual Virtues Fostered by Humor

By fostering a playful attitude toward new and unusual experiences in early humans, humor eventually promoted several intellectual virtues. One is open-mindedness. Even today, people who are not open to new information and perspectives not only perceive themselves as not humorous,[3] but even need more time to recognize something as an instance of humor.[4] Openness to new experiences also makes people more adaptable to change and more accepting of what we now call diversity.

Another virtue fostered by humor is divergent or creative thinking. As Edward de Bono has commented, "Humor is by far the most significant behavior of the human brain. . . . Humor . . . shows how perceptions set up in one way can suddenly be reconfigured in another way. This is the essence of creativity."[5] In the research of Alice Isen and of Avner Ziv, people who engaged in humor exercises before doing "brainstorming" thought up more solutions and more varied solutions to problems. Those who had *experienced* something funny, such as a comedy video-tape, were more creative than a control group, and those who had *generated* humor – as by thinking up captions for cartoon drawings – were more creative yet.[6]

Humor promotes divergent thinking in two ways. First, it blocks negative emotions such as fear, anger, and sadness, which suppress creativity by steering thought into familiar channels. Secondly, humor is a way of appreciating cognitive shifts: when we are in a humorous frame of mind, we are automatically on the lookout for unusual ideas and new ways of putting ideas together.

A third intellectual virtue fostered by humor is critical thinking. In looking for incongruity in society, we look for discrepancies between what people should do, what they say they do, and what they actually do. From the days of the ancient Greeks, comedy has focused on self-deception, pretense, and hypocrisy. Indeed, Plato said that the essence of the comic is thinking of oneself as better than one actually is. In looking for the comic, then, we look beneath appearances and do not accept what people say at face value.

In a humorous frame of mind, therefore, we are not as likely to blindly follow leaders, or do something merely because "we've always done it this way." The humorous person may be irreverent and even disrespectful toward those in authority, but that can be beneficial, especially if leaders are deceiving people. Political satirists like Jon Stewart and Bill Mahar encourage us to think twice before accepting any political message.

It is useful for even honest, well-intentioned leaders to have people think for themselves and ask challenging questions. That prevents what Irving Janis calls "Groupthink."[7] Spurring critical thinking through humor was even institutionalized in the traditional role of the court jester.[8] From the imperial courts of ancient Egypt and China to nineteenth-century European palaces, monarchs had jesters to tell them what no one else dared. When the Chinese Emperor Er Shi came to the throne in 209 BCE, he announced that he wanted to lacquer the Great Wall. Twisty Pole, his jester, said:

> That's a splendid idea. If you hadn't mentioned it, Your Majesty, I'd certainly have suggested it myself. It might mean an awful lot of toil and trouble for the ordinary people, but all the same it's a magnificent project. Lacquer the Great Wall all smooth and shiny, then it'll be too slippery for any invaders to climb over. Now, let's get down to the practical side of the job. The lacquering's easy enough, but building the drying room may present a problem or two.

At that point, the court record says, the emperor burst out laughing and quietly shelved the project.[9]

Several American presidents could have profited from having someone like Twisty Pole in their cabinets. When John Kennedy came into office in 1961, for example, he inherited from the Eisenhower administration a deeply flawed plan to invade Cuba. He presented the plan to his new Cabinet, and they all dutifully agreed with it; therefore the invasion was launched. Had Mort Sahl or George Carlin been Jester General, Kennedy would have heard some criticism of the plan, and the Bay of Pigs fiasco might have been avoided.

Democracy requires critical thinking and discussion, and so it's no accident that both democracy and comedy were born in fifth-century Athens. Before the American Revolution, too, there were over 530 satires in print in the colonies, many about the king. The leaders of the Revolution often used humor to make their case. At the signing of the Declaration of Independence, Ben Franklin said to his colleagues, "Gentlemen, we must all hang together, or, most assuredly, we will all hang separately."

Since the Revolution, political humor has often kept a critical, democratic spirit alive in the United States. Consider the cartoons of Thomas Nast in the nineteenth century, and of Tom Toles and Gary Trudeau today. During President Reagan's military build-up in the 1980s, *The Pentagon Catalog*[10] was published. It featured items such as a $640 toilet seat and a $7,622 coffee maker that military contractors had sold to the Defense Department. Protruding through a hole in the cover of the catalog is a half-inch steel nut ($.08 at a hardware store). "Buy this Catalog for Only $4.95 and Get this $2,043 Nut for Free," the blurb says. That's the price at which the McDonnell-Douglas Corporation sold such nuts to the Department of the Navy, describing them as "hexiform rotatable surface compression units."

Other satirical publications from the 1980s are *The Wit and Wisdom of George Bush*, *The Quayle Quarterly*, and *The Clothes Have No Emperor: A Chronicle of the American 80s.*[11] The last book includes this item from January 20, 1983 about Reagan's Secretary of the Interior:

> In an interview with *Business Week*, James Watt compares environmentalists to Nazis. "Look what happened to Germany in the 1930s," he says. "The dignity of man was subordinated to the powers of Nazism . . . Those are the forces that this can evolve into."

Even the business world has caught on to the value of humor in blocking Groupthink and encouraging critical thinking. An example is the Canadian Imperial Bank of Commerce, which, like many corporations, produces a monthly video for its employees. On most corporate videos, leaders present themselves as omniscient and infallible, but on the CIBC videos, a wisecracking hand puppet shows up to ask the CEO tough questions about recent decisions and policies. Employees love this feature of the videos, because the humor allows everyone to talk about issues in an open, honest way. That not only empowers them but leads to a wider range of ideas than would be forthcoming under Groupthink.

Moral Virtues Fostered by Humor

All these intellectual virtues are intertwined with moral virtues. A basic moral skill is self-transcendence: rising above personal concern to appreciate the interests of others. Inversely, egocentrism is a basic form of amorality and immorality. A person who could think only of here/now/me would be either infantile or sociopathic, in either case lacking the moral point of view.

The call for self-transcendence is found not just in philosophical moral systems, but in the ethics of religions as diverse as Buddhism, Confucianism, Judaism, and Christianity.

Humor, at its best, has moral and religious significance, Peter Berger has argued, because it involves this self-transcendence.[12] It liberates us from the narrow perspective of fight-or-flight emotions and helps us, as the old Candid Camera jingle put it, to see ourselves as other people do.

In almost any situation where we begin to respond with self-focused emotions, the virtuous thing to do will involve overcoming those emotions. When moral systems emphasize "self-control," what they mean is largely the ability to override the motivation of emotions. And for overriding emotions, nothing beats humor, especially humor about oneself. C. W. Metcalf described an interview with a cancer patient whose many surgeries had reduced him from a beefy 210 pounds to a weight under 100 pounds. "They could make another old fart from the pieces they've taken out of me," the man quipped.[13]

The ability to laugh at oneself not only fosters several virtues, as we will see, but is essential to the development of any moral perspective. As Robert C. Roberts put it, "A sense of humor about one's *own* foibles is a capacity of character-transcendence; but character-transcendence is basic to the very concept of a moral virtue."[14]

Seeing oneself objectively is also important in being honest with oneself instead of rationalizing one's shortcomings. Thus humor can contribute to self-knowledge, integrity, and mental health. Many psychiatrists now use humor to get patients out of their own heads to see their problems more objectively. In a technique called "Paradoxical Therapy," for example, the therapist responds to a patient's complaint that their nose is too big, for example, by adding, "And look at those *feet!*"[15]

Because all moral codes want us to transcend our "here/now/me" perspective, they encourage us to avoid anger, fear, and other self-focused emotions. Understanding the virtues that humor promotes is largely a matter of seeing which emotions humor reduces.

We can start with patience. Looking at things "in the big picture" with a sense of humor, we do not expect events to happen at just the speed we prefer. On vacation in New York State's Finger Lakes one summer, my family and I drove to a casual fish restaurant at the head of a beautiful lake for dinner. As we walked in, we noticed how crowded the place was, but the platters going by looked and smelled so good that we sat down and placed our order. Then we waited – 15 minutes, 17 minutes, 20 minutes. In looking around for the waiter, to complain, I noticed a sign on the wall:

WE PROMISE TO SERVE YOU IN FIVE MINUTES.
OR EIGHT OR NINE.
OR RELAX AND HAVE ANOTHER BEER –
IT CAN'T BE THAT MUCH LONGER.

I read the sign aloud, and we laughed. The management knew what they were doing, I realized, and they were moving as quickly as they could. So who was I to complain on this lovely day with a gorgeous lake right outside the window? I stopped looking at my watch and ordered another beer, as we struck up a conversation with the people at the next table. When our fish arrived, it was hot, tasty, and well worth the wait. That funny sign had completely changed our experience by eliciting our patience.

Allied with patience is acceptance of other people's shortcomings, and here too, humor can help. Humor is correlated with open-mindedness, as we said, and the willingness to see things in new ways makes us more understanding of other people, what they think, and how they act. In that way, humor can reduce social friction. Sammy Basu has examined how humor fosters religious tolerance.[16] In a more mundane setting, as I mentioned in Chapter 2, when I find myself in the first stages of road rage, I repeat George Carlin's quip, "Did you ever notice on the highway that everybody going faster than you is a maniac, and everyone going slower than you is a moron?"

Keeping our sense of humor makes us not only more tolerant of people's differences, but more gracious. Consider how Arizona Senator Barry Goldwater became a member of the Phoenix Country Club in the 1960s. Because his father was Jewish, the club initially rejected his application. Instead of getting angry or filing a lawsuit, Goldwater called the club president to ask a question. "Since I'm only *half*-Jewish, can I join if I just play *nine* holes?" The man laughed heartily and immediately let him in. Goldwater's humor had gently opened his eyes to the absurdity of the club's anti-Semitism and had given him an easy way to change its policy.

Graciousness is kindness that allows the other person – even someone who is morally blameworthy – to relax and not feel threatened. A person who is corrected with graciousness is more likely to listen to the message and act on it. A practical application of this principle is with debt collection letters. In their usual form – threatening the debtor with legal action or a bad credit rating – these letters often make people become defensive, unreasonable, and even hostile. But consider this middle paragraph from a debt collection letter: "We appreciate your business, but, please, give us a break. Your account is overdue ten months. That means we've carried you longer than your mother did." This message shows respect for the reader, but uses playful humor to persuade them to be reasonable and pay up.

Another application of the principle that humor makes criticism nonthreatening is with the defensive driving courses that traffic offenders are sent to by judges. Driving schools have long known that people resent having to take these courses, but until the 1980s no one had a systematic way to overcome this resentment. Then one driving school in Los Angeles hired a stand-up comedian to teach a defensive driving course. His funny approach to the lessons not only overcame students' resentment, but drew rave reviews from them. Many said that they actually looked forward to class. Today there are a dozen driving schools in California that have only professional comedians as instructors.

Humor not only reduces defensiveness but defuses conflict. That's why a number of police departments have trained their officers in using humor. In Troy, New York, one program involved having two officers answer calls to family fights. One was dressed in a standard uniform, and the other in a Daffy Duck costume. San Francisco police officer Adelle Roberts completed humor training with flying colors, and two weeks later answered a call for a family fight. Pulling up to the house in her car, she heard loud yelling and banging. As she approached the front door, a TV set came crashing through the front window. She knocked loudly.

A voice from inside bellowed, "Who is it?" "TV Repair," Roberts called out. The couple stopped fighting and came to the door with smiles on their faces.

Lives have been saved by humor. The most famous was that of Abraham Lincoln. A few years before becoming President, Lincoln was challenged to a duel. He agreed, provided that he could specify the weapons and the distance at which they would stand. The other gentleman agreed. Lincoln said, "Cow shit at five paces." And that was the end of the argument.

Not only did Lincoln's humor reduce his own negative emotion, so that he could act rationally, but it did the same for his opponent. His anti-bravado was also a clever way to admit that he was a poor shot and an even worse swordsman. It showed the virtue of humility. Looking for the humor in any situation is usually looking for human shortcomings, and, as Lincoln tacitly admitted, we can find plenty within ourselves.

The Most Rev Robert Runcie, Archbishop of Canterbury, told of how he once boarded a train to discover that the rest of the passengers in his car were mental patients going on a field trip. An attendant from the mental hospital came into the car to make sure he had everybody. "One, two, three, four, five," he counted. When he got to Runcie, he asked, "Who are you?" "I'm the Archbishop of Canterbury," Runcie said. The attendant smiled, pointed at him, and continued, "Six, seven, eight . . ."[17] Runcie's ability to see himself the way the hospital attendant saw him, and take delight in that perspective, showed humility of the first order.

Even etiquette sometimes prescribes humorous humility. The politest way to accept praise is to poke fun at yourself. When John Kennedy met with a group of schoolchildren at the White House, one asked, "Mr. President, how did you become a war hero?" Kennedy answered, "It was completely involuntary – they sank my boat." In making a joke to distract attention from his courage, Kennedy showed a higher kind of virtue.

When humility combines with patience, people can show considerable perseverance, another virtue fostered by humor. If we see our failures and mistakes with a comic eye, we are less likely to be overcome by feelings of frustration. In inventing the light bulb, Thomas Edison tried some 10,000 combinations of materials. When asked if he was upset by all his failed attempts, he said, "No, I just learned thousands of ways not to make a light bulb." His storage battery took almost 25,000 attempts. But with his sense of humor, he kept going. At his death, Edison had patented 1,093 inventions. In his desk were found slips of paper on which he had written notes to himself. One said: "Remember Jonah. He came out all right."

When perseverance operates in situations of danger, it becomes courage, and as we saw with Churchill's announcement about Italy's declaration of war, humor can promote courage by reducing fear. Medicine is a field in which fear is common and humor just as common as an antidote, as we saw in Chapter 3 with Erma Bombeck's reaction to her breast cancer.

Humor during the Holocaust

To further illustrate the value of humor, I would like to conclude this chapter by considering humor during the Holocaust. The very idea may at first seem jarring – incongruous but not funny! In Western culture there is a long tradition of prejudice against humor, especially in connection with anything as tragic as the Holocaust. Tragedy, on stage or in real life, is serious, even sublime, while humor and comedy are "light." When comedy appears within tragedy, as it often does in Shakespeare, it is usually discounted as mere "comic relief."

But the ancient Greeks, Shakespeare, and other dramatists took their comedy more seriously than that. They realized that comedy is not "time out" from the real world; rather it provides another perspective on that world. And that other perspective is no less valuable than the tragic perspective. As Conrad Hyers has suggested, comedy expresses a "stubborn refusal to give tragedy . . . the final say."[18] And that was certainly the case during the Holocaust.

In this period, humor had three main benefits. First was its critical function: humor focused attention on what was wrong and sparked resistance to it. Second was its cohesive function: it created solidarity in those laughing together at the oppressors. And third was its coping function: it helped the oppressed get through their suffering without going insane.

We can start with the critical function. During the rise of Hitler and the Third Reich, humorists were among the first to call attention to what was going wrong. The earliest criticisms of the Nazis came not from politicians or clergy, but from cabaret entertainers and newspaper cartoonists. At a time when most Americans did not want to know what was going on in Europe, Charlie Chaplin's *The Great Dictator* called our attention to Hitler's insanity.

In the ghettoes, Hitler's "masterpiece" was referred to as *Mein Krampf* (My Cramp). His theory of the Master Race was the butt of dozens of jokes. There are two kinds of Aryans, one went: non-Aryans and barb-Aryans. Others mocked the disparity between the icon of the tall, blond, muscular Aryan and the actual physiques of Hitler, Goebbels, and Goering.

This critical spirit worked against the Nazi propaganda machine. Research on brainwashing, indeed, has shown that wisecracking humor may be the single most effective way to block indoctrination. Psychiatrist William Sargent claims that if at any point in the brainwashing procedure, the subject laughs, "the whole process is wrecked and must be begun all over again."[19]

Because humor interfered with their propaganda and revealed the awful truth about the Nazis, they were quite afraid of it. Hitler, wrote one biographer, had "a horror of being laughed at."[20] When well-known figures made fun of him, Hitler viciously attacked them. Bertold Brecht, for example, was declared an enemy of the Reich, stripped of his citizenship, and forced to flee Germany.

One of the first actions of the new Nazi government in 1933 was the creation of a "Law against treacherous attacks on the state and party and for the protection of the party uniform." As Hermann Goering reminded the Academy of German Law, telling a joke could be an act against the Führer and the state. Under this law, circulating and listening to anti-Nazi jokes were acts of treason. Several people were even put on trial for naming dogs and horses "Adolf." Between 1933 and 1945, 5,000 death sentences were handed down by the "People's Court" for treason, a large number of them for anti-Nazi humor.

One of those executed was Josef Müller, a Catholic priest who had told two of his parishioners the following story: "A fatally wounded German soldier asked his chaplain to grant one final wish. 'Place a picture of Hitler on one side of me, and a picture of Goering on the other side. That way I can die like Jesus, between two thieves.'" The indictment against Müller called this joke "one of the most vile and most dangerous attacks directed on our confidence in our Führer. . . . It is a betrayal of the people, the Führer, and the Reich."[21]

Despite the trials and executions, anti-Nazi jokes flourished. There were even jokes about the prosecution of joke tellers, like the story of the comedian who was locked in solitary confinement until he had recited every anti-Nazi joke he knew. His internment, of course, lasted years.

Some of the jokes wore their hostility on their face, but many were more subtle, like the story of the Jewish father teaching his son how to say grace before meals:

"Today in Germany the proper form of grace is 'Thank God and Hitler.'"
"But suppose the Führer dies?" asked the boy.
"Then you just thank God."

Besides the jokes, there were even a few occasions for humor in dealing directly with the Nazis. Early in the Third Reich, Peter Lorre, who had become famous as the murderer in the movie *M*, was living in Vienna. Goebbels, not knowing that Lorre was Jewish, asked him to come to Germany. Lorre answered with a telegram: "There isn't room in Germany for two murderers like Hitler and me."[22]

Some of the best humor against the Nazis went right over their heads. Sigmund Freud was living in Vienna when the Germans marched into the city. They arrested him but then offered to let him leave the country if he signed a statement saying he had not been mistreated. Freud sat down and wrote the following note:

To Whom It May Concern:
I can heartily recommend the Gestapo to anyone.
Sigmund Freud

Sabotage and other acts of resistance were often funny. When the Nazis rolled into many cities, they found street signs and traffic warning signs switched around. Cooks pressed into service by the invaders sometimes stirred laxatives into the food for the German troops. Pavel Fantl, a physician forced to work in Gestapo headquarters in Czechoslovakia, sabotaged the files and smuggled food to Jews being held by the secret police. In 1942 he was sent to the Theresienstadt concentration camp, where he produced several paintings depicting Hitler in a clown's costume along with gawky, goose-stepping German soldiers.[23]

Outside of Europe, of course, people had more freedom to satirize Hitler. In 1935 the annual Purim Ad Loloyada parade in Tel Aviv featured cars disguised as Nazi tanks and marchers wearing mock Nazi uniforms. In Jerusalem during the war, Stanislaw Dobrzynski published a book of cartoons about Hitler. In one, a bloated Führer floats above Berlin, made airborne by absorbing his own hot air. Another sketch, "Sein Kampf" (His Struggle), showed wolves and vultures scavenging in a field of skeletons.[24]

The second benefit of humor lay in its cohesive function. Humor of the kind we have been discussing draws a line between an in-group and an out-group. Here the out-group, the target of the joking, was the Nazis and their collaborators. The in-group was those opposed to the Nazis. The Jews of Europe were the most obvious group in which this humor produced solidarity, as illustrated by this story.

As Hitler's armies faced more and more setbacks, he asked his astrologer, "Am I going to lose the war?"

"Yes," the astrologer said.
"Then, am I going to die?" Hitler asked.
"Yes."
"*When* am I going to die?"
"On a Jewish holiday."
"But on *what* holiday?"
"*Any* day you die will be a Jewish holiday."

But humor also created a wider solidarity among all those who resisted the Nazis. Cartoonist David Low, who drew anti-Nazi cartoons from the 1920s through the war, commented that, "If Hitler has not succeeded in establishing his New Order in Europe, certainly he has established the United Nations of Cartoonists."

Many Christians swallowed Hitler's ideas about a Master Race, but some saw its absurdity and felt solidarity with the persecuted Jews. That is illustrated in this story:

Several storm troopers enter an Evangelical Church during a Sunday morning service.

"My fellow Germans," begins their leader. "I am here in the interest of racial purity. We have tolerated non-Aryans long enough, and must now get rid of them. I am ordering all those here whose fathers are Jews to leave this church at once."

Several worshipers get up and leave.

"And now I am ordering out all those whose mothers are Jewish."

At this, the pastor jumps up, takes hold of the crucifix, and says, "Brother, now it's time for you and me to get out."

One of the first places to see the solidarity promoted by humor among those opposed to Hitler was in the cabarets. Long before the Nazis took full control of Germany in 1933, there were cabaret performers doing satirical sketches about Hitler and his storm troopers. If the German people had paid heed to the early warnings of these comedians, they would never have made him Führer.

In Munich, cabaret performer Weiss Ferdl would bring out large photographs of Hitler, Goering, and other Nazi leaders, and then think out loud, "Now should I hang them, or line them up against the wall?"

Several cabaret comedians had a simple routine in which they walked onto the stage with a gag over their mouth, sat on a chair silent for several minutes, then stood up and walked off the stage. Then the master of ceremonies would say, "Ladies and gentlemen, now that the political part of our program is over, we come to the entertainment."[25]

The popular comedian Werner Finck had his cabaret closed, reopened, and re-closed several times by the Nazis. When someone did not like his political material and shouted from the audience, "Dirty Jew," Finck would respond, "I only look this intelligent!" When he spotted Gestapo observers in the audience, he would ask them, "Am I speaking too fast for you?"

Eventually, the Nazis closed all the cabarets. Many of the performers were sent to prison camps, but cabaret humor reappeared there. Even in Dachau, a play satirizing the Nazis was performed for six weeks in the summer of 1943. The lead character, Count Adolar, was a thinly disguised Hitler. The SS were seated at the front as "honored guests." Rudolf Kalmar, the writer of the play, survived the camp and became a popular actor in East Germany after the war. Another survivor described the effect of this satire on the camp inmates:

> Many of them, who sat behind the rows of the SS each night and laughed with a full heart, didn't experience the day of freedom. But most among them took from this demonstration strength to endure their situation. . . . They had the certainty, as they lay that night on their wooden bunks: We have done something that gives strength to our comrades. We have made the Nazis look ridiculous.[26]

Theresienstadt in Czechoslovakia was the camp with the most developed cabaret and theater. Poets, actors, and musicians entertained with songs, skits, and music, doing special performances for the sick. As Rabbi Erich Weiner, spiritual leader of the prisoners, observed, the cabaret "strengthened their will to survive as well as infused their power to resist."[27]

The third function of humor during the Holocaust was that it helped oppressed people cope with suffering without going insane. Emil Fackenheim, philosopher and survivor of Auschwitz, put it simply, "We kept our morale through humor."[28] The emotional disengagement of humor was often enhanced by imagination. In the Lodz ghetto, for example, many of the jokes were about the shortage of food. "Before the war we ate ducks and walked like horses; now we eat horses and waddle like ducks."[29] If someone was seen running, people would say, "He eats race-horses."[30] In the concentration camps, bombs being dropped were called "Matzah balls," Soviet planes overhead were "red hens."[31]

In *Man's Search for Meaning*, psychiatrist Viktor Frankl described how he coached a fellow Auschwitz prisoner, a surgeon, in the survival value of humor. He proposed to his comrade that every day they would tell each other at least one funny story about something that might happen after their liberation. Other prisoners also invented "amusing dreams about the future." One imagined that when he had returned home, he would be at a dinner party and would beg the hostess to ladle the soup "from the bottom."

Not all of the coping humor was based on fantasy. Frankl described being in a group who were shaved of every hair and then herded into showers:

> The illusions some of us still held were destroyed one by one, and then, quite unexpectedly, most of us were overcome by a grim sense of humor. We knew that we had nothing to lose except our ridiculously naked lives. When the showers started to run, we all tried very hard to make fun, both about ourselves and about each other. After all, real water did flow from the sprays![32]

According to a tale in the Talmud, the prophet Elijah said that there will be reward in the next world for those who bring laughter to others in this one.[33] Now during the Holocaust, Jewish humor was somewhat different from earlier times. Traditional comic figures like the schnorrer (beggar), the schlmazl (fallguy), and the shlmiel (klutz), for example, were absent. But the functions of humor were much the same as before: it was a vehicle for critical thinking; it promoted group solidarity; and it helped people survive in a hostile world. This joke from the period shows all three:

> Goebbels was touring German schools. At one, he asked the students to call out patriotic slogans.
>
> "Heil Hitler," shouted one child.
> "Very good," said Goebbels.
> "*Deutschland über alles*," another called out.
> "Excellent. How about a stronger slogan?"
> A hand shot up, and Goebbels nodded.
> "Our people shall live forever," the little boy said.
> "Wonderful," exclaimed Goebbels. "What is your name, young man?"
> "Israel Goldberg."

Chapter 7

Homo Sapiens and
Homo Ridens

Philosophy and Comedy

"By God, for a minute there it suddenly all made sense!"

Was Socrates the First Stand-up Comedian?

In Chapters 1 and 5 we looked at assessments of humor by some traditional philosophers, and in Chapters 2 and 6 we discussed the benefits of humor. In this chapter, we will bring together philosophy and the benefits of humor. I'll argue that from the beginning of philosophy, its practitioners should have appreciated the value of humor, since most of its benefits are benefits of philosophy too.

One contemporary form of humor, stand-up comedy, has at least eight similarities to philosophy. First, it is conversational. Comedians typically present their observations as half of a dialogue, and they often work comments from the audience into their routine. In philosophy, the dialogue has been a standard form since Plato, and philosophical essays are sometimes addressed to a reader, with readers' possible comments worked into the discussion.

Secondly, stand-up comedy and philosophy are typically reflections on everyday experiences, especially puzzling ones. We awake from a vivid dream, for instance, not sure what has really occurred or what is occurring. We live for years under "democratic" leaders we vociferously opposed from the start.

A standard opening move is to ask questions about such experiences, which is a third similarity between stand-up comedy and philosophy. The most basic format in both comedy and philosophy is, "X – what's up with that?" If while dreaming we see what isn't there, then how can we trust our vision? Can we even be sure that we aren't dreaming right now? And what's so good about democracy if it forces tens of millions of us to live under a government we voted *against*?

These two questions may be too familiar from the writings of humor-impaired philosophers to sound promising as comedy, but consider the question, "Might I be a brain in a vat?" or Thomas Nagel's "What is it like to be a bat?," both of which could easily be routines by Robin Williams. With its footnotes removed, Ned Block's article " ¿umoᗡ/dU ʇoN ʇuᗺ ʇɥƃᴉᴚ/ʇɟǝꞀ ǝsɹǝʌǝᴚ sɹoɹɹᴉW oᗡ ʎɥM"[1] could be a script for Rita Rudner or Bill Cosby. And questions like these are not new, but go back to ancient philosophy. In Aristotle's notebook *Problems*, he asks:

> Why do all men, barbarians and Greeks alike, count up to ten and not up to any other number, saying for example, "2, 3, 4, 5" and then repeating them, "one-five, two-five," just as they say "eleven, twelve"?

Why is it that things of unpleasant odor do not seem to have an odor to those who have eaten them?
Why does a large choir keep better time than a small one?
Why are drunks more easily moved to tears?
Why is it that no one can tickle himself?

A fourth similarity is that as comedians and philosophers explore questions arising from everyday experiences, they are practically detached from those experiences. In philosophizing about something or joking about it, we view it from a higher perspective than our normal one. The perspective and disengagement in philosophizing long ago became an extended meaning of "philosophical": "rational; sensibly composed; calm, as in a difficult situation." And the same perspective and disengagement have characterized comedians for centuries. Think of Erma Bombeck, Oscar Wilde, or Mark Twain.

Fifthly, both comedians and philosophers search out new perspectives and surprising thoughts, and so they relish cognitive shifts. As Simon Critchley put it, both ask you to "look at things as if you had just landed from another planet."[2] William James noted that, "Philosophy, beginning in wonder, as Plato and Aristotle said, is able to fancy everything different from what it is. It sees the familiar as if it were strange, and the strange as if it were familiar."[3] Bertrand Russell said that, "The point of philosophy is to start with something so simple as not to seem worth stating, and to end with something so paradoxical that no one will believe it."[4]

In the parlance of the 1960s, both comedy and philosophy play with our heads. To consider the possibility that I might be dreaming now, or that I am a brain in a vat, is to extend thinking well beyond ordinary limits. Comedians stretch our thinking in similar ways. In a stand-up routine about women and men, for example, Rita Rudner had this observation: "I just read that women reach their sexual peak at age 35. Men reach theirs at 18. Do you get the feeling that God is into practical jokes? We reach our sexual peak just as they're coming to realize they have a favorite chair."

Though Bertrand Russell never performed stand-up comedy, with a little training, he could have. Consider these lines:

It has been said that man is a rational animal. All my life I have been searching for evidence which could support this.

Many people would sooner die than think; In fact, they do so.

The time you enjoy wasting is not wasted time.

I would never die for my beliefs because I might be wrong.

This is patently absurd; but whoever wishes to become a philosopher must learn not to be frightened by absurdities.[5]

The sixth similarity is that both comics and philosophers think critically. They encourage us to be honest with ourselves, and to reject rationalization and lazy conformism. They pay careful attention to words, their meanings, and their uses. A standard procedure in both comedy and philosophy is to bring up a widely accepted idea and ask the three C questions: Is it *clear* – what exactly are those who believe this saying? Is it *coherent* – do its parts fit with each other and with other ideas of the people who hold it? And is it *credible* – do we have good reasons to accept it? Comedy and philosophy thrive on "No" answers to these questions – on confusion, fallacies, and other incongruities in the way people think, speak, and write.

When their critical thinking is about politics or religion, comedians and philosophers don't defer to authority and tradition – which is a seventh similarity. Both oppose blind belief and unquestioning obedience, and in robust comedy and philosophy, nothing is sacred. That's why Socrates was tried and executed. So were dozens of German cabaret comics in the 1930s, as we have seen.

Comedy and philosophy work against the natural human predisposition to indoctrination. Most of the time, most of us do what we are told, and think what we are told. In Milgram's experiments on obedience, two-thirds of male subjects were willing to inflict a potentially fatal electric shock on a person simply because the experimenter with the clipboard told them to.[6] To repeat Russell's quip, "Most people would sooner die than think. In fact, they do so."[7]

In a February 1989 poll, 44 percent of participants said that the Cabinet appointments President George H. W. Bush had just made were "Good" or "Excellent." But 81 percent of respondents could not name any member of Bush's cabinet. That's material for philosophy or comedy. More recently, Bush's son was criticized by comedians like Jon Stewart and by philosophers like Peter Singer.[8] Had Bush been granted the powers given Hitler, Stewart and Singer might have shared a cell.

Lastly, comedians and philosophers often think in counterfactuals, mentally manipulating possibilities as easily as most people think about realities. Thought experiments have been standard in comedy and philosophy since ancient Athens. What if women got fed up with war and held a sex strike to force men to make peace? That's Aristophanes'

Lysistrata. If you define justice as giving people what belongs to them, then what about the neighbor who gives you his sword for safe keeping, and later, in a wild rage, asks for it back? That's Socrates in Plato's *Republic*.

In my Philosophy of Religion course, when we discuss the many conflicting doctrines that have been taught under the banner of Christianity, I point out that according to the *World Christian Encyclopedia*, there are now over 34,000 sects calling themselves "Christians." Maybe, I suggest, we might better speak of "Christianities" than "Christianity." Then I ask, "What if there were 34,000 Chemistries?"

As we discuss the Ontological Argument in the same course, I compare Anselm's "that than which none greater can be conceived" to a new product, "Perfecto Paint – the best possible paint for all uses." I ask students to imagine that they have bought a gallon and painted their room with it. If it required three coats, and it dissolved the bristles of your brush, I ask, would you have the right to complain that this was not the perfect paint? Of course, they say. But what if Perfecto Paint is still in the planning stages and hasn't been manufactured yet? Would you have a similar right to complain that it was not the perfect paint, since it lacked the most basic perfection any paint should have – existence? At that point, most students laugh.

I also ask the students to imagine a dialogue between a newly married couple who are on a tight budget and so wary of having children.

A: If we have a child, she won't have nice clothes or toys.
B: But if we don't have a child, she won't have any clothes or toys at all.

More laughter.

What's funny in these thought experiments is the incongruous way the notion of existence is being used – as a property lacked or possessed by an individual thing. And the improper use is obvious. The same misuse of the concept of existence is at the heart of the Ontological Argument, I suggest to students, only there it is less obvious. Over the years I have noticed that an occasional bright student will detect that misuse on first hearing Anselm's argument, and laugh, as students laugh at my thought experiments.

Humor and the Existentialists

Considering how humor often embodies the critical, imaginative attitude prized by philosophers, it's surprising how few of them have expressed appreciation for it. Some philosophers have shown wit in argumentation. J. L. Austin's title for his attack on sense data theory – *Sense and Sensibilia* – comes to mind here. But humor as a personal virtue is not common among philosophers.

One group of philosophers that seem as if they would have had to have a rich sense of humor is the existentialists. Themes such as the conflict between the individual and the group are custom-made for comic treatment. "Hell is other people," one of Sartre's characters says in *No Exit*. "People – they're the worst," quips Elaine on *Seinfeld*.

More generally, comedy and existentialism emphasize the problematic side of life. Mark Twain wrote that, "The secret source of humor itself is not joy but sorrow. There is no humor in heaven."[9] His contemporary, Nietzsche, said that humans are the only animals that laugh because they alone suffer so deeply.

Perhaps the biggest theme shared by existentialism and comedy is absurdity: that of individual experiences in life, and of the whole human condition. The basic situation in many Charlie Chaplin films, for instance, is similar to what Heidegger calls "thrownness" – finding ourselves in a situation we did not choose but in which we have to act. Without a script to follow, we, like Charlie, make it up as we go along.

Two themes of existentialism have even become theories of humor. One is the inability of reason to adequately capture the world of lived experience. That's the gist of Schopenhauer's analysis of humor as based on a discrepancy between concepts and perceptions.[10] The pleasure of amusement lies in the triumph of perception over conception, in seeing "that strict, untiring, troublesome governess, the reason," fall flat on her face.

The other existentialist theme that became a theory of humor is the categorical difference between a person and a thing, and the inauthenticity of a person acting like a thing. That is Henri Bergson's formula in *Laughter*: what we laugh at is mechanical inelasticity where we expect to find the living flexibility of a human being.[11] The function of laughter, according to Bergson, is to humiliate the inflexible person into acting humanly once more.

In the nineteenth century, the two major thinkers first called "existentialists" – Kierkegaard and Nietzsche – showed considerable appreciation of the connections between humor and philosophy. Kierkegaard speaks of humor as "the joy which has overcome the world," and he distinguishes the "three spheres of existence" – the aesthetic, the ethical, and the religious – using humor and its close relative, irony. "Humor is the last stage of existential awareness before faith," he writes in the *Concluding*

Unscientific Postscript.[12] He even classifies himself as "essentially a humorist." In discussing Hegel, for example, he writes that for all his world-historical categories and grand philosophical system, Hegel went on Fridays to pick up his pay like everyone else. Like today's stand-up comedians, Kierkegaard used techniques such as irony, indirect communication, and speaking through personae.

Well aware of the standard philosophical prejudices against laughter and humor, he criticizes the emphasis on seriousness in philosophy. It is just as mistaken, he insists, to be serious in the wrong place as it is to laugh in the wrong place.

The primary element in the comic Kierkegaard calls "contradiction," by which he means a violation of the way we expect things to be. Life is full of such events and so full of possibilities for humor. The more thoroughly we exist, Kierkegaard says, the more we discover the comic. Tragedy, like comedy, focuses on problems, but while the comic perspective sees a way out, the tragic perspective despairs of a way out.[13]

Nietzsche, like Kierkegaard, shows considerable humor in his writing and advocates an ironic stance toward the human condition. In *Thus Spoke Zarathustra*, laughter marks the liberated attitude of Zarathustra, who can affirm eternal recurrence and say a joyous "Yes" to life despite all its suffering. In his speech to the higher men, Zarathustra calls himself "the laughing prophet" and urges them to "learn to laugh at yourselves as a man ought to laugh."[14] The enemy Zarathustra must destroy is the Spirit of Gravity, which one kills not by anger but by laughter. We are still in the age of tragedy, an age of morals and religions, Nietzsche says, and the comedy of existence has not become apparent, but he looks forward to an age of lightness when there will be only wisdom united with laughter – joyful wisdom. He represents this spirit of lightness with several images connected to laughter, especially dancing, singing, and flying.

While these early existentialists showed a considerable appreciation of humor, later existentialists, especially Sartre and Camus, did not. In his biography of Flaubert,[15] Sartre adopts a view of humor like Bergson's, only with more emphasis on the offensiveness of laughter. For Sartre, as for Bergson, the incongruity in humor is between vitalism and mechanism. People are laughable, he says, when they think they are the source of their actions, while in fact their actions simply follow from previous circumstances and external factors. They are objects pretending to be subjects, being *en-soi* masquerading as being *pour-soi*.

People hate to be laughed at, Sartre says, because laughter is an attack against which there is little defense or retaliation. It is a substitute for lynching or banishment. In laughing at people, we treat them as objects and break solidarity with them. Laughter's function is to put the ridiculed person outside the group, allowing those laughing to maintain their own noble conception of what it is to be a human being. That's why, Sartre says, it is perverse to offer oneself as the butt of other people's laughter. The clown or comic actor is a traitor to himself!

What is striking about this account of laughter is how it includes no element of play, but treats humor as another form of serious interaction. Indeed, in Sartre's view, humor has as its purpose to save the spirit of seriousness. Ridicule denounces false seriousness in the name of true seriousness. Laughter is a panic reaction, he says, like shock, flight, or terror, which blows the whistle on subhumans pretending to be human. Even stage comedy is merely the institutionalization of savage laughter, the characters with their thing-like behavior providing practice targets for our scorn.

Albert Camus showed even less appreciation of humor than Sartre. In *The Rebel* and "The Myth of Sisyphus," Camus champions "metaphysical rebellion," protest against one's own state and the whole world, as the most authentic response to the absurdity of the human condition. There is no fate, he says, that cannot be surmounted by scorn.

The trouble with Camus's valorization of scorn is that while defiance might make sense against the Greek gods, it makes little sense against an impersonal universe. Protesting the human condition, at least for an atheist like Camus, seems like a petulant two-year-old shouting at the door in which he has pinched his fingers. Are we mistreated by the universe? Are we owed more than a human life? If absurdity, groundlessness, the lack of a script, is an inherent feature of our life, and it is what makes our freedom and dignity possible, then defiance and resentment against it seem silly and inauthentic. For a moment, defiance may evoke positive feelings of strength, pride, or courage. But such self-assuaging is unrealistic and self-indulgent. It is childish posturing at best, and self-deception at worst. As Thomas Nagel has suggested, if the universe is absurd and nothing matters objectively, then that fact does not matter either, and dramatic protests against one's fate betray a failure to appreciate the cosmic unimportance of our situation.[16] That unimportance, indeed, is more reasonably treated as comic than as tragic.

Grave responses to absurdity like Camus's seem to be anachronistic vestiges of ancient heroic and tragic traditions, combined with egocentric romanticism. Nietzsche's higher men, by contrast, will be joyful, dancing heroes who transcend the tragic stance; the lesson they offer is that facing a world without epistemological or ethical foundations, our highest and most authentic response is not pointless rebellion, but laughter.

If we are to take the absurdity of the human condition seriously, then, paradoxically, we must take it lightly.

The Laughing Buddha

A nice contrast to twentieth-century existentialism and other humor-challenged philosophies is the Eastern tradition that uses humor in its pursuit of mental liberation – Zen Buddhism, especially the tradition of Rinzai (Lin-chi), the ninth-century master. Unlike most Western philosophies, which are systems of explanation built on arguments and governed by rationalistic assumptions, Zen is not a system of explanations and arguments, makes no assumptions like the Principle of Sufficient Reason, and is generally anti-intellectual. The koans and mondos for which it is famous, indeed, are often directed against the very kinds of questions Western thinkers take seriously. Despite its differences with Western rationalism, however, Zen is still a systematic way of looking at the world and living in it, and so is a philosophy.

Let me sharpen the contrast between Zen and Western attitudes toward humor by citing a quotation from an eighteenth-century German philosopher, Georg Friedrich Meier, followed by three examples of Zen humor.

> There are things so great and important in themselves, as never to be thought of and mentioned but with much sedateness and solemnity. Laughter on such occasions is criminal and indecent. . . . For instance, all jests on religion, philosophy, and the like important subjects.[17]

> Rinzai would often reply, no matter what the question, by shouting "Kwatz," a meaningless sound.

> When a monk asked the Zen master Ummon (Yün-men) "What is the Buddha?" he answered, "A wiping stick of dried shit!"

> If you meet the Buddha, kill him.

For someone raised on Western thought, the last three items may sound shocking. Not only do they mix humor into religious and philosophical inquiry, but they countenance a disrespect for the institutions of religion and philosophy. How could someone claiming to be a Zen master carry on like that?

The tradition of humor in Buddhism pre-dates Zen, and goes back at least to Chuang Tzu; his philosophical legacy helped change Buddhism from the speculative metaphysics it had been in India to the more practical philosophy it became in China and Japan. In Indian Buddhism, humor had been frowned upon much as in Western thought. In scholastic style, Indian Buddhists had distinguished six kinds of laughter, with only the mildest forms of smiling acceptable for monks, and only the barely perceptible smile (no teeth showing) attributable to the Buddha.[18] But that attitude was to change radically under the Zen masters. As in Chuang Tzu, their humor was no mere teaching device; it sprang from their realization of an essential connection between the liberating power of humor and the central goal of Buddhism – to eliminate attachment and all forms of mental bondage.

Before we are enlightened, according to Zen, we try to get control over things and people, but our attachment to them gives them power over us. To reach *satori*, enlightenment, we need to liberate ourselves from attachment. Now many Western philosophers, especially in the Stoic and Christian traditions, have also preached liberation from attachment, and so they would presumably appreciate some Zen humor, as in this poem by Masahide:

> My barn burned down.
> Now I have a better view
> Of the rising moon.

But Zen masters also discuss a more radical kind of attachment than attachment to material things. They teach that one's attitude towards Buddhism itself can be a form of attachment, if Buddhism is thought of as a creed to accept or a set of rituals to follow. And so in Zen there are no rituals, scriptures, doctrines, or sacred figures – not even the Buddha – to whom the follower should become attached. Even the idea of non-attachment is not something to become attached to! This importance of non-attachment explains the irreverence and iconoclasm that pervades Zen, as seen in the examples above about the Buddha.

In Zen there is another kind of non-attachment that usually sounds strange to Western philosophers – non-attachment to words, concepts, logic, and rational thinking. We are attached, according to Zen, when we treat rational thinking as a form of power and control over the world, when through our words and concepts we try to "capture" or "master" things. This attitude, of course, has been the dominant one in the West, as seen in the relation between science and technology. "Knowledge is power," we often say.

Understanding the world through concepts is seen in Zen as inferior in at least three ways. First, it is a mediated kind of knowledge, while Zen seeks direct experience. Secondly, concepts are static, while reality is in flux. And thirdly, conceptual thinking works by making distinctions, especially between opposites – mind/matter, subject/object, good/bad – while reality is essentially a unity. Our rational mind, to be sure, will always form concepts and through them attempt to freeze and divide up the world. But we must remind ourselves that any conceptual system, however useful in a particular situation, is at best a tool and not a direct contact with reality. According to Zen, we must constantly challenge our conceptual systems and "break up" our concepts, to prevent ourselves from thinking that they give us an objective grasp of things.

This non-attachment to concepts and conceptual systems is related to an even more important kind of liberation, indeed the central liberation in Zen: from the mind itself treated as a metaphysical substance. The most basic attachment we must break is to the "I," the empirical self, thought of as an enduring subject distinct from the rest of reality. In Zen the empirical ego is not the person and is not an independent substance. The enlightenment sought is an intuitive awareness of the nothingness of the separate "mind" I normally think of as my self. In being liberated from that mistaken attachment to the self, I overcome the core of the problem of all attachment.

It is in helping to break our attachments to doctrines, to conceptual understanding, and to the delusory self, that humor is valuable in Zen, for it involves the clash of perception and conception, the reversal of perspectives, and the frustration of reason. And like enlightenment, of which it is sometimes a form, humor hits us abruptly and unexpectedly, in a flash. The sudden "Aha!" of enlightenment is close to the "Ha-ha!" of getting a joke. The fifteenth-century master Kukoku (K'ung-ku) observed that enlightenment is a "grand overturning of the whole system of consciousness,"[19] a comment that applies to much of the best humor, as well.

As long as rational thinking is going smoothly, we tend not to question the nature of thought and of the self, just as when our car is running well, we tend not to look under the hood. But humor throws a monkey wrench into the cognitive processing of the rational mind, and thus prompts us to question its nature. That is why incongruity of all kinds is so useful in Zen. Interchanges between masters and students, for example, often involve illogical cognitive shifts, as when Tozan (Tung-shan) was asked, "What is the Buddha?" and he answered, "Three pounds of flax." Contradictions are used in the same way, to frustrate the rational mind, and thus call attention to it. And answers to students' questions need not have any meaning at all, as in Rinzai's indiscriminately replying to questions with the sound "Kwatz!" or the practice of responding to students by striking them with sticks, slapping them, and twisting their noses. The purpose of all this nonsense and slapstick is to derail the train of thought, so that the student shifts to a more basic level of awareness, seeing the true nature of reality and the illusoriness of the individual substantial self. In this way, humor in Zen represents the ultimate form of critical thinking. We saw earlier a parallel in Western thought – Schopenhauer's comment that part of the fun of humor is our delight at discovering the shortcomings of conceptual thinking: "It must therefore be diverting to us to see that strict, untiring, troublesome governess, the reason, for once convicted of insufficiency."[20]

Schopenhauer and a few others aside, there is a sharp contrast between Western philosophy and Zen on the value of "breaking up" conceptual thinking and logic. The individual, substantial, self-aware ego, which in Zen is the fundamental illusion and the butt of joking, is the foundation stone of Descartes's rationalism and the philosophies which it spawned. For this tradition, the existence of the self-conscious "I" as a special kind of substance distinct from the rest of the world, is the one certitude with which I can begin to think, and on which I can base all other knowledge. Needless to say, this "I" is taken absolutely seriously in rationalism, much as God is taken absolutely seriously in Christianity and Islam.

Judged from a Zen perspective, the Cartesian *cogito* looks like trouble from the start, for it produces both the illusory idea of the individual substantial mind and the exaggerated trust in reason. If my essence is to think, after all, then things had better be thinkable. Relying on the *cogito* as a starting point is also, I think, largely responsible for the humorlessness of so many Western philosophers. They take everything too seriously because they take themselves too seriously, and they take themselves too seriously because they take their *selves* too seriously.

Working under rationalistic assumptions, Western philosophers usually react with distress when major unresolvable incongruities appear in life, as we saw earlier. When their substantial egos seem threatened by the thought that their death might be the end of their egos, for example, they react with evasion, despair, or defiance.

Zen thinkers, by contrast, have none of the problems Western thinkers have with absurdity, because the basic stance in Zen is already an ironic one. And because Zen has set up no expectation that the world be a rational system tailored to the requirements of my understanding, it is ready when things cannot be explained. Someone who can contemplate the unreality of the individual substantial mind, who, indeed, seeks that realization as the highest enlightenment, is, unlike the Western rationalist, ready for anything.

The discrepancy between our desires and what is possible is likewise no problem for Zen, because Zen seeks the elimination of desires. The person who is non-attached about material possessions can experience their loss with a smile, as in the poem above about seeing the moon better after the barn has burned down. Non-attachment to the self, similarly, allows laughter at oneself. As Thomas Merton says of the Zen student reaching illumination in the study of koans, "his own total acceptance of his own nothingness, far from constituting a problem, is the source and center of inexpressible joy."[21]

Not only can humor be used to produce enlightenment, then, but the experience of enlightenment, with its sudden realization of the illusory nature of the self, can itself be a profound kind of amusement. The biggest joke I shall ever experience is me. And once I am liberated from attachment to my ego and can see myself with humor, the humor in all experience comes easily.

In this examination of Zen's attitude toward humor, I have, of course, been adopting a Zen perspective. But what we have found here holds important lessons for thinkers in other traditions as well. Zen calls our attention to the neglected values of humor mentioned at the beginning of this section, especially its fostering of conceptual and practical liberation. The irreverent attitude in Zen would be healthy in any system of thought, for it keeps the critical spirit alive, preventing blind discipleship and other kinds of intellectual conformism. Also important is Zen's insistence that rational thought is only part of our lives, even of our mental lives, and that it has no absolute value.

But the most important feature of Zen's attitude toward humor is the most important aspect of Zen itself: its emphasis on non-attachment. Any comprehensive philosophy will have ways of responding to the little absurdities of everyday life, and to the big absurdities built into the human condition. Now most philosophers will admit that stepping back in amusement is an acceptable response to the little absurdities. That view has been common since Aristotle described comedy as laughter at *minor* flaws and misfortunes. But when it comes to the big absurdities, most Western philosophers think that only a serious response is appropriate – they reject a disengaged response like amusement. Think, for example, of Heidegger's insistence that we think hard and often about death. What the non-attached stance in Zen shows is the possibility of a disengaged response to *any* absurdity.

Thomas Nagel argues that this possibility should have been clear in Western philosophy all along.[22] Our noticing absurdity in the first place, after all, is based on our ability to see any situation in a larger context, from a distance. We are listening to a politician's speech in favor of X, for instance, but suddenly remember the speech she gave last month against X. Nagel shows that our capacity for stepping back and looking at things from a distance has no bounds. Just as we can dispassionately watch an ant struggle with a grain of sand, we can look at our lives or even the history of the universe *sub specie aeternitatis.*

But if it is permissible to take one step back and notice the incongruity in our lives, why would it somehow be inauthentic to take a second step back and laugh at that incongruity, especially if it is some permanent feature of the human condition about which nothing can be done? Under most circumstances, we have to take our children's hunger seriously; finding that amusing would be reprehensible. But what about the inevitability of death? And how about what Stephen Leacock calls "the incongruous contrast between the eager fret of our life and its final nothingness"?[23] Do we have to take those seriously?

Imagine that in the morning paper we read that a huge meteor on a collision course with Earth will end all life on this planet by the weekend. Would there be anything wrong with finding that funny? Is there some more engaged and responsible attitude we should adopt instead?

As things stand, of course, most of us have more than a few days left, but in some finite number of days our planet is still going to come to an end, and long before that so is each of our lives. In cosmic terms, neither event is so important as to transcend the possibility of humor. Indeed, seen from sufficient distance, either might be funny, much as disasters in old silent films are. In fact, it was the silent film comedian Charlie Chaplin who said that life is a tragedy in close-up but a comedy in long-shot. If, as is often claimed, philosophers have the most cosmic perspective, then they should also have the greatest appreciation of humor, for the comic view of the world is the most cosmic view of all.

Chapter 8

The Glass Is Half-Empty *and* Half-Full

Comic Wisdom

"I heard a bit of good news today. We shall pass this way but once."

As Philosophy 101 students learn the first day, the discipline gets its name from the Greek words for "love" and "wisdom." And from the beginning, philosophers have said that wisdom includes the knowledge of how to live well. As Robert Nozick puts it, "Wisdom is practical; it helps. Wisdom is what you need to understand in order to live well and cope with the central problems and avoid the dangers in the predicament(s) human beings find themselves in."[1]

Life is complicated, and so wisdom includes knowing many things. Nozick lists 15:

1. The most important goals and values of life – the ultimate goal, if there is one.
2. What means will reach these goals without too great a cost.
3. What kinds of dangers threaten the achieving of these goals.
4. How to recognize and avoid or minimize these dangers.
5. What different types of human beings are like in their actions and motives (as this presents dangers or opportunities).
6. What is not possible or feasible to achieve (or avoid).
7. How to tell what is appropriate when.
8. When certain goals are sufficiently achieved.
9. What limitations are unavoidable and how to accept them.
10. How to improve oneself and one's relationships with others or society.
11. What the true and unapparent value of various things is.
12. When to take a long-term view.
13. What the variety and obduracy of facts, institutions, and human nature are.
14. What one's real motives are.
15. How to cope and deal with the major tragedies and dilemmas of life, and with the major good things too.[2]

If my assessment of humor is close to right, then having a good sense of humor contributes to these kinds of knowledge. We don't typically engage in humor *in order to* increase our wisdom,[3] of course, any more than we play the piano in order to improve our math skills. But in cultivating our sense of humor, we develop our knowledge of how to "live well and cope with the central problems and avoid the dangers in the predicament(s) human beings find themselves in."

We've explored many of the benefits of humor. In Chapter 3 we saw how its emotional disengagement promotes rationality and mental flexibility. The contrast of comedy with tragedy in Chapter 4 showed how comedy fosters a more rational, critical, and creative attitude that serves us better in the modern world. It makes us sensitive to the complexity of life; it enhances our ability to deal with novelty and disorder; and it challenges elitism, militarism, and sexism. In Chapter 6 we examined some intellectual and moral virtues promoted by humor: open-mindedness, divergent thinking, critical thinking, self-transcendence, honesty with oneself, patience, tolerance, graciousness, humility, perseverance, and courage. Then in Chapter 7 we compared humor to philosophy in promoting a curious, imaginative, critical attitude in which we see our lives in perspective.

Many of these benefits overlap with the kinds of knowledge in Nozick's list. To see how, we can summarize and extend the discussion of comedy in Chapters 3 and 4. There I suggested that laughter evolved from play signals accompanying mock-aggressive activities like rough-and-tumble play, tickling, and chasing games. Humorous amusement evolved when early humans began to enjoy cognitive shifts – sudden changes in their perceptions and thoughts. In the dangerous world they lived in, False Alarm situations may have provided their first humor, as what looked threatening turned out not to be so. Like the laughter in mock-aggressive play, humorous laughter signaled an emotionally disengaged, playful attitude. As the group relaxed and enjoyed the cognitive shift, their shared delight strengthened their social bonds. As with any pleasurable experience, too, they wanted to enjoy it again. So they came to re-enact situations that had amused them. Then they added dramatic elements like exaggeration to boost the effect. Eventually, they invented situations from scratch to produce enjoyable cognitive shifts.

The big milestone in the development of humor was language. It allowed early humans to *describe* mentally jolting situations and events, without having to *create* them physically. It also made the emotional disengagement of humor easier to achieve. With words, they could tell stories about remembered funny events, and could make up funny stories, with little risk of triggering fight-or-flight emotions. One format that became popular was stories that shift from one interpretation of a phrase to a contrasting interpretation, such as the narrative joke. Another was playful question-and-answer interchanges, such as the funny riddle.

In the fifth century BCE, these and other techniques came together in Greece to become dramatic comedy. Later, comedy was distinguished into satire, parody, farce, burlesque, comedy of manners, romantic comedy, black comedy, etc. Other artistic media such as novels, poetry, drawing, painting, photography, music, and dance eventually developed comic forms, too. And so today we have limericks, cartoons, Le Ballet Trockadero, and

Weird Al Yankovic. "Comedy" in the broad sense is all the arts designed to elicit amusement.

To see how comedy fosters wisdom, consider some of its oldest characters and situations. Within a century of comedy's birth, human shortcomings – physical, psychological, and moral – had become standard triggers of cognitive shifts. And so in the fourth century BCE, Aristotle could say that comedy "is an imitation of people who are worse than average."[4] Plato focused on one kind of comic vice – self-delusion, as in the braggart, the pedant, the windbag, and the hypocrite, who reveal that they're not as strong, talented, smart, generous, etc. as they think they are. The essential object of amusement, Plato said, is "that kind of vice which can be described by the opposite of the inscription at Delphi . . . 'Know not thyself.'"[5]

In watching the performances of these stock characters, we learn our first lesson in living well:

1. Don't be like these comic butts. Instead, be honest about your strengths and weaknesses, and show integrity in how you talk and act.

In Shakespeare's time this lesson was touted by Ben Jonson and Sir Philip Sidney, who described comedy as a kind of negative moral training for audiences. Today John Cleese, of *Monty Python* fame, has become the world's largest producer of training videos largely through such negative learning. In videos like "Meetings, Bloody Meetings," Cleese acts out common mistakes in a funny way, so that trainees relax, laugh, and learn what to avoid.

From Aristophanes on, many comic butts have been figures who are usually taken seriously, such as political and military leaders. They are often portrayed as misleading people and causing harm under the guise of noble ideals like patriotism. From the beginning, comedy has questioned militarism, patriarchy, and the whole ethos of heroism. The lesson for life here is:

2. Think critically about authorities and institutions, especially ones that ask you to kill or die for honor.

In addition to deceptive leaders, comedy has many lower-level tricksters, flatterers, and swindlers. From them we learn to:

3. Be wary of people trying to persuade you to think or act in a way that will benefit them.

Comedy teaches lessons not just through its comic butts but through the protagonists we laugh *with*, instead of *at*. Like tragic heroes, they have to handle big problems. But unlike tragic heroes, they are able to solve most of their problems because they have a different approach in which intelligence trumps emotions. From Lysistrata to Hawkeye Pierce in *M*A*S*H*, comic protagonists have *thought* their way, rather than *felt* their way, out of trouble. To reinforce this contrast, comedies often present melodramatic and heroic characters as comic butts. The lesson here is:

4. When you face a problem, avoid anger, resentment, and self-pity. Keep your cool and *think*.

A related lesson is about the kind of thinking that is most promising in solving problems, and in living a satisfying life. In comedy, what saves the day is not convergent thinking based on applying standard formulas. That wouldn't be funny. It's clever, divergent thinking. Comic protagonists are role models for mental flexibility, and comic butts, as Bergson said, are role models for mental rigidity. So:

5. The more complex the situation, the more likely it will require thinking in a new way. Don't get locked into mental ruts but stay mentally flexible.

This promotion of mental flexibility is supported by comedy's social ethos. While the heroic genres of tragedy and epic glorify the elite upper classes, comedy celebrates diversity. Many of its cognitive shifts are power reversals, as servants outwit their masters, housewives outsmart generals, and midgets save the day. The lesson for life is that:

6. Each person counts for one. Everybody has a perspective, a story to tell, and a contribution to make.

Reinforcing this egalitarianism in comedy is an emphasis on humans' need for each other. While the basic unit in tragedy is the individual, the basic unit in comedy is the couple, the family, the village, the bunch of friends, or the gang at work. And groups find it much easier to handle problems. Many situations that would be emergencies for one person are fun for two or more. To emphasize human interdependence, too, comedies from Shakespeare to *Seinfeld* often feature simultaneous interlinked plots. From all this we learn that:

7. Humans belong in communities. We get by with a little help from our friends. Life isn't a solitary struggle, but a social adventure.

In celebrating community, comedy doesn't deny the prevalence of social conflict. As in tragedy, most problems in comedy are social. But the standard comic ways of handling conflict are quite different from tragic ways. Instead of confronting opponents head-on, comic protagonists use indirect tactics. They cajole, don disguises, enlist their opponent's friends, change their plans, and even run away. As the Irish saying goes, you're only a coward for a moment, but you're dead for the rest of your life. And once the conflict has been resolved, comic protagonists forgive and forget. The lesson here is:

8. Violence should be a last resort. Ruses and compromise usually work much better. And harboring a grudge benefits no one.

There is another big contrast between tragedy and comedy. Tragedy emphasizes the greatness and nobility of humanity – "What a piece of work is a man! How noble in reason! How infinite in faculties!" (*Hamlet*, Act II, Scene 2). Many of the Greek tragic heroes were even descended from the gods. Comedy, on the other hand, emphasizes human limitations. Partly, that's because comic butts are so prominent. It's also because comedy is embedded in the biological world of hunger, thirst, and sexual desire. While it's inconceivable that Hamlet would deliver a monologue gnawing on a leg of mutton, Sir John Falstaff might well do that. As Nathan Scott observes, "The major purpose of the comedian is to remind us of how deeply rooted we are in all the tangible things of this world."[6] Unlike tragic heroes, comic protagonists are at home in this world and live comfortably with their own limitations and those of their friends. Again, think of Falstaff. The lesson here:

9. It's no surprise that humans turn out to be 98 percent genetically identical to chimpanzees. Our fundamental needs have always been for food, drink, companions, and sex. There's a lot to enjoy in living the life of rational *animals*.

Beyond all these detailed lessons in living well, comedy teaches a general lesson by taking us through all its twists and turns, mistaken identities, miscommunication, screw-ups, and last-minute rescues. What we learn from enjoying these shifts is that:

10. Life is complicated and unpredictable. Whatever way you think about something now, someone else has a different way, and in a minute you may too. The big picture – if there is one – is not at all clear. As Albert Einstein said, "Our situation on this earth seems strange. Every one of us appears here, involuntarily and uninvited, for a short stay, without knowing the why and the wherefore."[7] So expect to be surprised, and look for the fun in it.

Comparing these 10 comic lessons with Nozick's 15 things known by the wise person, the overlap is clear, especially with his (5) what different types of human beings are like, (9) what limitations are unavoidable and how to accept them, (12) when to take a long-term view, and (15) how to cope and deal with the major tragedies and dilemmas of life, and with the major good things too.

The overall comic strategy for living well is versatility, which Aristotle and Thomas Aquinas called *eutrapelia*, "turning well." Especially important is the ability to turn to a play mode when a surprise doesn't require immediate attention. Often with "bad news" there's nothing to do to improve the situation – except to disengage from it emotionally so that it's funny rather than tragic. Remember the dying words of Oscar Wilde: "This wallpaper is atrocious. One of us has to go."

Die laughing. It's the ultimate comic relief.

Notes

Preface

1 See John Morreall, "The Rejection of Humor in Western Thought," *Philosophy East and West* 39 (1989), 243–65.

Chapter 1: No Laughing Matter

1 Ingvild Gilhus, *Laughing Gods, Weeping Virgins: Laughter in the History of Religion* (New York: Routledge, 1997), 80–8.

2 H. Paul Grice, "Logic and Conversation," in *Syntax and Semantics*, vol. 3, ed. Peter Cole and Jerry Morgan (New York: Academic Press, 1975), 41–58.

3 George Carlin, *Brain Droppings* (New York: Hyperion, 1997), 173.

4 Victor Raskin, *Semantic Mechanisms of Humor* (Dordrecht: Reidel, 1984).

5 Epictetus, *Enchiridion*, 33, in *The Philosophy of Laughter and Humor*, ed. John Morreall (Albany: State University of New York Press, 1987), 255.

6 Plato, *Republic*, 388e.

7 Ibid.

8 Ronald de Sousa, "When Is It Wrong to Laugh?" in *The Philosophy of Laughter and Humor*, ed. John Morreall (Albany: State University of New York Press, 1987), 238.

9 Plato, *Philebus*, 48–50, in *The Philosophy of Laughter and Humor*, ed. John Morreall (Albany: State University of New York Press, 1987), 10–13.

10 See John Morreall, *Comedy, Tragedy, and Religion* (Albany: State University of New York Press, 1999), 150–4, and John Morreall, "Comic Vices and Comic Virtues," *Humor: International Journal of Humor Research*, forthcoming.

11 Basil the Great, *The Long Rules*, trans. M. Wagner, *The Fathers of the Church Series*, vol. 9 (Washington: Catholic University of America, 1950), 271.

12   John Chrysostom, *On the Priesthood: Ascetic Treatises; Select Homilies and Letters; Homilies on the Statues*, vol. 9 of *A Select Library of the Nicene and Post-Nicene Fathers of the Christian Church*, ed. Philip Schaff (New York: Christian Literature Co., 1889), 442.

13   Neil Adkin, "The Fathers on Laughter," *Orpheus* 6/1 (1985), 151–2.

14   Gilhus, *Laughing Gods and Weeping Virgins*, 65.

15   Irwin Resnick, "Risus Monasticus: Laughter and Medieval Monastic Culture," *Revue Benedictine* 97/1–2 (1987), 95.

16   P. S. Frank, *Angelikos Bios* (Munster: Aschendorffsche: Verlagsbuchhandlung, 1964), 145.

17   William Prynne, *Histrio-Mastix: The Players Scourge or Actors Tragaedie* (London, 1633).

18   Thomas Hobbes, *Leviathan*, in his *Works*, ed. W. Molesworth (London: Bohn, 1839), vol. 3, ch. 11.

19   Thomas Hobbes, *Philosophical Rudiments Concerning Government and Society* (London: R. Royston, 1651), ch. 1, section 12.

20   Thomas Hobbes, *Leviathan*, Part I, ch. 6, in *The Philosophy of Laughter and Humor*, ed. John Morreall (Albany: State University of New York Press, 1987), 19.

21   Roger Scruton, "Laughter," in *The Philosophy of Laughter and Humor*, ed. John Morreall (Albany: State University of New York Press, 1987), 168.

22   Raskin, *Semantic Mechanisms of Humor*, 40.

23   Jerrold Levinson, "Humour," *Routledge Encyclopedia of Philosophy*, ed. E. Craig (London: Routledge, 1998), 564.

24   Plato, *Laws* 7: 816e.

25   Plato, *Laws* 11: 935e.

26   Sir Philip Sidney, *The Defense of Poesie* (1595), Ponsonby edition, British Museum.

27   Henri Bergson, *Laughter: An Essay on the Meaning of the Comic*, in *The Philosophy of Laughter and Humor*, ed. John Morreall (Albany: State University of New York Press, 1987), 124.

28   Francis Hutcheson, "Reflections upon Laughter" (Glasgow, 1750), in *The Philosophy of Laughter and Humor*, ed. John Morreall (Albany: State University of New York Press, 1987), 26–40.

29   Lambert Deckers, "On the Validity of a Weight-Judging Paradigm for the Study of Humor," *Humor: International Journal of Humor Research* 6 (1993), 43–56.

30   Hutcheson, in *The Philosophy of Laughter and Humor*, 29.

31   For a fuller discussion of the Incongruity Theory, see John Morreall, *Taking Laughter Seriously* (Albany: State University of New York Press, 1983), ch. 3.

32   Robert L. Latta, *The Basic Humor Process: A Cognitive-Shift Theory and the Case against Incongruity* (Berlin: Mouton de Gruyter, 1999), chs. 7–11.

33   Latta, *The Basic Humor Process*, 104.

34   Horace, *Satires, Epistles and Ars Poetica*, trans. H. Rushton Fairclough. Loeb Classical Library (Cambridge, MA: Harvard University Press, 1929), 451.

35   Paul McGhee, *Humor: Its Origin and Development* (San Francisco: W. H. Freeman, 1979), 10.

36   Cicero, *On the Orator*, trans. E. W. Sutton and H. Rackham. Loeb Classical Library (Cambridge, MA: Harvard University Press, 1942), Book II, ch. 63.

37   Immanuel Kant, *Critique of Judgment*, in *The Philosophy of Laughter and Humor*, ed. John Morreall (Albany: State University of New York Press, 1987), 47.

38   James Beattie, "An Essay on Laughter and Ludicrous Composition," in *Essays*, 3rd ed. (London: 1779), 318.

39   Beattie, "An Essay on Laughter and Ludicrous Composition," 320.

40   Arthur Schopenhauer, in *The Philosophy of Laughter and Humor*, ed. John Morreall (Albany: State University of New York Press, 1987), 52.

41   Ibid., 58.

42   Søren Kierkegaard, *Concluding Unscientific Postscript*, in *The Philosophy of Laughter and Humor*, ed. John Morreall (Albany: State University of New York Press, 1987), 85–6.

43   John Lippitt, *Humour and Irony in Kierkegaard's Thought* (London: Macmillan, 2000).

44   Michael Clark, "Humor and Incongruity," in *The Philosophy of Laughter and Humor*, ed. John Morreall (Albany: State University of New York Press, 1987), 139–55.

45   Mike Martin, "Humour and the Aesthetic Enjoyment of Incongruities," in *The Philosophy of Laughter and Humor*, ed. John Morreall (Albany: State University of New York Press, 1987), 176.

46   Kant, *Critique of Judgment*, in *The Philosophy of Laughter and Humor*, 48–9.

47   George Santayana, *The Sense of Beauty*, in *The Philosophy of Laughter and Humor*, ed. John Morreall (Albany: State University of New York Press, 1987), 92–3.

48   Richard Taylor, *Metaphysics*, 3rd ed. (Englewood Cliffs: Prentice-Hall, 1983), 91.

49   Barry Barnes, "The Comparison of Belief Systems: Anomaly versus Falsehood," in *Modes of Thought*, ed. Robin Horton and Ruth Finnegan (London: Faber and Faber, 1973), 190.

50   Leon Festinger, *A Theory of Cognitive Dissonance* (Stanford: Stanford University Press, 1957), 3.

51   Thomas Schultz, "A Cognitive-Developmental Analysis of Humor," in *Humor and Laughter: Theory, Research and Applications*, ed. Tony Chapman and Hugh Foot (New York: Wiley, 1976), 12–13. See also Jerry Suls, "A Two-Stage Model for the Appreciation of Jokes and Cartoons: An Information-Processing Analysis," in *The Psychology of Humor*, ed. Jeffrey Goldstein and Paul McGhee (New York: Academic Press, 1972), 81–99; and

Jerry Suls, "Cognitive Processes in Humor Appreciation," *Handbook of Humor Research*, ed. Paul McGhee and Jeffrey Goldstein (New York: Springer-Verlag, 1983), 39–58

52 John Locke, *An Essay Concerning Human Understanding*, Book III (London: 1690), ch. 9, para. 16.

53 Lord Shaftesbury, "The Freedom of Wit and Humour," *Characteristicks*, 4th ed. (London, 1727).

54 Herbert Spencer, "On the Physiology of Laughter," in *Essays on Education, Etc.* (London: J. M. Dent, 1911), 299.

55 Spencer, "On the Physiology of Laughter," 302.

56 Ibid., 303.

57 Ibid., 304.

58 Ibid., 307.

59 John Dewey, "The Theory of Emotion (I): Emotional Attitudes," *Psychological Review* 1 (1894), 558–9.

60 Sigmund Freud, *Jokes and Their Relation to the Unconscious*, trans. James Strachey (New York: Penguin, 1974). See also Sigmund Freud, "Humor," in *The Philosophy of Laughter and Humor*, ed. John Morreall (Albany: State University of New York Press, 1987), 111–16. Originally published in the *International Journal of Psycho-analysis* 9 (1928), 1–6.

61 For a fuller discussion of the Relief Theory, see Morreall, *Taking Laughter Seriously*, ch. 4.

62 Freud, *Jokes and Their Relation to the Unconscious*, 254.

63 Ibid., 293.

64 Ibid., 295.

65 William Fry, personal communication. See also Charmaine Liebertz, "A Healthy Laugh," *Scientific American*, September 2005.

66 http://www.mc.vanderbilt.edu/reporter/index.html?ID=4030.

67 Ogden Nash, *Best of Ogden Nash* (Chicago: Ivan R. Dee, 2007).

68 Spencer, "On the Physiology of Laughter," 307.

69 Latta, *The Basic Humor Process*, 47.

70 H. J. Eysenck, Foreword to Jeffrey H. Goldstein and Paul E. McGhee, eds., *The Psychology of Humor* (New York: Academic Press, 1972), xvi.

71 Freud, *Jokes and Their Relation to the Unconscious*, 255.

72 Ibid., 257.

73 Ibid., 300.

74 Aristotle, *Nicomachean Ethics*, 4, 8, in *The Philosophy of Laughter and Humor*, ed. John Morreall (Albany: State University of New York Press, 1987), 14–16.

75 Thomas Aquinas, *Summa Theologiae*, 2a2ae, Q. 168, Volume 44, *Well-Tempered Passion*, trans. Thomas Gilby (New York: McGraw-Hill, 1972), 211–27.

76 Aquinas, *Summa Theologiae*, 2a2ae, Q. 168, Article 2, 217.

77 Ibid.

78   Aquinas, *Summa Theologiae*, 2a2ae, Q. 168, Article 4, 225–7.
79   Latta, *The Basic Humor Process*.
80   Ibid., 44.
81   Ibid., 38.
82   Ibid., 103.

Chapter 2: Fight or Flight – or Laughter

1   In the older usage, a *humor* was a fluid, especially one of the four bodily fluids thought to control moods – blood, phlegm, yellow bile, and black bile.

2   See John Morreall, "Humor and Emotion," *American Philosophical Quarterly* 20/3 (1983), 297–304, reprinted in *The Philosophy of Laughter and Humor*, ed. John Morreall (Albany: State University of New York Press 1987), 212–24; John Morreall, "Funny Ha-Ha, Funny Strange, and Other Reactions to Incongruity," in *The Philosophy of Laughter and Humor*, ed. John Morreall (Albany: State University of New York Press, 1987), 188–207; and John Morreall, "Enjoying Incongruity," *Humor: International Journal of Humor Research* 2/1 (1989), 1–18.

3   See Jerome Shaffer, "An Assessment of Emotion," *American Philosophical Quarterly* 20 (1983), 161–73.

4   See, for example, Colin Radford, "How Can We Be Moved by the Fate of Anna Karenina?" *Proceedings of the Aristotelian Society*, suppl. vol. 69 (1975), 67–80; and Robert J. Yanal, *Paradoxes of Emotion and Fiction* (University Park: Pennsylvania State University Press, 1999).

5   Robert C. Roberts, "Is Amusement an Emotion?" *American Philosophical Quarterly* 25 (1988), 273.

6   Roger Scruton, in *The Philosophy of Laughter and Humor*, ed. John Morreall (Albany: State University of New York Press, 1987), 165.

7   Henri Bergson, *Laughter*, in *The Philosophy of Laughter and Humor*, ed. John Morreall (Albany: State University of New York Press, 1987), 118.

8   Horace Walpole, letter to Horace Mann, December 31, 1769.

9   Roberts, "Is Amusement an Emotion?," 296.

10 Wallace Chafe, *The Importance of Not Being Earnest: The Feeling Behind Laughter and Humor* (Amsterdam: John Benjamins, 2007), 23.

11 See Johann Huizenga, *Homo Ludens: A Study of the Play-Element in Human Culture* (Boston: Beacon, 1955).

12 George Santayana, *The Sense of Beauty* (New York: Charles Scribner's Sons, 1896), 27.

13 Thomas Aquinas, *Summa Theologiae*, 2a2ae, 168, 2, 217.

14 Victor Raskin, *Semantic Mechanisms of Humor* (Dordrecht: D. Reidel, 1985).

15 Owen Aldis, *Play Fighting* (New York: Academic Press, 1975), 139, and Jaak Panksepp, "Rough and Tumble Play: A Fundamental Brain Process," in

Parent–Child Play, ed. Kevin MacDonald (Albany: State University of New York Press, 1993), 150.

16 Jan van Hooff, "A Comparative Approach to the Phylogeny of Laughter and Smiling," in *Non-Verbal Communication*, ed. Robert A. Hinde (Cambridge: Cambridge University Press, 1972), 209–11. See also Jane Goodall, "The Behavior of Free-Living Chimpanzees in the Gombe Stream Reserve," *Animal Behavior Monographs* 1 (1968), 165–311; and Robert Provine, *Laughter: A Scientific Investigation* (Harmondsworth: Penguin, 2000).

17 Van Hooff, "A Comparative Approach to the Phylogeny of Laughter and Smiling," 212–13.

18 Ibid., 217.

19 Aldis, *Play Fighting*; Jane Goodall, "The Behavior of Free-Living Chimpanzees in the Gombe Stream Reserve," 165–311; Provine, *Laughter: A Scientific Investigation*, 75–6.

20 See R. Andrew, "The Origins and Evolution of the Calls and Facial Expressions of the Primates," *Behaviour* 20 (1963), 1–109; William Fry, "A Comparative Study of Smiling and Laughter," Paper at Western Psychological Association, San Francisco, April 1971; William F. Fry, "The Appeasement Function of Mirthful Laughter: A Comparative Study," Paper at the International Conference on Humour and Laughter, Cardiff, Wales, July 1976.

21 Provine, *Laughter: A Scientific Investigation*, ch. 5.

22 Marvin Harris, *Our Kind* (New York: Harper and Row, 1989), 77.

23 Robert Provine and K. R. Fischer, "Laughing, Smiling and Talking: Relation to Sleeping and Social Context in Humans," *Ethology* 83 (1989), 295–305; Provine, *Laughter: A Scientific Investigation*, 45.

24 Provine, *Laughter: A Scientific Investigation*, 42.

25 Ibid., 40.

26 Ibid., 40–1.

Chapter 3: From Lucy to "I Love Lucy"

1 Robert Provine, *Laughter: A Scientific Investigation* (Harmondsworth: Penguin, 2000), 86; Jennifer Gamble, "Humor in Apes," *Humor: International Journal of Humor Research* 14/2 (2001), 169; William Fry, "The Biology of Humor," *Humor: International Journal of Humor Research* 7/2 (1994), 111–26.

2 Immanuel Kant, in *The Philosophy of Laughter and Humor*, ed. John Morreall (Albany: State University of New York Press, 1987), 46, 48.

3 See Paul McGhee, *Humor: Its Origin and Development* (San Francisco: W. H. Freeman, 1979).

4 Jean Piaget, *Play, Dreams, and Imitation in Childhood*, trans. C. Gattegno and F. M. Hodgson (London: Routledge and Kegan Paul, 1991), 91.

5 Piaget, *Play, Dreams, and Imitation in Childhood*, 92.

6   In McGhee, *Humor: Its Origin and Development*, 66.

7   Piaget, *Play, Dreams, and Imitation in Childhood*, 96.

8   In McGhee, *Humor: Its Origin and Development*, 68. See Piaget *Play, Dreams, and Imitation in Childhood*, 120.

9   Kornei Chukovsky, *From Two to Five*, trans. Miriam Morton (Berkeley: University of California Press, 1963), 601.

10 V. S. Ramachandran and Sandra Blakeslee, *Phantoms in the Brain* (New York: William Morrow, 1998), 206.

11 Wallace Chafe, *The Importance of Not Being Earnest: The Feeling Behind Laughter and Humor* (Amsterdam: John Benjamins, 2007), 23.

12 An early version of this account of laughter is in Donald Hayworth, "The Social Origin and Function of Laughter," *Psychological Review* 35 (1928), 367–85. A contemporary version is in Provine, *Laughter: A Scientific Investigation*.

13 Ramachandran and Blakeslee, *Phantoms in the Brain*, p. 205.

14 Kendall Walton, *Mimesis as Make-Believe: On the Foundations of the Representational Arts* (Cambridge: Harvard University Press, 1990).

15 Provine, *Laughter: A Scientific Investigation*, 87.

16 See John Morreall, *Taking Laughter Seriously* (Albany: State University of New York, 1983), 70–2.

17 Paul Radin, *The Trickster: A Study in American Indian Mythology* (New York: Random House, 1972), 6.

18 Beatrice Otto, *Fools Are Everywhere: The Court Jester Around the World* (Chicago: University of Chicago Press, 2001).

19 Gamble, "Humor in Apes," 163–79; Francine Patterson and Eugene Linden, *The Education of Koko* (New York: Holt, Rinehart and Winston, 1985), ch. 16; McGhee, *Humor: Its Origin and Development*, 110–20; Provine, *Laughter: A Scientific Investigation*, ch. 5.

20 Francine Patterson, "Koko: Conversations with Herself," *Gorilla*, 10 (December 1989).

21 Provine, *Laughter: A Scientific Investigation*, 94.

22 Patterson, "Koko: Conversations with Herself," ch. 1.

23 Provine, *Laughter: A Scientific Investigation*, 95.

24 Woody Allen, *Getting Even* (New York: Random House, 1971), 33.

25 Aristotle, *Poetics*, 5, 1449a, in *The Philosophy of Laughter and Humor*, ed. John Morreall (Albany: State University of New York Press, 1987), 14.

26 Mark Twain, *Following the Equator: A Journey around the World* (New York: Harper and Brothers, 1906), ch. 10.

27 Victor Raskin, *Semantic Mechanisms of Humor* (Dordrecht: Reidel, 1984), 107–14.

28 Søren Kierkegaard, *Either/Or*, trans. W. Lowrie, Vol. II (Garden City, NY: Anchor Books, 1959), 331–2.

29 Henri Bergson, *Laughter*, in *The Philosophy of Laughter and Humor*, ed. John Morreall (Albany: State University of New York Press, 1987), 119.

30 Willibald Ruch, *Die Emotion Erheiterung: Alusdrucksformen und Bedingungen* [The Emotion of Exhilaration: Forms of Expression and Eliciting Conditions], unpublished habilitations thesis, Department of Psychology, University of Düsseldorf, 1990.

31 Immanuel Kant, *Critique of Judgment*, in *The Philosophy of Laughter and Humor*, ed. John Morreall (Albany: State University of New York Press, 1987), 45–7.

32 Ibid., 47.

33 Aristotle, *Nicomachean Ethics*, 4, ch. 8, in *The Philosophy of Laughter and Humor*, ed. John Morreall (Albany: State University of New York Press, 1987), 15.

34 Cf. Harvey Mindess, *Laughter and Liberation* (Los Angeles: Nash, 1971).

35 Arthur Schopenhauer, *The World as Will and Idea*, trans. R. B. Haldane and J. Kemp (London: Routledge and Kegan Paul, 1964), 2: 280.

36 Dave Barry, *Dave Barry's Guide to Life* (New York: Wings Books, 1991), 215.

37 Sigmund Freud, "Humor," *International Journal of Psychoanalysis* 9 (1928), 1–6.

38 Richard Brautigan, *Sombrero Fallout: A Japanese Novel* (New York: Simon and Schuster, 1976), 80.

39 Enid Welsford, *The Fool: His Social and Literary History* (Garden City, NY: Doubleday Anchor, 1961), 223.

40 Qian Suoqiao, "Translating 'Humor' into Chinese Culture," *Humor: International Journal of Humor Research* 20 (2007), 277–95.

41 Jerrold Levinson, "Humour," *Routledge Encyclopedia of Philosophy*, ed. E. Craig (London: Routledge, 1998), 565.

42 Ibid.

43 Noël Carroll, "Humour," *The Oxford Handbook of Aesthetics* (Oxford: Oxford University Press, 2003), 353. See Levinson, "Humour," 562–7.

44 Carroll, "Humour," 355.

45 Ibid., 354.

46 Ibid., 354–5.

47 Ibid., 354.

48 Ibid.

49 For many of these ideas about the adaptive value of humor, I am indebted to Brian Boyd, "Laughter and Literature: A Play Theory of Humor," *Philosophy and Literature* 28 (2004), 1–22. See also Gordon Burghardt, *The Genesis of Animal Play: Testing the Limits* (Cambridge, MA: MIT Press, 2005). For a critique of the claims made for the benefits of play, see Brian Sutton-Smith, *The Ambiguity of Play* (Cambridge: Harvard University Press, 1997), 24–6.

50 Robert Fagen, "Animal Play, Games of Angels, Biology, and the Brain," in *The Future of Play Theory: A Multidisciplinary Inquiry into the Contributions of Brian Sutton-Smith*, ed. Anthony D. Pellegrini (Albany: State University of New York Press, 1995), 35; and Stuart Brown, "Play as an Organizing

Principle: Clinical Evidence and Personal Observations," in *Animal Play: Evolutionary, Comparative, and Ecological Perspectives*, ed. Marc Bekoff and J. A. Byers (Cambridge: Cambridge University Press, 1998), 243–59.

51 Brown, "Play as an Organizing Principle," 248. See also Sutton-Smith, *The Ambiguity of Play*, 40.

52 Marek Spinka et al., "Mammalian Play: Training for the Unexpected," *Quarterly Journal of Biology* 76 (2001), 141–68.

53 Michael Lewis, "Play as Whimsy," in *Does Play Matter? Functional and Evolutionary Aspects of Animal and Human Play*, ed. P. K. Smith, *The Behavioral and Brain Sciences* 5/1 (1982), 166.

54 Kant, *Critique of Judgment*, in *The Philosophy of Laughter and Humor*, ed. John Morreall, 46.

55 See Thomas Nagel, *The View from Nowhere* (New York: Oxford University Press, 1989).

56 On the similarities between humor, science, and art, see Arthur Koestler, *The Act of Creation* (London: Hutchinson, 1964).

57 Herbert Lefcourt and Rod A. Martin, *Humor and Life Stress: Antidote to Adversity* (New York: Springer-Verlag, 1986); Herbert M. Lefcourt, *Humor: The Psychology of Living Buoyantly* (New York: Plenum, 2001); Rod A. Martin et al., "Humor, Coping with Stress, Self-Concept, and Psychological Well-Being," *Humor: International Journal of Humor Research* 6/1 (1993), 89–104; Rod A. Martin, "The Situational Humor Response Questionnaire (SHRQ) and Coping Humor Scale (CHS): A Decade of Research Findings," *Humor: International Journal of Humor Research* 9/3–4 (1996), 251–72.

58 Max Eastman, *Enjoyment of Laughter* (New York: Halcyon House, 1936), 45.

59 John Morreall, *Humor Works* (Amherst, MA: Human Resource Development Press, 1997), 59–90.

60 Erma Bombeck, "Me Have Cancer?" *Reader's Digest* 142 (April 1993), 96–8.

61 On the psychological and physical benefits of humor, see the special number of *Humor: International Journal of Humor Research* on Humor and Health, 17/1–2 (2004). Also, Lefcourt and Martin, *Humor and Life Stress: Antidote to Adversity*; Lefcourt, *Humor: The Psychology of Living Buoyantly*; Martin et al., "Humor, Coping with Stress, Self-Concept, and Psychological Well-Being," 89–104; Martin, "The Situational Humor Response Questionnaire (SHRQ) and Coping Humor Scale (CHS)," 251–72; Rod A. Martin, *The Psychology of Humor: An Integrative Approach* (Amsterdam: Elsevier Science: 2006), chs. 6, 9, 10, 11.

Chapter 4: That Mona Lisa Smile

1 E. H. Gombrich, "Huizinga and 'Homo Ludens,'" review of *Homo Ludens: A Study of the Play Element in Culture*, by Johan Huizenga, *Times Literary Supplement*, October 4, 1976, 1089.

2   Plato, *Philebus*, 48–50, in *The Philosophy of Laughter and Humor*, ed. John Morreall (Albany: State University of New York Press, 1987), 10–13; Aristotle, *Nicomachean Ethics*, 4, 8, in *The Philosophy of Laughter and Humor*, ed. John Morreall (Albany: State University of New York Press, 1987), 14–16.

3   Sigmund Freud, *Jokes and Their Relation to the Unconscious, Standard Edition of the Complete Psychological Works of Sigmund Freud*, trans. James Strachey (New York: W. W. Norton, 1963), chs. 3–4.

4   Cf. Mike Martin, "Humor and the Aesthetic Enjoyment of Incongruities," in *The Philosophy of Laughter and Humor*, ed. John Morreall (Albany: State University of New York Press, 1987), 183.

5   Martin, "Humor and the Aesthetic Enjoyment of Incongruities," 176.

6   See John Morreall, "Funny Ha-Ha, Funny Strange, and Other Reactions to Incongruity," in *The Philosophy of Laughter and Humor*, ed. John Morreall (Albany: State University of New York Press, 1987), 204–5; Noël Carroll, "The Nature of Horror," *Journal of Aesthetics and Art Criticism* 46 (1987), 51–9; and Noël Carroll, *The Philosophy of Horror* (New York: Routledge, 1990).

7   Carroll, "The Nature of Horror," 51–9; and Carroll, *The Philosophy of Horror*.

8   André Breton, *First Surrealist Manifesto* (Paris: Éditions du Sagittaire, 1924).

9   Quoted in James Thrall Soby, *René Magritte* (New York: The Museum of Modern Art, Doubleday), 15.

10   Quoted in Soby, *René Magritte*, 9.

11   See John Morreall, *Comedy, Tragedy, and Religion* (Albany: State University of New York Press, 1999), ch. 4.

12   Noël Carroll, "Art and Ethical Criticism: An Overview of Recent Directions of Research," *Ethics* 110 (2000), 350–1.

13   See James Robson, *Humour, Obscenity, and Aristophanes* (Tubingen: Gunter Narr Verlag, 2006).

14   Edward L. Galligan, *The Comic Vision in Literature* (Athens: University of Georgia Press, 1984), 190.

15   See Morreall, *Comedy, Tragedy, and Religion*, ch. 4.

16   Galligan, *The Comic Vision in Literature*, 36.

17   Conrad Hyers, *And God Created Laughter: The Bible as Divine Comedy* (Atlanta: John Knox Press, 1987), 115–16.

18   Warren St. John, "Seriously, the Joke is Dead," *New York Times*, May 22, 2005, Section 9.

19   B. F. Skinner, *Beyond Freedom and Dignity* (New York: Bantam, 1976), 49.

Chapter 5: Laughing at the Wrong Time

1   In I. Hausherr, *Penthos: La doctrine de la componction dans l'Orient cretien* (coll. Orientalia Christiana Analecta, 132) (Rome: Pontificum Institutum Orientalium Studiorum, 1944).

2   Gregory of Nyssa, *Opera*, vol. 5, ed. J. McDonough and P. Alexander (Leiden: Brill, 1962), 310.

3   John Climacus, *The Ladder of Divine Ascent* (Mahwah, NJ: Paulist Press, 1982), 192.

4   Anthony Ludovici, *The Secret of Laughter* (New York: Viking, 1933), 12–13, 11.

5   William Prynne, *Histrio-Mastix: The Players Scourge or Actors Tragaedie.* (London, 1633).

6   Quoted in *The Sayings of the Desert Fathers*, ed. Benedicta Ward (Oxford: Mowbrays, 1981), 893.

7   Climacus, *The Ladder of Divine Ascent*, 140.

8   Michael Philips, "Racist Acts and Racist Humor," *Canadian Journal of Philosophy* 14 (1984): 75.

9   Christie Davies, *Ethnic Humor around the World* (Bloomington: Indiana University Press, 1996); *Jokes and Their Relations to Society* (New York: Mouton de Gruyter, 1998); and *The Mirth of Nations* (New Brunswick, NJ: Transaction, 2002).

10 Ronald de Sousa, in *The Philosophy of Laughter and Humor*, ed. John Morreall (Albany: State University of New York Press, 1987), 239.

11 Ibid.

12 Ibid.

13 Ibid.

14 See Roger Scruton, in *The Philosophy of Laughter and Humor*, ed. John Morreall (Albany: State University of New York Press, 1987), 170–1.

15 Ludovici, *The Secret of Laughter*, 11–13.

16 Thomas Hobbes, *English Works of Thomas Hobbes*, 11 vols. (London: Bohn, 1845), vol. 4, 455.

17 Henri Bergson, *Laughter: An Essay on the Meaning of the Comic*, trans. by C. Brereton and F. Rothwell (New York: Macmillan, 1913), 139.

18 Stanley Milgram, *Obedience to Authority: An Experimental View* (New York: HarperCollins, 1974). For a videorecording of this laughter response, see: http://www.chass.ncsu.edu/langure/ethics/php816/modules/human_subjects/laugh.mov.

19 Peter Jones, "Laughter," in *Proceedings of the Aristotelian Society*, Supplementary Volume 56 (1982), 225.

20 Philips, "Racist Acts and Racist Humor," 76.

21 Ibid., 77.

22 Richard Mohr, "Fag-ends and Jokes' Butts," from "Gays and Equal Protection," unpublished manuscript.

23 For an historical examination of the use of humor to keep American blacks "in their place," see Joseph Boskin, *Sambo: Rise and Demise of an American Jester* (Oxford: Oxford University Press, 1986).

24 Joseph Boskin, "The Complicity of Humor: The Life and Death of Sambo," in *The Philosophy of Laughter and Humor*, ed. John Morreall (Albany: State University of New York Press, 1987), 250–63.

Chapter 6: Having a Good Laugh

1 Thomas Aquinas, *Summa Theologiae*, 2a2ae, Q. 168, Article 2, 219.
2 Brian Boyd, "Laughter and Literature: A Play Theory of Humor," *Philosophy and Literature* 28/1 (2004), 1–22.
3 Paul N. Dixon et al., "Relating Social Interest and Dogmatism to Happiness and Sense of Humor," *Individual Psychology Journal of Adlerian Theory, Research, and Practice* 42 (1986), 421–7.
4 Gerald R. Miller and Bacon, P., "Open- and Closed-Mindedness and Recognition of Visual Humor," *Journal of Communication* 21 (1971), 150–9.
5 Edward de Bono, *Serious Creativity: Using the Power of Lateral Thinking to Create New Ideas* (New York: HarperCollins, 1992), 8.
6 Alice Isen, "Some Perspectives on Positive Feelings and Emotions: Positive Affect Facilitates Thinking and Problem Solving," in *Feelings and Emotions: The Amsterdam Symposium*, ed. Anthony Manstead et al. (New York: Cambridge University Press, 2004), 263–81. Avner Ziv, "Using Humor to Develop Creative Thinking," *Journal of Children in Contemporary Society* 20 (1988), 99–116.
7 Irving Janis, *Groupthink: Psychological Studies of Policy Decisions and Fiascoes*, 2nd ed. (Boston: Houghton Mifflin, 1982).
8 Beatrice Otto, *Fools Are Everywhere: The Court Jester around the World* (Chicago: University of Chicago Press, 2001).
9 Otto, *Fools Are Everywhere*, 128.
10 Christopher Cerf and Henry Beard, *The Pentagon Catalog: Ordinary Products at Extraordinary Prices* (New York: Workman, 1986).
11 Paul Slansky, *The Clothes Have No Emperor: A Chronicle of the American 80s* (New York: Fireside, 1989).
12 Peter Berger, *Redeeming Laughter: The Comic Dimension of Human Experience* (New York: Walter de Gruyter, 1997).
13 C. W. Metcalf and Roma Felible, *Lighten Up: Survival Skills for People under Pressure* (New York: Addison-Wesley, 1992), 30.
14 Robert C. Roberts, "Humor and the Virtues," *Inquiry* 31 (1988), 127.
15 See Allen Fay, *Making Things Better by Making Them Worse* (New York: Hawthorn, 1978).
16 Sammy Basu, "'Woe Unto You Who Laugh Now!': Humor and Toleration in Overton and Shaftesbury," in *Religious Toleration: "The Variety of Rites" from Cyrus to Defoe*, ed. John Christian Laursen (New York: St. Martin's Press, 1999), 147–72.
17 Robert Runcie, *Seasons of the Spirit* (Grand Rapids, MI: Eerdmans, 1983).
18 M. Conrad Hyers, "The Dialectic of the Sacred and the Comic," in *Holy Laughter: Essays on Religion in the Comic Perspective*, ed. M. Conrad Hyers (New York: Seabury, 1969), 232.
19 William Sargent, in Joyce O. Herzler, *Laughter: A Socio-Scientific Analysis* (New York: Exposition Press, 1970), 143.

20 Robert Waite, *The Psychopathic God: Adolf Hitler* (New York: Basic Books, 1977), 13.

21 Harry Trimhorn, "Did Hitler's Hanging Judges Act Illegally?" *Toronto Star*, August 31, 1980.

22 Steve Lipman, *Laughter in Hell: The Use of Humor during the Holocaust* (Northvale, NJ: Jason Aronson, 1991), 103.

23 Hana Greenfield, "Fighting Back with Satire," *Jerusalem Post Entertainment Magazine*, April 27, 1990.

24 Stanislaw Dobrzynski, *Sein Kampf: 41 Caricatures politiques* (Jerusalem: Wydawnictwo "W Drodze," 1944), 46.

25 B. D. Shaw, ed., *Is Hitler Dead? and Best Anti-Nazi Humor* (New York: Alcaeus House, 1939), 10–11.

26 Uwe Naumann, *Zwischen Tränen und Gelächter* (Cologne: Pahl-Rugenstein Verlag, 1983), 226–7.

27 Ulrike Migdal, *Und die Musik spielt dazu: Chansons und Satiren aus dem KZ Theresienstadt* (Munich: Piper, 1986), 24.

28 Konnelyn Feig, *Hitler's Death Camps: The Sanity of Madness* (New York: Holmes & Meier, 1979), 77.

29 Lucjan Dobroszycki, ed., *The Chronicle of the Lodz Ghetto 1941–1944* (New Haven: Yale University Press, 1984), 327.

30 Robert Moses Shapiro, "Yiddish Slang under the Nazis," *The Book Peddler*, Summer 1989, 30.

31 Shapiro, "Yiddish Slang under the Nazis," 31.

32 Viktor Frankl, *Man's Search for Meaning* (New York: Simon & Schuster, 1959), 54–6.

33 *Talmud*, Tanit 22a.

Chapter 7: Homo Sapiens and Homo Ridens

1 Ned Block, "Why Do Mirrors Reverse Left/Right but Not Up/Down?" *Journal of Philosophy* 71 (1974), 259–77.

2 Simon Critchley, interview on http://www.onegoodmove.org, November 18, 2002.

3 William James, *Some Problems of Philosophy*, in *William James: The Essential Writings*, ed. Bruce Wilshire (New York, Harper, 1971), 2.

4 Bertrand Russell, *The Philosophy of Logical Atomism* (London: Allen and Unwin, 1918), 53.

5 All quotes are from http://www.quotationspage.com/quotes/Bertrand_Russell.

6 Stanley Milgram, *Obedience to Authority: An Experimental View* (New York: HarperCollins, 1974).

7 Bertrand Russell, *The ABC of Relativity* (London: Kegan Paul, Trench, Trubner & Co., 1925), 166.

8 Peter Singer, *The President of Good and Evil* (New York: Dutton, 2004).

9   Mark Twain, *Following the Equator: A Journey around the World* (New York: Harper and Brothers, 1906), ch. 10.

10 Arthur Schopenhauer, in *The Philosophy of Laughter and Humor*, ed. John Morreall (Albany: State University of New York Press, 1987), ch. 9.

11 Henri Bergson, *Laughter*, in *The Philosophy of Laughter and Humor*, ed. John Morreall (Albany: State University of New York Press, 1987), 120–1.

12 Søren Kierkegaard, *Concluding Unscientific Postscript*, tr. David Swenson and Walter Lowrie (Princeton: Princeton University Press, 1941), 259.

13 Kierkegaard, *Concluding Unscientific Postscript*, 83–4.

14 Friedrich Nietzsche, *Thus Spoke Zarathustra*, tr. Walter Kaufmann (New York: Penguin, 1978), ch. 73, section 15.

15 Jean-Paul Sartre, *The Family Idiot: Gustave Flaubert 1821–1857*, tr. Carol Cosman, 3 vols. (Chicago: University of Chicago Press, 1981).

16 Thomas Nagel, "The Absurd," *Journal of Philosophy* 68 (1971), 716–27.

17 Georg Friedrich Meier, *Thoughts on Jesting*, ed. Joseph Jones (Austin: University of Texas Press, 1947), 55–6.

18 Conrad Hyers, *Zen and the Comic Spirit* (Philadelphia: Westminster John Knox Press, 1975), 34.

19 D. T. Suzuki, *Essays in Zen Buddhism* (London: Rider, 1948–53), vol. 2, 97.

20 Arthur Schopenhauer, *The World as Will and Idea*, trans. Haldane and Kemp (London: Routledge and Kegan Paul, 1964), 2: 280.

21 Thomas Merton, *Mystics and Zen Masters* (New York: Delta, 1967), 228.

22 Nagel, "The Absurd," 716–27.

23 Stephen Leacock, *Humor and Humanity* (New York: Henry Holt, 1938), 219–20.

Chapter 8: The Glass Is Half-Empty *and* Half-Full

1   Robert Nozick, *The Examined Life: Philosophical Meditations* (New York: Touchstone, 1989), 267.

2   Nozick, *The Examined Life*, 269.

3   One exception is the members of the Association of Applied and Therapeutic Humor who incorporate "humor interventions" into their therapeutic sessions.

4   Aristotle, *Poetics*, 5, 1449a, in *The Philosophy of Laughter and Humor*, ed. John Morreall (Albany: State University of New York Press, 1987), 14.

5   Plato, *Philebus* 48–50, in *The Philosophy of Laughter and Humor*, ed. John Morreall (Albany: State University of New York Press, 1987), 11.

6   Nathan Scott, "The Bias of Comedy and the Narrow Escape into Faith," in *Holy Laughter: Essays on Religion in the Comic Perspective*, ed. M. Conrad Hyers (New York: Seabury, 1969), 57.

7   Albert Einstein, "My Credo," Speech to the German League of Human Rights, Berlin, 1932.

Bibliography

Adkin, Neil. "The Fathers on Laughter," *Orpheus* 6/1 (1985): 149–52.

Aichele, George. *Theology as Comedy*. Lanham, MD: University Press of America, 1980.

Aldis, Owen. *Play Fighting*. New York: Academic Press, 1975.

Allen, Woody. *Getting Even*. New York: Random House, 1971.

Andrew, R. J. "The Origins and Evolution of the Calls and Facial Expressions of the Primates," *Behaviour* 20 (1963): 1–109.

Aquinas, Thomas. *Summa Theologiae*. Volume 44. *Well-Tempered Passion*, trans. Thomas Gilby. New York: McGraw-Hill, 1972.

Aristotle. *The Basic Works of Aristotle*, ed. Richard McKeon. New York: Random House, 1941.

Armstrong, A. MacC. "The Idea of the Comic," *British Journal of Aesthetics* 25 (1985): 232–8.

Ascione, Lou. "Dead Sharks and Dynamite Ham: The Philosophical Use of Humor in *Annie Hall*." In *Woody Allen and Philosophy: You Mean My Whole Fallacy is Wrong*? ed. Mark T. Conard. Chicago: Open Court, 2004.

Auden, W. H. "Notes on the Comic," *Thought* 27(1952): 57–71.

Bailey, John. *Intent on Laughter*. New York: Quadrangle, 1976.

Bain, Alexander. *The Emotions and the Will*, 3rd ed. London: Longmans and Green, 1875.

Barnes, Barry. "The Comparison of Belief Systems: Anomaly versus Falsehood." In *Modes of Thought*, ed. Robin Horton and Ruth Finnegan, 182–98. London: Faber and Faber, 1973.

Barry, Dave. *Dave Barry's Guide to Life*. New York: Wings Books, 1991.

Basil the Great. *The Long Rules*, trans. M. Wagner. *The Fathers of the Church Series*, vol. 9. Washington: Catholic University of America, 1950.

Basu, Sammy. "Dialogic Ethics and the Virtue of Humor," *Journal of Political Philosophy* 7 (1999): 378–403.

Basu, Sammy. "'Woe Unto You Who Laugh Now!': Humor and Toleration in Overton and Shaftesbury." In *Religious Toleration: "The Variety of Rites" from*

Cyrus to Defoe, ed. John Christian Laursen, 147–72. New York: St. Martin's Press, 1999.

Baudelaire, Charles. "The Essence of Laughter." In *The Essence of Laughter and Other Essays, Journals, and Letters*, trans. Charles Pierre, ed. Peter Quennell. New York: Meridian Books, 1956.

Beattie, James. "An Essay on Laughter and Ludicrous Composition." In *Essays*, 3rd ed. London, 1779.

Bekoff, Marc and Byers, J. A. *Animal Play: Evolutionary, Comparative, and Ecological Perspectives*. Cambridge: Cambridge University Press, 1998.

Bell, Jason. "The Laughing Animal: An Inquiry into the Ethical and Religious Implications of Humor," *Kinesis: Graduate Journal in Philosophy* 30 (2003): 4–22.

Benatar, David. "Prejudice in Wit: When Racial and Gender Humor Harms," *Public Affairs Quarterly* 13 (1999): 191–203.

Berger, Peter. *Redeeming Laughter: The Comic Dimension of Human Experience*. New York: De Gruyter, 1997.

Bergler, Edmund. *Laughter and the Sense of Humor*. New York: Intercontinental Medical Book Company, 1956.

Bergmann, Merrie. "How Many Feminists Does It Take to Make a Joke: Sexist Humor and What's Wrong with It," *Hypatia* 1 (1986): 63–82.

Bergson, Henri. *Laughter: An Essay on the Meaning of the Comic*, trans. Cloudesley Brereton and Fred Rothwell. London: Macmillan, 1913.

Bierman, Arthur K. "Socratic Humor: Understanding the Most Important Philosophical Argument," *Apeiron: A Journal for Ancient Philosophy and Science* 5 (1971): 23–42.

Block, Ned. "Why Do Mirrors Reverse Left/Right but Not Up/Down?" *Journal of Philosophy* 71 (1974): 259–77.

Bombeck, Erma. "Me Have Cancer?" *Reader's Digest* 142 (April 1993): 96–98.

Boskin, Joseph. "The Complicity of Humor: The Life and Death of Sambo." In *The Philosophy of Laughter and Humor*, ed. John Morreall, 250–63. Albany: State University of New York Press, 1987. Originally published in *Philosophical Forum* 9 (1977–8): 371–82.

Boskin, Joseph. *Sambo: Rise and Demise of an American Jester*. Oxford: Oxford University Press, 1986.

Boston, Richard. *An Anatomy of Laughter*. London: Collins, 1974.

Boullart, Karel. "Laughing Matters or 'Comodia Naturalis,'" *Philosophica* 38 (1986): 5–26.

Boyd, Brian. "Laughter and Literature: A Play Theory of Humor," *Philosophy and Literature* 28 (2004): 1–22.

Brautigan Richard. *Sombrero Fallout: A Japanese Novel*. New York: Simon and Schuster, 1976.

Bremond, André. "Hints on Risibility," *Modern Schoolman* 17 (1940): 29–30.

Breton, André. *First Surrealist Manifesto*. Paris: Éditions du Sagittaire, 1924.

Brottman, Mikita. *Funny Peculiar: Gershon Legman and the Psychopathology of Humor.* Hillsdale, NJ: Analytic Press, 2004.

Brown, Deborah J. "What Part of 'Know' Don't You Understand?" *Monist* 88/1 (2005): 11–35.

Brown, Stuart. "Play as an Organizing Principle: Clinical Evidence and Personal Observations." In *Animal Play: Evolutionary, Comparative, and Ecological Perspectives*, ed. Marc Bekoff and J. A. Byers, 243–59. Cambridge: Cambridge University Press, 1998.

Buckham, John W. "Humor at a Time Like This," *Personalist* 27 (1946): 413–24.

Buckley, Francis. H. *The Morality of Laughter.* Ann Arbor: University of Michigan Press, 2003.

Burghardt, Gordon. *The Genesis of Animal Play: Testing the Limits.* Cambridge, MA: MIT Press, 2005.

Carlin, George. *Brain Droppings.* New York: Hyperion, 1997.

Carpino, Joseph J. "On Laughter," *Interpretation* 13 (1985): 91–102.

Carroll, Noël. "Art and Ethical Criticism: An Overview of Recent Directions of Research," *Ethics* 110 (2000): 350–87.

Carroll, Noël. "Humor," *The Oxford Handbook of Aesthetics*, ed. Jerrold Levinson, 344–65. Oxford: Oxford University Press, 2003.

Carroll, Noël. "Horror and Humor," *Journal of Aesthetics and Art Criticism* 57 (1999): 145–60.

Carroll, Noël. "Intimate Laughter," *Philosophy and Literature* 24 (2000): 435–50.

Carroll, Noël. "The Nature of Horror," *Journal of Aesthetics and Art Criticism* 46 (1987): 51–9.

Carroll, Noël. "On Jokes," *Midwest Studies in Philosophy* 16 (1991): 280–301.

Carroll, Noël. *The Philosophy of Horror.* New York: Routledge, 1990.

Carroll, Noël. "Two Comic Plot Structures," *Monist* 88 (2005): 154–83.

Cave, Peter. "Humour and Paradox Laid Bare," *Monist* 88 (2005): 135–53.

Cavell, Stanley. *Pursuits of Happiness: The Hollywood Comedy of Re-Marriage.* Cambridge, MA: Harvard University Press, 1984.

Cerf, Christopher and Beard, Henry. *The Pentagon Catalog: Ordinary Products at Extraordinary Prices.* New York: Workman, 1986.

Chafe, Wallace. *The Importance of Not Being Earnest: The Feeling behind Laughter and Humor.* Amsterdam: John Benjamins, 2007.

Chapman, Anthony, and Foot, Hugh, eds. *Humor and Laughter: Theory, Research and Applications.* New York: Wiley, 1976.

Chapman, Anthony, and Foot, Hugh, eds. *It's a Funny Thing, Humour.* Oxford, NY: Pergamon, 1977.

Chrysostom, John. *On the Priesthood: Ascetic Treatises; Select Homilies and Letters; Homilies on the Statues*, vol. 9 of *A Select Library of the Nicene and Post-Nicene Fathers of the Christian Church*, ed. Philip Schaff. New York: Christian Literature Co., 1889.

Chukovsky, Kornei. *From Two to Five*, trans. Miriam Morton. Berkeley: University of California Press, 1963.

Cicero, Quintus Tullius. *On the Orator*, Book II, trans. E. W. Sutton and H. Rackham. Loeb Classical Library. Cambridge, MA: Harvard University Press, 1942.

Claiborne, John. "Laughter and the Theory of Action," *Southern Journal of Philosophy* 10: 343–52.

Clark, Michael. "Humor and Incongruity." In *The Philosophy of Laughter and Humor*, ed. John Morreall, 139–55. Albany: State University of New York Press, 1987. Originally published in *Philosophy* 45 (1970): 20–32.

Clark, Michael. "Humor, Laughter, and the Structure of Thought," *British Journal of Aesthetics* 27 (1987): 238–46.

Climacus, John. *The Ladder of Divine Ascent*. Mahwah, NJ: Paulist Press, 1982.

Cohen, Ted. "Humor." In *The Routledge Companion to Aesthetics*, ed. Berys Gaut and Dominic M. Lopes, 375–82. New York: Routledge, 2001.

Cohen, Ted. "Jokes." In *Pleasure, Preference and Value: Studies in Philosophical Aesthetics*, ed. Eva Schaper, 120–36. Cambridge: Cambridge University Press, 1983.

Cohen, Ted. *Jokes: Philosophical Thoughts on Joking Matters*. Chicago: University of Chicago Press, 1999.

Conard, Mark, and Skoble, Aeon, eds. *Woody Allen and Philosophy: You Mean My Whole Fallacy is Wrong?* Chicago: Open Court, 2004.

Condren, Conal. "Between Social Constraint and the Public Sphere: On Misreading Early Modern Political Satire," *Contemporary Political Theory* 1 (2002): 79–101.

Conolly, Oliver, and Haydar, Bashshar. "The Good, the Bad and the Funny," *Monist* 88 (2005): 121–34.

Cooper, Lane. *An Aristotelian Theory of Comedy, With an Adaptation of the Poetics and a Translation of the "Tractatus Coislinianus."* New York: Harcourt Brace, 1922.

Critchley, Simon. *On Humour*. New York: Routledge, 2002.

Darwin, Charles. *The Expression of Emotions in Man and Animals*. Chicago: University of Chicago Press, 1965.

Dauer, Francis W. "The Picture as the Medium of Humorous Incongruity," *American Philosophical Quarterly* 25 (1988): 241–51.

Davenport, Manuel. "An Existential Philosophy of Humor," *Southwestern Journal of Philosophy* 7 (1976): 169–76.

Davies, Christie. *Ethnic Humor around the World*. Bloomington: Indiana University Press, 1996.

Davies, Christie. *Jokes and Their Relations to Society*. New York: Mouton de Gruyter, 1998.

Davies, Christie. *The Mirth of Nations*. New Brunswick, NJ: Transaction, 2002.

Davis, William H. "The Beautiful, the Amusing, and the Right," *Philosophy Today* 27 (1983): 269–72.

De Bono, Edward. *Serious Creativity: Using the Power of Lateral Thinking to Create New Ideas*. New York: HarperCollins, 1992.

Deckers, Lambert. "On the Validity of a Weight-Judging Paradigm for the Study of Humor," *Humor: International Journal of Humor Research* 6 (1993): 43–56.

De Sousa, Ronald. "When Is It Wrong to Laugh?" In *The Philosophy of Laughter and Humor*, ed. John Morreall, 226–49. Albany: State University of New York Press, 1987.

Descartes, René. "The Passions of the Soul." In *The Philosophy of Laughter and Humor*, ed. John Morreall, 21–5. Originally published in Elizabeth Haldane and G. R. T. Ross, trans., *The Philosophical Works of Descartes*, vol. 1 (Cambridge: Cambridge University Press, 1911).

Dewey, John. "The Theory of Emotion," *Psychological Review* 1 (1894): 553–69.

Dixon, Paul N. et al. "Relating Social Interest and Dogmatism to Happiness and Sense of Humor," *Individual Psychology Journal of Adlerian Theory, Research, and Practice* 42 (1986): 421–7.

Dobroszycki, Lucjan, ed. *The Chronicle of the Lodz Ghetto 1941–1944.* New Haven: Yale University Press, 1984.

Dobrzynski, Stanislaw. *Sein Kampf: 41 Caricatures politiques.* Jerusalem: Wydawnictwo "W Drodze," 1944.

Dolitsky, Marlene. "Humor and the Unsaid," *Journal of Pragmatics* 7 (1983): 39–48.

Dziemidok, Bohdan. *Comical: A Philosophical Analysis*, trans. Marek Janiak. Dordrecht, Holland: Kluwer, 1992.

Eastman, Max. *Enjoyment of Laughter*. New York: Simon and Schuster, 1936.

Eastman, Max. *The Sense of Humor*. New York: Scribner's, 1921.

Egenberger, Stefan. "The Poetic Representation of the Religious in Kierkegaard's Postscript: Climacus's Humoristic Style against the Backdrop of E. T. A. Hoffmann's Understanding of Humor," *Kierkegaard Studies*, 2005 Yearbook: 113–36.

Einstein, Albert. "My Credo." Speech to the German League of Human Rights, Berlin, 1932.

Else, Gerald F. "Comedy." In *Plato and Aristotle on Poetry*, ed. Peter Burian, 185–95. Chapel Hill: University of North Carolina Press, 1986.

Erasmus. *In Praise of Folly*, trans. Hoyt Hopewell Hudson. Princeton: Princeton University Press, 1941.

Evans, C. Stephen. "Kierkegaard's View of Humor: Must Christians Always Be Solemn?" *Faith and Philosophy* 4 (1987): 176–86.

Eysenck, H. J. Foreword to *The Psychology of Humor*, ed. Jeffrey H. Goldstein and Paul E. McGhee. New York: Academic Press, 1972.

Fagen, Robert. *Animal Play Behavior*. New York: Oxford University Press, 1981.

Fagen, Robert. "Animal Play, Games of Angels, Biology, and the Brain." In *The Future of Play Theory: A Multidisciplinary Inquiry into the Contributions of*

Brian Sutton-Smith, ed. Anthony D. Pellegrini, 23–44. Albany: State University of New York Press, 1995.

Fay, Allen. *Making Things Better by Making Them Worse.* New York: Hawthorn, 1978.

Feig, Konnelyn. *Hitler's Death Camps: The Sanity of Madness.* New York: Holmes & Meier, 1979.

Festinger, Leon. *A Theory of Cognitive Dissonance.* Stanford: Stanford University Press, 1957.

Fisher, Fred. "Musical Humor: A Future as Well as a Past?" *Journal of Aesthetics and Art Criticism* 32 (1974): 375–83.

Flewelling, Ralph T. "The Animal Capable of Laughter," *Personalist* 25 (1944): 341–53.

Frank, P. S. *Angelikos Bios.* Munster: Aschendorffsche: Verlagsbuchhandlung, 1964.

Frankl, Victor. *Man's Search for Meaning.* New York: Simon and Schuster, 1959.

Franzwa, Gregg. "Some Thoughts on Funniness," *Southwest Philosophical Studies* 5 (1980): 77–80.

Freud, Sigmund, *Jokes and Their Relation to the Unconscious. Standard Edition of the Complete Psychological Works of Sigmund Freud,* vol. 5, trans. James Strachey. New York: W. W. Norton, 1963.

Freud, Sigmund. "Humor," trans. Joan Rivière. In *The Philosophy of Laughter and Humor,* ed. John Morreall, 111–16. Originally published in the *International Journal of Psycho-Analysis* 9 (1928): 1–6.

Froeschels, Emil. *Philosophy of Wit.* New York: Philosophical Library, 1948.

Fry, William, "The Biology of Humor," *Humor: International Journal of Humor Research* 7 (1994): 111–26.

Fry, William. *Sweet Madness.* Palo Alto: Pacific, 1963.

Fuller, Benjamin A. G. "Is Reality Really Comic?" *Journal of Philosophy* 43 (1946): 589–98.

Galligan, Edward L. *The Comic Vision in Literature.* Athens: University of Georgia Press, 1984.

Gamble, Jennifer. "Humor in Apes," *Humor: International Journal of Humor Research* 14 (2001). 163–79.

Gaut, Berys. "Just Joking: The Ethics and Aesthetics of Humor," *Philosophy and Literature* 22 (1998): 51–68.

Gayman, Cynthia. "Not So Funny: A Deweyan Response," *Contemporary Pragmatism* 2 (2005): 85–91.

Gelven, Michael. *Truth and the Comedic Art.* Albany: State University of New York Press, 2000.

Gibbs, Paul. "A Psychoanalytic Interpretation of the Effectiveness of Humor for Teaching Philosophy," *Journal of Thought* 32 (1997): 123–33.

Gilhus, Ingvild. *Laughing Gods, Weeping Virgins: Laughter in the History of Religion.* New York: Routledge, 1997.

Gilman, Bradley. "The Ethical Element in Wit and Humor," *International Journal of Ethics* 19 (1909): 488–94.

Gilman, Sander L. "Is Life Beautiful? Can the Shoah Be Funny?" *Critical Inquiry* 26 (2000): 279–308.

Giora, Rachel. "On the Cognitive Aspects of the Joke," *Journal of Pragmatics* 16 (1991): 465–85.

Golden, Leon. *Aristotle on Tragic and Comic Mimesis.* Atlanta: Scholars Press, 1992.

Goldstein, Jeffrey, and Paul McGhee, eds. *The Psychology of Humor.* New York: Academic Press, 1972.

Goldstein, Laurence. "Humor and Harm," *Sorites* 3 (November 1995): 27–42.

Goldstein, Laurence, Editor's Introduction, *Monist* 88/1 (2005). Special issue on Humor.

Gombrich, E. H. "Huizinga and 'Homo Ludens.'" Review of *Homo Ludens: A Study of the Play Element in Culture,* by Johan Huizenga, *Times Literary Supplement,* October 4, 1976, 1089.

Goodall, Jane. "The Behavior of Free-Living Chimpanzees in the Gombe Stream Reserve," *Animal Behavior Monographs* 1 (1968): 165–311.

Gordon, Jeffrey. "A Bolt in the Summer Sky: In Quest of the Essence of Humor," *Southwest Philosophical Studies* 7 (1982): 142–6.

Gracia, Jorge J. E. "The Secret of Seinfeld's Humor: The Significance of the Insignificant." In *Seinfeld and Philosophy: A Book about Everything and Nothing,* ed. William Irwin, 148–59. Chicago: Open Court, 1999.

Gregory of Nyssa. *Opera,* ed. J. McDonough and P. Alexander. Leiden: Brill, 1962.

Gregory, Joel C. *The Nature of Laughter.* New York: Harcourt Brace, 1924.

Greig, John Y. T. *The Psychology of Laughter and Comedy.* New York: Rowman and Littlefield, 1969.

Grice, H. Paul. "Logic and Conversation." In *Syntax and Semantics,* vol. 3, ed. Peter Cole and Jerry Morgan, 41–58. New York: Academic Press, 1975.

Grotjahn, Martin. *Beyond Laughter: Humor and the Subconscious.* New York: McGraw-Hill, 1966.

Gruneberg, R. "Humor in Music," *Philosophy and Phenomenological Research* 30 (1969): 122–5.

Gruner, Charles R. *The Game of Humor: A Comprehensive Theory of Why We Laugh.* New Brunswick, NJ: Transaction, 1999.

Gruner, Charles R. *Understanding Laughter: The Workings of Wit and Humor.* New York: Rowman and Littlefield, 1979.

Gunter, Pete A. Y. "Nietzschean Laughter," *Sewanee Review* 77 (1968): 493–506.

Gunter, Pete A. Y. "Whitehead, Bergson, Freud: Suggestions toward a Theory of Laughter," *Southern Journal of Philosophy* 4 (1966): 55–60.

Gutwirth, Marcel. *Laughing Matter: An Essay on the Comic.* Ithaca: Cornell University Press, 1993.

Hanks, Donald. "Self-Deprecating Humor in Relation to Laughter," *Contemporary Philosophy* 23 (2001): 29–33.

Hanley, Richard, ed. *South Park and Philosophy: Bigger, Longer, and More Penetrating.* Chicago: Open Court, 2007.

Hanna, Thomas. "The Compass Points of the Comic and Pathetic," *British Journal of Aesthetics* 8 (1968): 284–94.

Harbsmeier, Christoph. "Humor in Ancient Chinese Philosophy," *Philosophy East and West* 39 (1989): 289–310.

Hardcastle, Gary L., and Reisch, George A., eds. *Monty Python and Philosophy: Nudge, Nudge, Think, Think!* Chicago: Open Court, 2006.

Harpham, Geoffrey. "The Grotesque: First Principles," *Journal of Aesthetics and Art Criticism* 34/4 (1976): 461–8.

Harris, Marvin. *Our Kind.* New York: Harper and Row, 1989.

Hartz, Glenn, and Hunt, Ralph. "Humor: the Beauty and the Beast," *American Philosophical Quarterly* 4 (1991): 299–309.

Harvey, Jean. "Humor as Social Act," *Journal of Value Inquiry* 29/1 (1995): 19–30.

Haskins, Casey. "Art, Morality, and the Holocaust: The Aesthetic Riddle of Benigni's *Life Is Beautiful,*" *Journal of Aesthetics and Art Criticism* 59 (2001): 373–84.

Hatab, Lawrence. "Laughter in Nietzsche's Thought: A Philosophical Tragicomedy," *International Studies in Philosophy* 20 (1988): 67–79.

Hausherr, Irenee. *Penthos: La doctrine de la componction dans l'Orient cretien* (coll. Orientalia Christiana Analecta, 132). Rome: Pontificum Institutum Orientalium Studiorum, 1944.

Hayworth, Donald. "The Social Origin and Function of Laughter," *Psychological Review* 35 (1928): 367–85.

Hazlitt, William. *Lectures on the English Comic Writers.* London: Oxford University Press, 1920.

Herzler, Joyce O. *Laughter: A Socio-Scientific Analysis.* New York: Exposition Press, 1970.

Heyd, David. "The Place of Laughter in Hobbes' Theory of Emotions," *Journal of the History of Ideas* 43 (1982): 285–95.

Hill, Carl. *The Soul of Wit: Joke Theory from Grimm to Freud.* Lincoln: University of Nebraska Press, 1993.

Hinde, Robert A., ed. *Non-Verbal Communication.* Cambridge: Cambridge University Press, 1972.

Hobbes, Thomas. *Human Nature. English Works*, vol. 4, ed. William Molesworth. London: Bohn, 1840.

Hobbes, Thomas. *Leviathan. English Works*, vol. 3, ed. William Molesworth. London: Bohn, 1839.

Hobbes, Thomas. *Philosophical Rudiments Concerning Government and Society.* London: R. Royston, 1651.

Hofstadter, Albert. "The Tragicomic: Concern in Depth," *Journal of Aesthetics and Art Criticism* 24 (1965): 295–302.

Holland, Norman. *Laughing: A Psychology of Humor.* Ithaca: Cornell University Press, 1982.

Hong, Howard V. "The Comic, Satire, Irony, and Humor: Kierkegaardian Reflections," *Midwest Studies in Philosophy* 1 (1976): 98–105.

Horace. *Satires, Epistles and Ars Poetica*, trans. H. Rushton Fairclough. Loeb Classical Library. Cambridge, MA: Harvard University Press, 1929.

Hösle, Vittorio. *Woody Allen: An Essay on the Nature of the Comical*. Notre Dame, IN: University of Notre Dame Press, 2007.

Huizenga, Johann. *Homo Ludens: A Study of the Play-Element in Human Culture*. Boston: Beacon, 1955.

Hume, Robert. "Some Problems in the Theory of Comedy," *Journal of Aesthetics and Art Criticism* 31 (1972): 87–100.

Hutcheson, Francis. *Reflections Upon Laughter, and Remarks Upon the Fable of the Bees*. Glasgow, 1750.

Hyers, Conrad, *And God Created Laughter: The Bible as Divine Comedy*. Atlanta: John Knox Press, 1987.

Hyers, Conrad. "The Dialectic of the Sacred and the Comic." In *Holy Laughter: Essays on Religion in the Comic Perspective*, ed. M. Conrad Hyers, 208–40. New York: Seabury, 1969.

Hyers, M. Conrad. *Holy Laughter: Essays on Religion in the Comic Perspective*. New York: Seabury, 1969.

Hyers, Conrad. "Humor in Zen: Comic Midwifery," *Philosophy East and West* 39 (1989): 267–77.

Hyers, Conrad. *The Comic Vision and the Christian Faith*. New York: Pilgrim Press, 1981.

Hyers, Conrad. *The Spirituality of Comedy: Comic Heroism in a Tragic World*. New Brunswick, NJ: Transaction, 1995.

Hyers, Conrad. *Zen and the Comic Spirit*. Philadelphia: Westminster Press, 1975.

Irwin, William, ed. *Seinfeld and Philosophy: A Book about Everything and Nothing*. Chicago: Open Court, 1999.

Irwin, William, Conard, Mark, and Skoble, Aeon, eds., *The Simpsons and Philosophy: The D'oh! of Homer*. Chicago: Open Court, 2001.

Isen, Alice. "Some Perspectives on Positive Feelings and Emotions: Positive Affect Facilitates Thinking and Problem Solving." In *Feelings and Emotions: The Amsterdam Symposium*, ed. Anthony Manstead et al., 263–81. New York: Cambridge University Press, 2004.

James, William. *Some Problems of Philosophy*. In *William James: The Essential Writings*, ed. Bruce Wilshire. New York: Harper, 1971.

Janis, Irving. *Groupthink: Psychological Studies of Policy Decisions and Fiascoes*, 2nd ed. Boston: Houghton Mifflin, 1982.

Janko, Richard. *Aristotle on Comedy: Towards a Reconstruction of Poetics II*. London: Duckworth, 1984.

Jones, Peter. "Laughter," *Proceedings of the Aristotelian Society*, suppl. vol. 56 (1982): 213–28.

Jones, Ward E. "The Function and Content of Amusement," *South African Journal of Philosophy* 25 (2006): 126–37.

Joubert, Laurent. *Treatise on Laughter*, trans. Gregory deRocher. Tuscaloosa: University of Alabama Press, 1980.

Kahn, Samuel. *Why and How We Laugh*. New York: Philosophical Library, 1975.

Kallen, Horace M. *Liberty, Laughter, and Tears: Reflections on the Relations of Comedy and Tragedy to Human Freedom*. DeKalb, IL: Northern Illinois University Press, 1968.

Kant, Immanuel. *Critique of Judgment*, trans. J. H. Bernard. London: Macmillan, 1892.

Karassev, Leonid V. *Filosofia Smekha / Philosophy of Laughter*. Moscow, Russia: R. G. G. U., 1996.

Kayser, Wolfgang. *The Grotesque in Art and Literature*, trans. Ulrich Weisstein. New York: McGraw Hill, 1966.

Khatchadourian, Haig. "Semantics and Humor," *Methodos* 10 (1958): 101–12.

Kierkegaard, Søren. *Concluding Unscientific Postscript*, trans. David Swenson and Walter Lowrie. Princeton: Princeton University Press, 1941.

Kierkegaard, Søren. *The Concept of Irony*, trans. Howard V. Hong and Edna H. Hong. Princeton: Princeton University Press, 1989.

Kierkegaard, Søren. *Either/Or*, trans. Walter Lowrie. Garden City, NY: Anchor Books, 1959.

Kincaid, James. *Dickens and the Rhetoric of Laughter*. Oxford: Oxford University Press, 1971.

Kivy, Peter. "Jokes Are a Laughing Matter," *Journal of Aesthetics and Art Criticism* 61 (2003): 5–15.

Knox, Israel. "The Comic, the Tragic, and the Cynical: Some Notes on Their Ethical Dimensions," *Ethics* 62 (1952): 210–14.

Knox, Israel. "Towards a Philosophy of Humor," *Journal of Philosophy* 48 (1951): 541–7.

Koestler, Arthur. *The Act of Creation*. London: Hutchinson, 1964.

Krishna Menon, V. K. *A Theory of Laughter*. London: Allen and Unwin, 1931.

Kuhlman, Thomas. *Humor and Psychotherapy*. Homewood, IL: Dow Jones-Irwin, 1984.

Kulka, Tomas. "The Incongruity of Incongruity Theories," *Estetika* 30 (1993): 1–10.

Kupperman, Joel. "Not in So Many Words: Chuang Tzu's Strategies of Communication," *Philosophy East and West* 39 (1989): 311–17.

LaFollette, Hugh, and Shanks, Niall. "Belief and the Basis of Humor," *American Philosophical Quarterly* 30/4 (1993): 329–39.

Lamarque, Peter. "How Can We Fear and Pity Fictions?" *British Journal of Aesthetics* 21 (1981): 291–304.

Langer, Suzanne. *Feeling and Form*. New York: Scribner, 1953.

Lash, Kenneth. "A Theory of the Comic as Insight," *Journal of Philosophy* 45 (1948): 113–20.

Latta, Robert L. *The Basic Humor Process: A Cognitive-Shift Theory and the Case against Incongruity*. Berlin: Mouton de Gruyter, 1999.

Leacock, Stephen. *Humor and Humanity*. New York: Holt, 1938.

Leacock, Stephen. *Humor: Its Theory and Technique*. New York: Dodd, Mead, 1935.

Lefcourt, Herbert M., and Martin, Rod A. *Humor and Life Stress: Antidote to Adversity*. New York: Springer-Verlag, 1986.

Lefcourt, Herbert M. *Humor: The Psychology of Living Buoyantly*. New York: Plenum, 2001.

Legman, Gershon. *No Laughing Matter: Rationale of the Dirty Joke*, 2nd series. New York: Breaking Point, 1975.

Legman, Gershon. *The Rationale of the Dirty Jokes: An Analysis of Sexual Humor*, 1st series. New York: Grove Press, 1968.

Lengbeyer, Lawrence. "Humor, Context, and Divided Cognition," *Social Theory and Practice: An International and Interdisciplinary Journal of Social Philosophy* 31 (2005): 309–36.

Levine, Jacob, ed. *Motivation in Humor*. New York: Atherton, 1969.

Levinson, Jerrold. "Humour." *Routledge Encyclopedia of Philosophy*, ed. E. Craig, 562–7. London: Routledge, 1998.

Lewis, Michael. "Play as Whimsy." In *Does Play Matter? Functional and Evolutionary Aspects of Animal and Human Play*, ed. P. K. Smith, 139–84. *The Behavioral and Brain Sciences* 5/1 (1982).

Lewis, Peter B. "Schopenhauer's Laughter," *Monist* 88 (2005): 36–51.

Liebertz, Charmaine. "A Healthy Laugh," *Scientific American* 16/3, September 2005.

Lipman, Steve. *Laughter in Hell: The Use of Humor during the Holocaust*. Northvale, NJ: Jason Aronson, 1991.

Lippitt, John. "A Funny Thing Happened to Me on the Way to Salvation: Climacus as Humorist in Kierkegaard's *Concluding Unscientific Postscript*," *Religious Studies: An International Journal for the Philosophy of Religion* 33 (1997): 181–202.

Lippitt, John. *Humor and Irony in Kierkegaard's Thought*. London: Macmillan, 2000.

Lippitt, John. "Humour." In *Companion to Aesthetics*, ed. David Cooper. Oxford: Blackwell, 1992.

Lippitt, John. "Is a Sense of Humour a Virtue?" *Monist* 88/1 (2005): 72–92.

Lippitt, John. "Laughter: A Tool in Moral Perfectionism?" In *Nietzsche's Futures*, ed. John Lippitt, 99–126. New York: Macmillan/St. Martin's, 1999.

Lippitt, John. "Nietzsche, Zarathustra, and the Status of Laughter," *British Journal of Aesthetics* 32/1 (1992): 39–49.

Locke, John. *An Essay Concerning Human Understanding*. London, 1690.

Lorenz, Konrad. *On Aggression*. New York: Bantam, 1963.

Ludovici, Anthony. *The Secret of Laughter*. New York: Viking, 1933.

Lutz, Cora. "Democritus and Heraclitus," *The Classical Journal* 49 (1954): 309–14.

Magada-Ward, Mary. "Helping Thought and Keeping It Pragmatical, or, Why Experience Plays Practical Jokes," *Contemporary Pragmatism* 2 (2005): 63–71.

Mandel, Oscar. "The Nature of the Comic," *Antioch Review* 30 (1970): 73–89.

Marmysz, John. *Laughing at Nothing: Humor as a Response to Nihilism.* Albany: State University of New York Press, 2003.

Martin, Mike W. "Humor and the Aesthetic Enjoyment of Incongruities." In *The Philosophy of Laughter and Humor*, ed. John Morreall, 172–86. Albany: State University of New York Press, 1987. Originally published in *British Journal of Aesthetics* 23 (1983): 74–85.

Martin, Rod A. *The Psychology of Humor: An Integrative Approach.* Amsterdam: Elsevier, 2006.

Martin, Rod A. "The Situational Humor Response Questionnaire (SHRQ) and Coping Humor Scale (CHS): A Decade of Research Findings," *Humor: International Journal of Humor Research* 9 (1996): 251–72.

Martin, Rod A., Kuiper, N. A., Olinger, L. J., and Dance, K. A. "Humor, Coping with Stress, Self–Concept, and Psychological Well-Being," *Humor: International Journal of Humor Research* 6/1 (1993): 89–104.

McDonald, Kevin, ed. *Parent–Child Play.* Albany: State University of New York Press, 1993.

McFadden, George. *Discovering the Comic.* Princeton: Princeton University Press, 1982.

McFadden, George. "The Quality of the Comic." In *Essays on Aesthetics: Perspectives on the Work of Monroe C. Beardsley*, ed. John Fisher, 261–77. Philadelphia: Temple University Press, 1983.

McGhee, Paul. *Humor: Its Origin and Development.* San Francisco: W. H. Freeman, 1979.

McGhee, Paul, and Goldstein, Jeffrey, eds. *Handbook of Humor Research.* New York: Springer-Verlag, 1983.

Meier, Georg Friedrich. *Thoughts on Jesting*, ed. Joseph Jones. Austin: University of Texas Press, 1947.

Merton, Thomas. *Mystics and Zen Masters.* New York: Delta, 1967.

Metcalf, C. W., and Felible, Roma. *Lighten Up: Survival Skills for People under Pressure.* New York: Addison-Wesley, 1992.

Metcalf, Robert. "Balancing the Senses of Shame and Humor," *Journal of Social Philosophy* 35 (2004): 432–47.

Migdal, Ulrike. *Und die Musik spielt dazu: Chansons und Satiren aus dem KZ Theresienstadt.* Munich: Piper, 1986.

Milgram, Stanley. *Obedience to Authority: An Experimental View.* New York: HarperCollins, 1974.

Miller, Gerald R., and Bacon, P. "Open- and Closed-Mindedness and Recognition of Visual Humor," *Journal of Communication* 21 (1971): 150–9.

Mills, Claudia. "Racist and Sexist Jokes: How Bad Are They (Really)?" *Report from the Center for Philosophy and Public Policy* 7 (1987): 9–12.

Mindess, Harvey. *Laughter and Liberation*. Los Angeles: Nash, 1971.

Mohr, Richard. "Fag-ends and Jokes' Butts," from "Gays and Equal Protection." Unpublished manuscript.

Monro, David H. *Argument of Laughter*. Melbourne: Melbourne University Press, 1951.

Morreall, John. *Comedy, Tragedy, and Religion*. Albany: State University of New York Press, 1999.

Morreall, John. "The Comic and Tragic Visions of Life," *Humor: International Journal of Humor Research* 11/4 (1998): 333–56.

Morreall, John. "Comic Vices and Comic Virtues," *Humor: International Journal of Humor Research*, forthcoming.

Morreall, John. "Enjoying Incongruity," *Humor: International Journal of Humor Research* 2 (1989): 1–18.

Morreall, John. "Fear without Belief," *Journal of Philosophy* 90/7 (1993): 359–66.

Morreall, John. "Funny Ha-Ha, Funny Strange, and Other Reactions to Incongruity." In *The Philosophy of Laughter and Humor*, ed. John Morreall, 188–207. Albany: State University of New York Press, 1987.

Morreall, John. "Humor and Aesthetic Education," *Journal of Aesthetic Education* 15/1 (1981): 55–70.

Morreall, John. "Humor and Emotion." In *The Philosophy of Laughter and Humor*, ed. John Morreall, 212–24. Albany: State University of New York Press, 1987. Originally published in *American Philosophical Quarterly* 20/3 (1983): 297–304.

Morreall, John. "Humor and Philosophy," *Metaphilosophy* 15 (1984): 305–17.

Morreall, John. "Humor and Work," *Humor: International Journal of Humor Research* 4 (1991): 359–73.

Morreall, John. *Humor Works*. Amherst, MA: Human Resource Development Press, 1997.

Morreall, John, ed. *The Philosophy of Laughter and Humor*. Albany: State University of New York Press, 1987.

Morreall, John. "The Rejection of Humor in Western Thought," *Philosophy East and West* 39 (1989): 243–65.

Morreall, John. "The Resistance of Humor during the Holocaust." In *Hearing the Voices: Teaching the Holocaust to Future Generations*, ed. Michael Hayse et al., 103–12. Merion Station, PA: Merion International, 1999.

Morreall, John. *Taking Laughter Seriously*. Albany: State University of New York Press, 1983.

Nagel, Thomas. "The Absurd," *The Journal of Philosophy* 68 (1971): 716–27.

Nagel, Thomas. *The View from Nowhere*. New York: Oxford University Press, 1989.

Nahm, Milton C. "Falstaff, Incongruity and the Comic: An Essay in Aesthetic Criticism," *Personalist* 49 (1968): 289–321.

Nash, Ogden. *Best of Ogden Nash*. Chicago: Ivan R. Dee, 2007.

Naumann, Uwe. *Zwischen Tränen und Gelächter*. Cologne: Pahl-Rugenstein Verlag, 1983.

Nevo, Ruth. "Toward a Theory of Comedy," *Journal of Aesthetics and Art Criticism* 21 (1963): 327–32.

Nietzsche, Friedrich. *Thus Spoke Zarathustra*, trans. Walter Kaufmann. New York: Penguin, 1978.

Nozick, Robert. *The Examined Life*. New York: Touchstone Press, 1989.

Nuñez-Ramos, Raphael, and Lorenzo, Guillermo. "On the Aesthetic Dimension of Humor," *Humor: International Journal of Humor Research* 10 (1997): 105–16.

O'Connell, Walter, and Peterson, Penny. "Humor and Repression," *Journal of Existentialism* 4 (1964): 309–16.

Otto, Beatrice K. *Fools Are Everywhere: The Court Jester Around the World*. Chicago: University of Chicago Press, 2001.

Panksepp, Jaak. "Rough and Tumble Play: A Fundamental Brain Process." In *Parent–Child Play*, ed. Kevin MacDonald, 147–84. Albany: State University of New York Press, 1993.

Pappas, Nickolas. "Morality Gags," *Monist* 88/1 (2005): 52–71.

Patterson, Francine. "Koko: Conversations with Herself," *Gorilla* 19 (December 1989).

Patterson, Francine and Linden, Eugene. *The Education of Koko*. New York: Holt, Rinehart and Winston, 1985.

Paulos, John Allen. *I Think, Therefore I Laugh: An Alternative Approach to Philosophy*. New York: Columbia University Press, 1985.

Pellegrini, Anthony D., ed. *The Future of Play Theory: A Multidisciplinary Inquiry into the Contributions of Brian Sutton-Smith*. Albany: State University of New York Press, 1995.

Percival, Philip. "Comic Normativity and the Ethics of Humour," *Monist* 88 (2005): 93–120.

Perkins, Robert L. "The Categories of Humor and Philosophy," *Midwest Studies in Philosophy* 1 (1976): 105–8.

Pfeifer, Karl. "Causal Capacities and the Inherently Funny," *Conceptus: Zeitschrift für Philosophie* 27 (1994): 149–59.

Pfeifer, Karl. "From Locus Neoclassicus to Locus Rattus: Notes on Laughter, Comprehensiveness, and Titillation," *Res Cogitans* 3 (2006): 29–46.

Pfeifer, Karl (1994). "Laughter and Pleasure," *Humor: International Journal of Humor Research* 7 (1994): 157–72.

Pfeifer, Karl. "Laughter, Freshness and Titillation," *Inquiry* 40 (1997): 307–22.

Pfeifer, Karl. "More on Morreall on Laughter," *Dialogue* 26 (1987): 161–6.

Philips, Michael. "Racist Acts and Racist Humor," *Canadian Journal of Philosophy* 14 (1984): 75–96.

Piaget, Jean. *Play, Dreams, and Imitation in Childhood*, trans. C. Gattegno and F. M. Hodgson. London: Routledge and Kegan Paul, 1991.

Piddington, Ralph. *The Psychology of Laughter*. London: Figurehead, 1933.

Plato. *The Collected Dialogues of Plato*, ed. Edith Hamilton and Huntington Cairns. Princeton: Princeton University Press, 1978.

Plessner, Helmuth. *Laughing and Crying*, trans. James Spence and Marjorie Grene. Evanston, IL: Northwestern University Press.

Porteous, Janice. "Humor and Social Life," *Philosophy East and West* 39 (1989): 279–88.

Potter, Nancy. "Is There a Role for Humor in the Midst of Conflict?" In *Social Philosophy Today: Communication, Conflict, and Reconciliation*, Volume 17, ed. Cheryl Hughes, 103–23. Charlottesville, VA: Philosophy Documentation Center, 2003.

Prado, Carlos G. "Why Analysis of Humor Seems Funny," *Humor: International Journal of Humor Research* 8 (1995): 155–66.

Provine, Robert. *Laughter: A Scientific Investigation*. Harmondsworth: Penguin, 2000.

Provine, Robert, and Fischer, K. R. "Laughing, Smiling and Talking: Relation to Sleeping and Social Context in Humans," *Ethology* 83 (1989): 295–305.

Prynne, William. *Histrio-Mastix: The Players Scourge or Actors Tragaedie*. London, 1633.

Purdie, Susan. *Comedy: The Mastery of Discourse*. Toronto: University of Toronto Press, 1993.

Qian Suoqiao. "Translating 'Humor' into Chinese Culture," *Humor: International Journal of Humor Research* 20 (2007): 277–95.

Quintilian. *Institutes of Oratory*, trans. John Selby Watson. London: George Bell and Sons, 1891.

Radford, Colin. "How Can We Be Moved by the Fate of *Anna Karenina*?" *Proceedings of the Aristotelian Society*, suppl. vol. 69 (1975): 67–80.

Radin, Paul. *Trickster: A Study in American Indian Mythology*. New York: Random House, 1972.

Rahner, Hugo. "Eutrapelia: A Forgotten Virtue." In *Holy Laughter*, ed. M. Conrad Hyers, 185–97. New York: Seabury Press, 1969.

Rahner, Hugo. *Man at Play*. New York: Herder and Herder, 1972.

Ramachandran, V. S., and Blakeslee, Sandra. *Phantoms in the Brain*. New York: William Morrow, 1998.

Randall, Francis B. "The Goofy in Art," *British Journal of Aesthetics* 11 (1971): 327–40.

Rapp, Albert. *The Origins of Wit and Humor*. New York: E. P. Dutton, 1951.

Raskin, Victor. "Humor and Truth," *The World and I* (August 1992): 670–2.

Raskin, Victor. *Semantic Mechanisms of Humor*. Dordrecht: Reidel, 1984.

Resnick, Irwin. "Risus Monasticus: Laughter and Medieval Monastic Culture," *Revue Benedictine* 97/1–2 (1987): 90–100.

Roberts, Robert C. "Humor and the Virtues," *Inquiry* 31(1988): 127–49.

Roberts, Robert C. "Is Amusement an Emotion?" *American Philosophical Quarterly* 25/3 (1988): 269–74.

Roberts, Robert C. "Sense of Humor as a Christian Virtue," *Faith and Philosophy* 7 (1990): 177–92.

Roberts, Robert C. "Smiling with God: Reflections on Christianity and the Psychology of Humor," *Faith and Philosophy* 4 (1987): 168–75.

Robson, James. *Humour, Obscenity, and Aristophanes.* Tubingen: Gunter Narr Verlag, 2006.

Roeckelein, *The Psychology of Humor: A Reference Guide and Annotated Bibliography.* Westport, CT: Greenwood, 2002.

Ruch, Willibald, ed. *The Sense of Humor: Explorations of a Personality Characteristic.* Berlin: Mouton de Gruyter, 1998.

Ruch, Willibald. *Die Emotion Erheiterung: Alusdrucksformen und Bedingungen* [The Emotion of Exhilaration: Forms of Expression and Eliciting Conditions]. Unpublished habilitations thesis, Department of Psychology, University of Düsseldorf, 1990.

Rudner, Rita. *I Still Have It . . . I Just Can't Remember Where I Put It: Confessions of a Fiftysomething.* New York: Random House, 2008.

Runcie, Robert. *Seasons of the Spirit.* Grand Rapids, MI: Eerdmans, 1983.

Russell, Bertrand. *The ABC of Relativity.* London: Kegan Paul, Trench, Trubner & Co., 1925.

Russell, Bertrand. *The Philosophy of Logical Atomism.* London: Allen and Unwin, 1918.

Russell, Olga Webster. *Humor in Pascal.* North Quincy, MA: Christopher, 1977.

Santayana, George. *The Sense of Beauty.* New York: Scribner's, 1896.

Sartre, Jean-Paul. *The Family Idiot: Gustave Flaubert 1821 1857,* trans. Carol Cosman, 3 vols. Chicago: University of Chicago Press, 1981.

Schopenhauer, Arthur. *The World as Will and Idea,* trans. R. B. Haldane and John Kemp. London: Routledge and Kegan Paul, 1964.

Schrempp, G. "Our Funny Universe: On Aristotle's Metaphysics, Oring's Theory of Humor, and Other Appropriate Incongruities," *Humor: International Journal of Humor Research* 8 (1995): 219–28.

Schultz, Thomas. "A Cognitive-Developmental Analysis of Humor." In *Humor and Laughter: Theory, Research and Applications,* ed. Tony Chapman and Hugh Foot, 12–13. New York: Wiley, 1976.

Scott, Nathan. "The Bias of Comedy and the Narrow Escape into Faith." In *Holy Laughter,* ed. M. Conrad Hyers, 45–74. New York: Seabury Press, 1969.

Scruton, Roger. "Laughter." In *The Philosophy of Laughter and Humor,* ed. John Morreall, 156–71. Albany: State University of New York Press, 1987. Originally published in *Proceedings of the Aristotelian Society,* suppl. vol. 56 (1982): 197–212.

Seward, Samuel. *The Paradox of the Ludicrous.* Stanford: Stanford University Press, 1930.

Shaffer, Jerome. "An Assessment of Emotion," *American Philosophical Quarterly* 20 (1983): 161–73.

Shaftesbury, Lord. "The Freedom of Wit and Humour," *Characteristicks*, 4th ed. London, 1727.

Shapiro, Robert Moses. "Yiddish Slang under the Nazis," *The Book Peddler* (Summer 1989): 30.

Sharpe, Robert A. "Seven Reasons Why Amusement Is an Emotion." In *The Philosophy of Laughter and Humor*, ed. John Morreall, 208–11. Albany: State University of New York Press, 1987. Originally published in *Journal of Value Inquiry* 9 (1975): 201–3.

Shaw, B. D. ed. *Is Hitler Dead? and Best Anti-Nazi Humor*. New York: Alcaeus House, 1939.

Shibles, Warren. *Humor: A Comprehensive Classification and Analysis*. Whitewater, WI: Language Press, 1978.

Sidis, Boris. *The Psychology of Laughter*. New York: Appleton, 1913.

Sidney, Philip. *The Defense of Poesie*, ed. Ponsonby. British Museum, 1595.

Singer, Peter. *The President of Good and Evil*. New York: Dutton, 2004.

Sjursen, Harold. "The Comic Apprehension," *Midwest Studies in Philosophy* 1 (1976): 108–13.

Skinner, B. F. *Beyond Freedom and Dignity*. New York: Bantam, 1976.

Slansky, Paul. *The Clothes Have No Emperor: A Chronicle of the American 80s*. New York: Fireside, 1989.

Söderquist, K. Brian. "Irony and Humor in Kierkegaard's Early Journal: Two Responses to an Emptied World," *Kierkegaard Studies*, 2003 Yearbook: 143–67.

Spencer, Herbert. "On the Physiology of Laughter," *Essays on Education, Etc.* London: Dent, 1911.

Spinka, Marek et al. "Mammalian Play: Training for the Unexpected," *Quarterly Journal of Biology* 76 (2001): 141–68.

Stearns, Frederic. *Laughing: Physiology, Pathophysiology, Psychology, Pathopsychology, and Development*. Springfield, IL: Thomas, 1972.

Steward, Julian. "The Ceremonial Buffoon of the American Indian," *Papers of the Michigan Academy of Science, Arts, and Letters* 14 (1931): 189–98.

Stolnitz, Jerome. "Notes on Comedy and Tragedy," *Philosophy and Phenomenological Research* 16 (1955): 45–60.

Sully, James. *An Essay on Laughter*. London: Longmans, Green, 1902.

Sully, James. "Prologomena to a Theory of Laughter," *Philosophical Review* 9 (1900): 365–83.

Suls, Jerry. "A Two-Stage Model for the Appreciation of Jokes and Cartoons: An Information-Processing Analysis." In *The Psychology of Humor*, ed. Jeffrey Goldstein and Paul McGhee, 81–99. New York: Academic Press, 1972.

Suls, Jerry. "Cognitive Processes in Humor Appreciation." In *Handbook of Humor Research*, ed. Paul McGhee and Jeffrey Goldstein, 39–58. New York: Springer-Verlag, 1983.

Sutton-Smith, Brian. *The Ambiguity of Play*. Cambridge, MA: Harvard University Press, 1997.

Suzuki, D. T. *Essays in Zen Buddhism.* London: Rider, 1948–53.

Swabey, Marie Collins. "The Comic as Nonsense, Sadism, or Incongruity," *Journal of Philosophy* 55 (1958): 819–32.

Swabey, Marie Collins. *Comic Laughter: A Philosophical Essay.* New Haven: Yale University Press, 1961.

Tapley, Robin. "Just Joking: The Ethics of Humour," *Yeditepe'de Felsege* 4 (2005) 171–98.

Tarozzi-Goldsmith, Marcella. *Nonrepresentational Forms of the Comic: Humor, Irony and Jokes.* New York: Peter Lang, 1991.

Taylor, Richard. *Metaphysics,* 3rd ed. Englewood Cliffs: Prentice-Hall, 1983.

Telfer, Elizabeth. "Hutcheson's *Reflections upon Laughter,*" *Journal of Aesthetics and Art Criticism* 53 (1995): 359–69.

Thomson, A. A. *Anatomy of Laughter.* London: Epworth, 1966.

Todorov, Tzvetan. *The Fantastic.* Ithaca, NY: Cornell University Press, 1970.

Twain, Mark. *Following the Equator: A Journey around the World.* New York: Harper and Brothers, 1906.

Van de Vate, Dwight. "Laughter and Detachment," *Southern Journal of Philosophy* 3 (1965): 163–71.

Van Hooff, J. A. R. A. M. "A Comparative Approach to the Phylogeny of Laughter and Smiling." In *Non-Verbal Communication,* ed. Robert A. Hinde, 209–41. Cambridge: Cambridge University Press, 1972.

Vasey, George. *The Philosophy of Laughter and Smiling,* 2nd ed. London: J. Burns, 1877.

Vogel, Susan. *Humor: A Semiogenetic Approach.* Bochum, Germany: Studieneur/ Brockmeyher, 1989.

Wahman, Jessica. "We Are All Mad Here: Santayana and the Significance of Humor," *Contemporary Pragmatism* 2 (2005): 73–83.

Waite, Robert. *The Psychopathic God: Adolf Hitler.* New York: Basic Books, 1977.

Walsh, J. J. *Laughter and Health.* New York: Appleton, 1928.

Walton, Kendall. *Mimesis as Make-Believe: On the Foundations of the Representational Arts.* Cambridge, MA: Harvard University Press, 1990.

Weeks, Mark. "Beyond a Joke: Nietzsche and the Birth of Super-Laughter," *Journal of Nietzsche Studies* 27 (2004): 1–17.

Welsford, Enid. *The Fool: His Social and Literary History.* Garden City, NY: Doubleday Anchor 1961.

White, Richard. "Hume's Dialogues and the Comedy of Religion," *Hume Studies* 14 (1988): 390–407.

Wieck, David Thoreau. "Funny Things," *Journal of Aesthetics and Art Criticism* 25 (1967): 437–47.

Wilson, Christopher. *Jokes: Form, Content, Use and Function.* New York: Academic Press, 1979.

Wisdo, David. *The Life of Irony and the Ethics of Belief.* Albany: State University of New York Press, 1993.

Wolf, Michael P. "A Grasshopper Walks into a Bar: The Role of Humor in Normativity," *Journal for the Theory of Social Behaviour* 32 (2002): 331–44.

Wolfenstein, Martha. *Children's Humor*. Glencoe, IL: Free Press, 1954.

Woodruff, Paul. "Rousseau, Moliere, and the Ethics of Laughter," *Philosophy and Literature* 1 (1977): 325–36.

Wright, Milton. *What's Funny and Why*. New York: McGraw-Hill, 1939.

Wurzer, Wilhelm S. "Culture Clowns on a Tour with Nietzsche and Heidegger," *Existentia: An International Journal of Philosophy* 11 (2001): 267–76.

Xu, Weihe. "The Confucian Politics of Appearance – and Its Impact on Chinese Humor," *Philosophy East and West* 54 (2004): 514–32.

Yanal, Robert J. *Paradoxes of Emotion and Fiction*. University Park: Pennsylvania State University Press, 1999.

Zemach, Shlomo. "A Theory of Laughter," *Journal of Aesthetics and Art Criticism* 17 (1959): 311–29.

Ziv, Avner. "Using Humor to Develop Creative Thinking," *Journal of Children in Contemporary Society* 20 (1988): 99–116.

Zucker, Wolfgang W. "The Giant Mouthless," *Journal of Aesthetics and Art Criticism* 19 (1960): 185–90.

Index